# WALT WHITMAN AND MODERN MUSIC
## WAR, DESIRE, AND THE TRIALS OF NATIONHOOD

EDITED BY
LAWRENCE KRAMER

GARLAND PUBLISHING, INC.
A MEMBER OF THE TAYLOR & FRANCIS GROUP
NEW YORK & LONDON
2000

Published in 2000 by
Garland Publishing, Inc.
A member of the Taylor & Francis Group
29 West 35th Street
New York, NY 10001

"Reclaiming Walt: Marc Blitzstein's Whitman Settings," by David Metzer, first published in *The Journal of the American Musicological Society,* © 1995 American Musicological Society. Reprinted by permission of University of Chicago Press.

10   9   8   7   6   5   4   3   2   1

**Library of Congress Cataloging-in-Publication Data**

Walt Whitman and modern music : war, desire, and the trials of nationhood / edited by Lawrence Kramer.
     p.  cm. — (Garland reference library of the humanities ; v. 2100. Border crossings ; v. 10.)
    Includes bibliographical references and index.
    ISBN 0-8153-3154-1 (acid-free paper)
    1. Whitman, Walt, 1819–1892—Musical settings—History and criticism.
2. United States—History—Civil War, 1861–1865—Music and the war.  3. Music and literature—History—20th century.  4. Modernism (Aesthetics)  5. Nationalism in music.  I. Kramer, Lawrence, 1946–  II. Garland reference library of the humanities ; vol. 2100.  III. Garland reference library of the humanities. Border crossings ; v. 10.
ML80.W5 W35 2000
782.43—dc21

                                        99-045480

Front cover: Holograph of "Dirge for Two Veterans" by Kurt Weill, set to a text by Walt Whitman, 1942. Photograph provided by the Weill-Lenya Research Center, New York. The original score is located in the Weill-Lenya Papers (Box 35, Folder 535), Yale University Music Library.

Printed on acid-free, 250-year-life paper.
Manufactured in the United States of America

# Contents

# Acknowledgments

Several people made indispensable contributions to the production of this volume. I would like to thank Christina Acosta for expert help in designing the layout of the manuscript, insuring continuity of style editing among the different contributions, and preparing the manuscript and associated disk file; Joan Heller for her tireless work in making the compact disc possible and of course for performing the songs; and Daniel Albright for initiating the project and enriching it with valuable suggestions.

David Metzer's essay "Reclaiming Walt" originally appeared in the summer 1995 issue of the *Journal of the American Musicological Society,* copyright 1995 by the American Musicological Society, and is reprinted by permission of the University of Chicago Press.

# Series Editor's Foreword

*Daniel Albright*

## The Need for Comparison Among the Arts

To study one artistic medium in isolation from others is to study an inadequacy. The twentieth century, so rich in literature, in music, and in the visual arts, has also been rich in criticism of these arts; but it is possible that some of the uglinesses and distortions in modern criticism have arisen from the consideration of each artistic medium as an autonomous field of development, fenced off from other media. It is hard for us to believe, but when, long ago, Horace said *Ut pictura poesis*—the poem should be like a picture—he meant it. Now that the twenty-first century has arrived, perhaps it will be possible to come near a total critique appropriate to the total artwork.

The twentieth century, perhaps more than any other age, has demanded a style of criticism in which the arts are considered as a whole. This is partly because the artists themselves insisted again and again upon the inextricability of the arts. Ezra Pound, for one, believed that, in antiquity, "music and poetry had been in alliance . . . that the divorce of the two arts had been to the advantage of neither, and that melodic invention had declined simultaneously and progressively with their divergence. The rhythms of poetry grew stupider." He thought that it was the duty of the poet to learn music, and the duty of the musician to study poetry. But we must learn to challenge the boundaries among the arts, not only because the artists we study demanded it, but because our philosophy demands it as well. The linguistics of Ferdinand de Saussure, the philosophy of Ludwig Wittgenstein and Jacques Derrida, tend to strip language of denotation, to make language a game of arbitrary signifiers; and as words lose connection to the world of hard objects, they become more and more like musical notes. Wittgenstein claimed, "To say that a word has meaning does not imply that it *stands for* or *represents* a thing. . . . The sign plus the rules of grammar applying to it is all we need [to make a language]. We need nothing further to make the connection with reality. If we did we should need something to connect that with reality, which would lead to an infinite regress." And, for Wittgenstein, the consequence of this disconnection was clear: "Understanding a sentence is much more akin to understanding a theme in music than one may think." To Horace, reading is like looking at a picture; to Wittgenstein, reading is like listening to music. The arts seem endlessly inter-permeable, a set of fluid systems of construing and reinterpreting, in which the quest for meaning engages all our senses at once. Thinking is itself looking, hearing, touching—even tasting, since such words as *savoir* are forms of the Latin *sapere,* to taste.

### The Term *Modernism*

*Modernism*—like any unit of critical terminology—is a fiction, but an indispensable fiction. It is possible to argue (as Vladimir Nabokov did) that each work of art in the universe is unique and incommensurable; that there is no such thing as a school of artists; that an idea such as *influence* among artists arises from sheer intellectual laziness. This line of argument, however, contradicts our intuition that certain works of art look like one another; that, among many works of art produced at the same time or in the same place, there are family resemblances. Such terms as modernism need have no great prestige: they're simply critical inductions convenient for describing certain family resemblances.

Furthermore, these terms denote not only kinship relations established by critics from outside, but also kinship relations determined by artists from within. The term modernism had tremendous potency for the modernists themselves: when Ezra Pound first read a poem by T. S. Eliot, he was thunderstruck that Eliot had managed to *modernize* his poetry all by himself, without any contact with other poets. Pound regarded modernism itself as a huge group project. To this extent, modernism isn't just a label attached by students of a period, but a kind of tribal affiliation, one of thousands of examples of those arbitrary loyalty groups that bedevil the human race. Nearly every early twentieth-century artist felt the need to define himself or herself as a modernist or otherwise. When Stravinsky at last met Rachmaninov in Hollywood, Stravinsky obviously greeted his colleague not simply as a fraternal fellow in the order of Russian expatriate composers, but as a (self-sacrificing) modernist condescending to a (rich and successful) romantic. The label *modernist* shaped the interactions of artists themselves—sometimes as a help, sometimes as a hindrance.

Of course, it is the task of criticism of the present age to offer a better account of modernism than the modernists themselves could. Stravinsky's ideas about Rachmaninov were wrong in several ways: not just because Rachmaninov's royalties weren't noticeably greater than Stravinsky's, but also because their music was somewhat more similar than Stravinsky would have liked to admit. For instance, compare the Easter finale from Rachmaninov's "Suite for Two Pianos," op. 5, with the carillon evoked by the piano in Stravinsky's song "Spring," op. 6 no. 1: they inhabit the same aesthetic realm.

A theory of the modernist movement that might embrace both Rachmaninov and Stravinsky, or Picasso and Balthus, could be constructed along the following lines: modernism is a *testing of the limits of aesthetic construction.* According to this perspective, the modernists tried to find the ultimate bounds of certain artistic possibilities: volatility of emotion (expressionism); stability and inexpressiveness (the new objectivity); accuracy of representation (hyperrealism); absence of representation (abstractionism); purity of form (neoclassicism); formless energy (neobarbarism); cultivation of the technological present (futurism); cultivation of the prehistoric past (the mythic method). These extremes have, of course, been arranged in pairs because aesthetic heresies, like theological ones, come in binary sets: each limit-point presupposes an opposite limit-point, a counter-extreme toward which the artist can push. Much of the strangeness, the stridency, the exhilaration of modernist art can be explained by this strong thrust toward the verges of the aesthetic experience: after the nineteenth century had established a remarkably safe, intimate center where the artist and the audience could dwell, the twentieth century has reached out to the freakish circumferences of art. The extremes of the aesthetic experience tend to converge: in the modernist movement, the most barbaric art tends to be the most up-to-date and sophisticated. For example, when T. S. Eliot first heard *The Rite of Spring,* he wrote that the music seemed to "transform the rhythm of the steppes into the scream of the motor-horn, the rattle of machinery, the grind of wheels, the beating of iron and steel, the roar of the underground railway, and the other barbaric noises of modern life." *The Waste Land* is itself written to the same recipe: the world of London, with its grime, boredom, and abortifacient drugs, overlays the antique world of primal rites for the rejuvenation of the land through the dismemberment of a god. In the modernist movement, things tend to coexist uncomfortably with their exact opposites.

Wallace Stevens referred to the story we tell ourselves about the world, about our presence in the world, and about how we attempt to configure pleasant lives for ourselves, as a Supreme Fiction; and similarly, critics live by various critical fictions, as they reconfigure the domain of similarities and differences in the arts. Modernism is just such a "high critical fiction."

## The Span of the Modernist Age

The use of a term such as modernism usually entails a certain restriction to a period of time. Such a restriction is rarely easy and becomes immensely difficult for the interdisciplinary student: the romantic movement, for example, will invariably mean one age for a musicologist, another (perhaps scarcely overlapping) for a student of British poetry. One might say that the modernist age begins around 1907–1909, because in those years Picasso painted *Les Demoiselles d'Avignon,* Schoenberg made his "atonal" breakthrough, and the international careers of Stravinsky, Pound, Stein, and Cocteau were just beginning or were not long to come. And one might choose 1951 for a terminus, since in that year Cage started using the *I Ching* to compose chance-determined music, and Samuel Beckett's trilogy and *Waiting for Godot* were soon to establish an artistic world that would have partly bewildered the early modernists. The modernists did not (as Cage did) abdicate their artistic responsibilities to a pair of dice; the modernists did not (as Beckett did) delight in artistic failure. Modernism was a movement associated with scrupulous choice of artistic materials, and with hard work in arranging them. Sometimes the modernists deflected the domain of artistic selection to unusual states of consciousness (trance, dream, etc.); but, except for a few Dadaist experiments, they didn't abandon artistic selection entirely—and even Tristan Tzara, Kurt Schwitters, and the more radical Dadaists usually attempted a more impudent form of non-sense than aleatory procedures can generate. The modernists *intended* modernism—the movement did not come into existence randomly.

But the version of modernism outlined here—a triumphalist extension of the boundaries of the feasible in art—is only *one* version of modernism. There exist many modernisms, and each version is likely to describe a period with different terminal dates. It isn't hard to construct an argument showing that modernism began, say, around 1886 (the year of the last painting exhibition organized by the Impressionists, at which Seurat made the first important show of his work). Nietzsche had privately published *Also Sprach Zarathustra* in 1885, and Mahler's first symphony would appear in 1889. And it is possible to construct arguments showing that modernism has only recently ended, since Beckett actualized certain potentialities in Joyce (concerning self-regarding language), and Cage followed closely after Schoenberg and Satie (Cage's *Cheap Imitation,* from 1969, is simply a note-by-note rewriting, with random pitch alterations, of the vocal line of Satie's 1918 *Socrate*).

And it is also possible that modernism hasn't ended at all: the term *postmodernism* may simply be erroneous. Much of the music of Philip Glass is a straightforward recasting of musical surface according to models derived from visual surface, following a formula stated in 1936 by an earlier American composer, George Antheil, who wrote of the "filling out of a certain time canvas with musical abstractions and sound material composed and contrasted against one another with the thought of time values rather than tonal values ... I used time as Picasso might have used the blank spaces of his canvas. I did not hesitate, for instance, to repeat one measure one hundred times." Most of the attributes we ascribe to postmodernism can easily be found, latently or actually, with the modernist movement: for another example, Brecht in the 1930s made such deconstructionist declarations as "*Realist* means: laying bare society's causal network / showing up the dominant viewpoint as the viewpoint of the dominators." It is arguable that in the 1990s we are still trying to digest the meal that the modernists ate.

If modernism can be said to reach out beyond the present moment, it is also true that modernism can be said to extend backwards almost indefinitely. Wagner, especially the Wagner of *Tristan und Isolde,* has been a continual presence in twentieth-century art: Brecht and Weill continually railed against Wagnerian narcosis and tried to construct a music theater exactly opposed to Wagner's; but Virgil Thomson found much to admire and imitate in Wagner—even though Thomson's operas sound, at first hearing, even less Wagnerian than Kurt Weill's. In some respects, the first modernist experiment in music theater might be said to be the Kotzebue-Beethoven *The Ruins of Athens* (1811), in which the goddess Minerva claps her hands over her ears at hearing the hideous music of the dervishes; chorus (blaring tritones, Turkish percussion): here is the conscious sensory assault, sensory overload, of Schoenberg's first operas. Modernism is partly confined to the first half of the twentieth century, but it tends to spill into earlier and later ages. Modernism created its own precursors; it made the past new, as well as the present.

### The Question of Boundaries

The revolution of the Information Age began when physicists discovered that silicon could be used either as a resistor or as a conductor of electricity. Modernist art is also a kind of circuit board, a pattern of yieldings and resistances, in which one art sometimes asserts its distinct, inviolable nature and sometimes yields itself, tries to imitate some foreign aesthetic. Sometimes music and poetry coexist in a state of extreme dissonance (as Brecht thought they should, in the operas that he wrote with Weill); but on other occasions music tries to *become* poetry, or poetry tries to *become* music. To change the metaphor, one might say that modernism investigates a kind of transvestism among the arts—what happens when one art stimulates itself by temporarily pretending to be another species of art altogether.

Modernist art has existed in an almost continual state of crisis concerning the boundaries between one art medium and another. Is a painting worth a thousand words, or is it impossible to find a verbal equivalent of an image, even if millions of words were used? Are music and literature two different things, or two aspects of the same thing? This is a question confronted by artists of every age, but the artists of the modernist period found a special urgency here. The literature of the period, with its dehydrated epics and other semantically supercharged texts, certainly resembles, at least to a degree, the music of the period, with its astonishing density of acoustic events. But some artists tried to erase the boundaries among music and literature and the visual arts, while other artists tried to build foot-thick walls.

Some of the modernists felt strongly that the purity of one artistic medium must not be compromised by the encroachment of styles or themes taken from other artistic media. Clement Greenberg, the great modernist critic, defended abstractionism on the grounds that an abstract painting is a pure painting: not subservient to literary themes, not enslaved to representations of the physical world, but a new autonomous object, not a copy of reality but an addition to reality. Such puritans among the modernists stressed the need for fidelity to the medium: the opacity and spectral precision of paint or the scarified, slippery feel of metal; the exact sonority of the highest possible trombone note; the spondaic clumps in a poetic line with few unstressed syllables. As Greenberg wrote in 1940, "The history of avant-garde painting is that of a progressive surrender to the resistance of its medium; which resistance consists chiefly in the flat picture plane's denial of efforts to 'hole through' it for realistic perspectival space." To Greenberg, the medium has a message: canvas and paint have a recalcitrant will of their own, fight against the artists' attempts to pervert their function. He profoundly approved of the modernist art that learned to love paint for paint's sake, not for its capacity to create phantoms of solid objects.

But this puritan hatred of illusions, the appetite for an art that possesses the dignity of reality, is only part of the story of modernism. From another perspective, the hope that art can overcome its illusory character is itself an illusion: just because a sculpture is hacked out of rough granite doesn't mean that it is real in the same way that granite is real. The great musicologist Theodor Adorno was as much a puritan as Greenberg: Adorno hated what he called *pseudomorphism,* the confusion of one artistic medium with another. But Adorno, unlike Greenberg, thought that all art was dependent on illusion, that art couldn't attempt to compete with the real world: as he wrote in 1948, it is futile for composers to try to delete all ornament from music: "Since the work, after all, cannot be reality, the elimination of all illusory features accentuates all the more glaringly the illusory character of its existence."

But, while the puritans tried to isolate each medium from alien encroachment, other, more promiscuous modernists tried to create a kind of art in which the finite medium is almost irrelevant. For them, modernism was *about* the fluidity, the interchangeability, of artistic media themselves. Here we find single artists, each of whom often tried to become a whole artistic colony— we see, for example, a painter who wrote an opera libretto (Kokoschka), a poet who composed music (Pound), and a composer who painted pictures (Schoenberg). It is as if artistic talent were a kind of libido, an electricity that could discharge itself with equal success in a poem, a sonata, or a sculpture. Throughout the modernist movement, the major writers and composers both enforced and transgressed the boundaries among the various arts with unusual energy—almost savage at times.

It is important to respect both the instincts for division and distinction among the arts, and the instincts for cooperation and unity. In the eighteenth century, Gotthold Lessing (in *Laokoon*) divided the arts into two camps, which he called the *nacheinander* (the temporal arts, such as poetry and music) and the *nebeneinander* (the spatial arts, such as painting and sculpture). A modernist *Laocoön* might restate the division of the arts as follows: not as a tension between the temporal arts and the spatial—this distinction has often been thoroughly flouted in the twentieth century—but as a tension between arts that try to retain the propriety, the apartness, of their private media, and arts that try to lose themselves in some pan-aesthetic whole. On one hand, *nacheinander* and *nebeneinander* retain their distinctness; on the other hand, they collapse into a single spatiotemporal continuum, in which both duration and extension are arbitrary aspects. Photographs of pupillary movement have traced the patterns that the eye makes as it scans the parts of a picture trying to apprehend the whole—a picture not only may suggest motion, but is constructed by the mind acting over time. Similarly, a piece of music may be heard so thoroughly that the whole thing coexists in the mind in a instant—as Karajan claimed to know Beethoven's fifth symphony.

There are, then, two huge contrary movements in twentieth-century experiments in bringing art media together: consonance among the arts, and dissonance among the arts. Modernism carries each to astonishing extremes. The dissonances are challenging; perhaps the consonances are even more challenging.

In the present series of books, each volume will examine some facet of these intriguing problems in the arts of modernism—the dissemblings and resistings, the smooth cooperations and the prickly challenges when the arts come together.

# Introduction

*Lawrence Kramer*

Walt Whitman's poetic response to nineteenth-century music was both ardent and well informed, but his impact on it was negligible. There is no tradition of nineteenth-century Whitman settings, despite the steady development of an international readership for his poetry. The reasons, I suspect, were less aesthetic than sociocultural. In Europe, the composition of art songs was a nationalist project; the leading centers of song, Germany and France, were focused intently, even aggressively, on their own languages and artistic ideologies.[1] Whitman might be read or translated there, but he would not be set. The United States was a more eclectic venue, always being drawn to nativize the tradition of high-art music that it otherwise prized for European cultivation. The American art-music culture of the era, however, was far too genteel to accommodate a poetry as uncouth, as egocentric, and as highly sexed as Whitman's. Even the more moderate, more "public," later poetry seemed too outrageous. Charles Ives characteristically made a point of attacking this high-minded gentility in his song "Walt Whitman," which begins by setting a provocative line from *Song of Myself:* "Who goes there? Hankering, gross, mystical, nude?" (389; there is even a pungent bad-boy *fortissimo* on "nude"). But Whitman was too much even for the ostensibly iconoclastic Ives, who wrote no other Whitman songs.

The musical reception of Whitman in the twentieth century was another story; it more than made amends for past neglect. Many modernist composers, representing many different types of modernism, turned to Whitman at important points in their careers. The modernisms involved, moreover, were strikingly international. Perhaps the first important Whitman settings came from British composers, notably Frederick Delius and Ralph Vaughan Williams. American composers such as Marc Blitzstein, Howard Hanson, Roger Sessions, and Ned Rorem followed in due course, but so, too, did such Germans as Paul Hindemith, Kurt Weill, Karl Amadeus Hartmann, and Hans-

Werner Henze. (The French, it is true, seem not to have taken the bait.) And although no single concept can organize the diverse responses of modernist music to Whitman without oversimplifying, there does seem to be a red thread running through the diversity. Tracing that thread is the intent of this volume.

The starting point is Whitman himself. Like most of his contemporaries, Whitman identified musical style with national origin:

> *All songs of current lands come sounding round me,*
> *The German airs of friendship, wine and love,*
> *Irish ballads, merry jigs and dances, English warbles,*
> *Chansons of France, Scotch tunes, and o'er the rest,*
> *Italia's peerless compositions.* ("Proud Music of the Storm," 71–75)[2]

At the same time, however, Whitman heard European music as the expression of a universal identity. Influenced in part by Hegel's philosophy of history, he understood this universality as the still-pending outcome of a great historical process, which in his case meant that it was supposed to be the outcome of democracy in the United States. In Whitman's poetry, all musical nationalisms funnel into the transcendental melting pot of American nationalism. "Foreign" music buoys up the American spirit and blends into the material vitality of the North American continent. The world-transforming mission of America finds its anthem when the new world receives the music of the old.

"Italian Music in Dakota" (1881) shows this process at work where two kinds of border coalesce: a geographical one between "whites" and "Indians," and a musical one between Italian opera arias and their arrangement for regimental band:

> *Through the soft evening air enwinding all,*
> *Rocks, woods, fort, cannon, pacing sentries, endless wilds,*
> *In dulcet streams, in flutes' and cornets' notes,*
> *Electric, pensive, turbulent, artificial,*
> *(Yet strangely fitting even here, meanings unknown before,*
> *Subtler than ever, more harmony, as if born here, related here,*
> *Not to the city's fresco'd rooms, not to the audience of the opera house,*
> *Sounds, echoes, wandering strains, as here really at home,*
> Somnambula's *innocent love, trios with* Norma's *anguish,*
> *And thy ecstatic chorus* Poliuto;)
> *Ray'd in the limpid yellow slanting sundown,*
> *Music, Italian music in Dakota.* (1–12)

Without ever ceasing to be "Italian," the music described here undergoes a kind of multiple emigration to the American frontier. It is removed from its usual venues in the opera house and "the city's fresco'd rooms"; it is pried away from its origin in the singing voice; it is even cut off from the material presence of the military instruments that are performing it, sight unseen, in a Dakota fort, suggestively marking and holding with music the borders of Indian territory. In this form, this distillation of itself to pure, migratory sound (the "wandering strains" literally wandering until they find themselves "as really at home"), the music both palpably fills the landscape—"Through the soft evening air enwinding all"—and gradually becomes indistinguishable from the landscape it fills: "Ray'd in the limpid yellow slanting sundown, / Music, Italian music in Dakota." The metaphorical fusion of music and sundown, Italy and Dakota, "enwinds" itself through both space and time: spatially, in the perceptual blend of music seen, sundown heard, and temporally, in the extended, boundless present suggested by the absence of verbs.

The more famous poem "To a Locomotive in Winter" (1876) carries a similar set of identifications to a startling pitch of extravagance. The links between Italian opera, modern democratic energy, and the vast span of American space and time here draw to a focus in a sustained metaphor equating the sounds emitted by a brawny steam engine chugging and churning across the snowy continent with the singing of an operatic soprano. The figure (in all its willful absurdity) is announced in the poem's opening line, at once an apostrophe and an act of election: "Thee for my recitative." The subsequent elaboration of the engine's potent fusion of mechanical and sensual energy all but submerges the operatic idea, which only flickers here and there in the repeated references to the sonority of the moving train. But the second half of the poem revives the idea with a new, erotically charged apostrophe, and this time homes in on it:

> *Fierce-throated beauty!*
> *Roll through my chant with all thy lawless music, thy swinging lamps at*
> *    night,*
> *Thy madly-whistled laughter, echoing, rumbling like an earthquake,*
> *    rousing all,*
> *Law of thyself, thine own track firmly holding,*
> *(No sweetness debonair of tearful harp or glib piano thine,)*
> *Thy trills of shrieks by rocks and hills return'd,*
> *Launch'd over prairies wide, across the lakes,*
> *To the free skies unpent and glad and strong.* (18–25)

Perhaps thinking of Lucia di Lammermoor, a favorite role, Whitman here transvalues the operatic mad scene and identifies its "lawless" spirit and high-flying vocal energies with the sound of the train whistle as it surges across the wide, free terrain. (The imagery is of the West, and the western movement of the train, with all its political and historical ramifications, goes without saying here.) The resulting soundscape becomes a material embodiment of the democratic ideal moving irresistibly on its way, ebullient and autonomous. Like the feminine character whose pyrotechnical voice carries her beyond the limits imposed by a feudal patriarchy, the Whitman persona in this poem, fused with that of the train and the singer, recognizes only its own power and motion. The poem takes special pains to disengage the operatic sound from that of sentimental parlor music; like the opera houses of Whitman's New York, especially those he remembered from the 1830s and 1840s, the continental landscape is a scene of "unpent" enjoyment, not of order or restraint. And in its reciprocity with the landscape, the sound of Italian opera at its most vocally and dramatically extravagant becomes the sound of American modernity, one of the strands in the far-reaching vocal fabric of which he wrote elsewhere: "I hear America singing, the varied carols I hear" ("I Hear America Singing," 1860).

In a sense, Whitman's conception of music as evidenced here finds its mirror image in the conception of Whitman that modernist composers most often brought to the setting of his poetry. The same power that Whitman found in music, modernist composers tended to find in him. In various ways, the Whitman persona in the twentieth century came to stand musically for the kind of transcendental collective identity that Whitman heard as the music, both literal and figurative, of nineteenth-century America. This all-embracing identity may be nationalist, as when the èmigrès Kurt Weill and Paul Hindemith respectively set texts from *Drum-Taps* and "When Lilacs Last in the Dooryard Bloom'd" to commemorate America's sacrifices in World War II, or it may be antinationalist, as when Ned Rorem sets Civil War vignettes from the prose miscellany *Specimen Days* to memorialize the dead on both sides of the Vietnam War. The identity may be cultural, as when Frederick Delius takes up "Out of the Cradle Endlessly Rocking" to affirm an impassioned sensualism at odds with Victorian highmindedness, or it may be sexual, as when Marc Blitzstein turns to Whitman's erotic—and, more specifically, his homoerotic—lyrics to reclaim them as a model and a legacy. As a rule (with the many exceptions duly noted), modernist Whitman settings project a real or desired transition from one collective identity to another, most often passing from a condition of oppression to one of liberation. In some cases, the character of this process is elegiac, as in Hindemith's "Lilacs" requiem, Ralph Vaughan Williams's "Toward the Unknown Region" (a "song" for chorus and orchestra based on Whitman's death-hymn "Darest Thou Now, O Soul"), and John Adams's *Drum-Taps* elegy "The Wound Dresser." In some cases, the process is erotic and ecstatic, as in Delius's lush "Idyll: Once I Pass'd Through a Populous City," or "The Explorers," the vast fresco on extracts from "A Passage to India"—Whitman's most programmatic statement of liberatory modernity—that stands as the finale of Vaughan Williams's "A Sea Symphony." Whitman's characteristic use of elegiac and erotic imagery to depict transformative processes thus seems repeatedly to have "struck a chord" in the modernist imagination, which found in elegy and in eros terms by which to resist the dehumanizing effects of modernity itself.

The essays collected here, arranged more or less in the chronological order of their topics, thus trace the transformation of Whitman's nineteenth-century texts into vehicles for confronting twentieth-century problems—aesthetic, social, and political. They demonstrate how, through the agency of modern music, a small group of Whitman's poems became exemplary means of dealing affirmatively with both the tragic and utopian faces of modernism. Especially prominent in this process are compositions focused on the themes of death in war, the possibilities of sexual love, and the relation of both to the idea of the modern nation. These themes also are reflected in the compact disc that accompanies the text, containing performances (by Joan Heller, soprano, and Thomas Stumpf, piano) of three complete song cycles and the first recording of four Whitman songs composed by Marc Blitzstein in the 1920s but never published.

## Notes

1. The leading exception to this statement proves the rule. German settings of texts by Scottish authors, notably Macpherson, Burns, and Scott, provided a mode of Romantic primitivism internal to, or at least on the margins of, Europe.

2. The text (here and subsequently) is from *Leaves of Grass,* Norton Critical Edition, ed. Sculley Bradley and Harold W. Blodgett (New York: Norton, 1973).

# Walt Whitman
# and Modern Music

# CHAPTER 1

# "Red War Is My Song"
## Whitman, Higginson, and Civil War Music

*John M. Picker*

Although both Thomas Wentworth Higginson and Walt Whitman produced invaluable records of their experiences during the Civil War, their relationship was marked by fierce animosity. Higginson often made clear in his essays and diaries that he could not stomach Whitman's poetry: "I encountered Whitman's 'Leaves of Grass' for the first time on my first voyage in an Azorian barque," Higginson wrote in 1905, "and it inspires to this day a slight sense of nausea, which it might, after all, have inspired equally on land."[1] In a famously damning review, he objected to the poetry's explicit sexual references, which he considered "nauseous passages": "Whitman's love, if such it can be called, is the sheer animal longing of sex for sex—the impulse of the savage, who knocks down the first woman he sees, and drags her to his cave. On the whole, the condition of the savage seems more wholesome, for he simply gratifies his brute lust and writes no resounding lines about it."[2] Higginson "concluded that Whitman lacked the stylistic control of a poet" and that reading his poems was like "bringing home a sackful of pebbles from the beach and asking you to admire the collected heap as a fine sea view."[3]

Most important, the colonel believed that *Drum-Taps,* Whitman's collection of Civil War poetry, was hypocritical and illegitimate. According to Higginson, Whitman "talks of labor as one who has never really labored; his 'Drum-Taps' proceed from one who has never personally responded to the tap of the drum."[4] While all of Whitman's poetry, wrote Higginson, displayed "a certain quality of hollowness," this was "nowhere more felt than in the strains called 'Drum-Taps'."[5] Higginson perceived as "hollow" the fact that Whitman's war poems emanated from one who had served his country as a nurse and not a soldier. "Hospital attendance is a fine thing, no doubt, yet if all men, South and North, had taken the same view of their duty that Whitman held, there would have been no occasion for hospitals on either side"—so Higginson commented in his memoirs, his traditional sense of military duty otherwise blinding him to the sheer sanity of such an outcome.[6] His deprecatory accusations finally manifested themselves in action when, in 1886, upholding the belief that Whitman had indeed avoided the true call to arms during the war, Higginson vehemently opposed an attempt to provide a pension for the poet.[7]

Whitman responded to such personal attacks less publicly but with equal fire. In a conversation with Horace Traubel in 1888, Whitman referred to Higginson "with his strict, straight notions of literary propriety" as one of his "enemies, creatures natively antipathetic."[8] "Oh! damn Higginson!" Whitman reportedly said to Traubel when told that the colonel was visiting Camden in 1890, ". . . that's my compliment to [*him*]!"[9] Whitman considered Higginson's relentless criticism of his poetry a threat to its radical experiments with form, and he rightly saw Higginson himself as an obstacle to his economic security.[10] In retaliation, the poet dismissed Higginson's literary judgments as "thin" and his "literary crowd" as "the good fellows who had an awful belief in respectability—an awful hunger to be gentlemen." He reserved particular bile for the colonel, designating him a "lady's man" who "amounts to nothing," who "has always been mere sugar and water. He lacks all else."[11]

Despite Higginson's and Whitman's mutual disgust, however, the authors' Civil War writings reveal a significant resemblance. Both *Drum-Taps* (1865) and *Army Life in a Black Regiment* (1870) invoke music as essential to the uniting of communities amid a war of national dissolution. In a wider sense, *Drum-Taps* and *Army Life* successfully bridge the gap between written and aural modes of representation. Yet this general resemblance ultimately gives way to the kind of deeper opposition one would expect between the two authors, for Whitman and Higginson treat a similar theme using contrary techniques. Each man's work foregrounds a different kind of interaction between Civil War texts and wartime music. Whereas Whitman constructs the poems of *Drum-Taps* as a musical expression of the war, Higginson in his *Army Life* transforms Civil War music into written text.

## The Music of *Drum-Taps*

The title *Drum-Taps* indicates that Whitman wants to draw attention to the musical structure of his collection and to the ways in which martial music can represent the contrary states of war. Just as the words "drum-taps" suggest both inspiring drumbeats and the somber bugle call of "taps," so the poems follow a particular movement from an opening "reveille tattoo" to the solemn music of mourning.[12] Although Michael Moon characterizes this movement between the poems of "hectic anticipation" and the later elegies and memorials as one between "discordant rhetorics," such a tonal division in fact achieves a certain unity when considered from a musical perspective.[13] In his article on the psychology of Civil War music, James Stone writes that military music serves its audience in two ways: either as a "lubricant," to rouse soldiers to march and fight, or as a "sedative," to occupy soldiers' less active moments and relieve them from thoughts of battle.[14] This division has particular significance for Whitman, because he captures martial music's abilities both to rouse and to soothe, to energize and to calm, in the title of his text as well as individual poems throughout *Drum-Taps.*

It is not surprising that Whitman assumes the role of singer in the volume: "I myself as connector, as chansonnier of a great future," he exclaims in "The Centenarian's Story" (96), and in "City of Ships" he tells us, "in peace I chanted peace, but now the drum of war is mine, / War, red war is my song" (16–17).[15] Throughout much of *Leaves of Grass,* of course, Whitman characterizes himself as a singer and his poems as songs, but this tactic has greater significance within *Drum-Taps,* for by using it here, Whitman traces for his project a lineage extending back to Virgil, who famously begins his *Aeneid,* "Of arms and a man I sing." Furthermore, it is important to consider that the songs that became popular during the Civil War often had powerful political significance. The Army of the Potomac, for instance, went so far as to ban "When This Cruel War Is Over" on the grounds that it caused desertion, and "the 'Marseillaise' was so identified with the Confederacy that when it was sung by a foreign troupe in New York the performers were thrown into jail as suspected secessionists."[16] Popular songs could serve as expressions of protest and pride in the Civil War much as they would a century later during the Vietnam War. Identifying himself as a wartime singer, then, Whitman superimposes the epic tradition of the past on the potentially dangerous popular role of the present. What is more, through his use of martial music, as I will show, Whitman moves beyond the role of singer to represent military-instrument performances and the sounds of battle themselves.

The opening poems of *Drum-Taps* feature rousing music suggestive of Whitman's eagerness for war. Even as he maintains his role as wartime bard, however, Whitman enters into another guise: "I have charged myself, heeded or unheeded, to compose a march for these States," he later claims ("Not The Pilot," 4), and he indeed serves through much of *Drum-Taps* as a march composer who commands "the drum of war." "First O Songs for a Prelude," the poem that begins the collection, shows how Whitman's Manhattan anticipates war in specifically musical terms, moving from the lull of opera to the pulse of the march:

> *How your soft opera-music changed, and the drum and fife were heard in*
> *    their stead,*
> *How you led to the war, (that shall serve for our prelude, songs of soldiers)*
> *How Manhattan drum-taps led.* (8–10)

Manhattan's rhythmic sounds are echoed in words that make extensive use of tense vowels and explosive stops: "Lightly strike on stretch'd tympanum pride and joy in my city," Whitman begins the poem (2). Whitman's manipulation of percussive sound allows this opening phrase to strike like drum-taps on eardrums.[17] The electric jolt of the war hits the city like a drumbeat:

> ... *unawares the lady of this teeming and turbulent city, ... suddenly,*
> *At dead of night at news from the south,*
> *Incens'd struck with clinch'd hand the pavement.* (12–16)

What is more, the transformation of the name of his home into percussive taps—"Mannahatta a-march—and it's O to sing it well!"—reveals martial music altering Whitman's own language (48). Whitman indicates that although the war comes unexpectedly and disrupts city life, it gives Manhattan a new tempo and the poet himself a new role: the singer as drumbeater, the "hectic" keeper of march-time.[18]

Whitman goes on to suggest that the movement from peace to war necessitates an equally radical shift in music and rhythm. This change involves the surrendering of speech to the sounds of war. In "First O Songs," Whitman indicates that the new bustle of "arming" leaves no room for the spoken word:

> *The tearful parting, the mother kisses her son, the son kisses his mother,*
> *(Loth is the mother to part, yet not a word does she speak to detain him,)*
> *The tumultuous escort, the ranks of policemen preceding, clearing the*
>     *way,*
> *The unpent enthusiasm, the wild cheers of the crowd for their favorites,*
> *The artillery, the silent cannons bright as gold, drawn along, rumble lightly*
>     *over the stones,*
> *(Silent cannons, soon to cease your silence,*
> *Soon unlimber'd to begin the red business;)*
> *All the mutter of preparation, all the determin'd arming ...* (36–43)

Manhattan's noisy war music, its "tumultuous escort," "wild cheers," and its cannons' rolling "rumble," relegate to mere parentheses the desires of the mother who holds back her words to her son. Whitman again shows the powerlessness of speech in "Beat! Beat! Drums!" when he urges readers to "Mind not the old man beseeching the young man, / Let not the child's voice be heard, nor the mother's entreaties" (18–19). Indeed, in the early poems of *Drum-Taps*, the voices of individuals no longer have an audience in a society dominated by the music of war. The human voice is displaced by the "rumble" of "preparation" and the song of the cannon: "[I] heard your determin'd voice launch'd forth again and again, / Year that suddenly sang by the mouths of the round-lipp'd cannon" ("Eighteen Sixty-One," 14–15). The "determin'd voice" of these poems does not murmur words so much as generate rhythm, nor does it chant peace so much as strike the beat of war. Whitman emphasizes the silencing of conversation and speech in these poems—indeed, they themselves mimic such silence in their percussive musicality—to suggest that rational dialogue has no place alongside "the mutter of preparation," the relentless rumbling forth of a seemingly inevitable military conflict.

In "Beat! Beat! Drums!" Whitman most insistently conveys the raw, explosive playing of martial drums and brass. The repetition of the heavily syncopated line "Beat! beat! drums!—blow! bugles! blow!" produces a rhythm of rising urgency over the poem's three stanzas (1, 8, 15). Whitman exhorts the music of bugles and drums to move swiftly, like a brush fire through a small town: "through the windows—through doors—burst like a ruthless force" (2). The concentrated, surging sonic force overpowers the church, school, home, and farm, tearing apart civilization in its path.[19] Yet Whitman urges it on, begging it literally to wake the dead:

> *Make no parley—stop for no expostulation, . . .*
> *Make even the trestles to shake the dead where they lie awaiting their*
>    *hearses,*
> *So strong you thump O terrible drums—so loud you bugles blow.*
>    (16, 20–21)

The poem's terrible enthusiasm for the destructive power of music distinguishes it as perhaps the most alarming representative in *Drum-Taps* of "the patriotic strains that Whitman sings with only the most troubled voice."[20] Ironically, it is precisely the poem's troubling dynamism that has given it a musical life quite independent of its critical status; Michael Hovland lists eleven published settings of "Beat! Beat! Drums!," including Ralph Vaughan Williams's celebrated treatment in *Dona Nobis Pacem* (1936) as well as those by Howard Hanson (1935) and Kurt Weill (1942).[21] Though problematic to a contemporary reader or listener, Whitman's enthusiasm mirrors the prevailing mood at the beginning of the war, when, as Kenneth Olson writes, "bands fanned the flames of patriotism and followed the recruit into service. Music resonated from everywhere and all were anxious to go."[22] The opening poems of *Drum-Taps* reflect this contagious excitement. In them, Whitman conspires with the initial music of war, drumming and blaring to impassion followers and recruits.

By the midpoint of the volume, however, Whitman's shift in attitude toward the war is marked by a corresponding shift in musical tone and role. In the transitional sequence from "Cavalry Crossing a Ford" to "By the Bivouac's Fitful Flame," the visual experience of "the brown-faced men, each group, each person a picture," takes precedence over "the musical clank" of soldiers on the march ("Cavalry," 2, 4). These pictorial poems privilege sight over sound, as if to suggest that acts of witnessing change the poet's perception of the war's musicality. Indeed, "the silence" of the army camp at night brings Whitman a disquieting moment of self-consciousness: "The shrubs and trees, (as I lift my eyes they seem to be stealthily watching me)" ("By the Bivouac's Fitful Flame," 4, 6). The snapshots of death in "A

March in the Ranks Hard-Prest" and "A Sight in the Camp in the Daybreak Gray and Dim" provide graphic images of the war's effects, in "the crowd of the bloody forms" awaiting surgery and the "three forms . . . on stretchers lying" ("A March," 16; "A Sight," 4). In light of these scenes, the ensuing musical charge of "Not the Pilot" ("I have charged myself . . . to compose a march for these States") comes to seem double-edged, as both Whitman's reminder to himself of his initial enthusiasm and his anxious realization of weighty responsibility (4). "Year that Trembl'd and Reel'd beneath Me" further reveals the poet's self-doubt as his excitement disintegrates under the weight of the war's casualties: "Must I change my triumphant songs? said I to myself, / Must I indeed learn to chant the cold dirges of the baffled? / And sullen hymns of defeat?" (4–6).

Immediately following this poem, near the beginning of "The Wound-Dresser," Whitman answers his own questions in the affirmative:

> *(Arous'd and angry, I'd thought to beat the alarum, and urge relentless war,*
> *But soon my fingers fail'd me, my face droop'd and I resign'd myself,*
> *To sit by the wounded and soothe them, or silently watch the dead;).* (4–6)

As they did with the mother's entreaties in "First O Songs," the parentheses suggest that one voice is muted to allow another to be heard: but while the mother had earlier stifled her protest against her son marching off to battle, the poet now allows his "angry" war chant to be subordinated to his nursing voice. The centerpiece of *Drum-Taps,* "The Wound-Dresser" suggests a significant shift in Whitman's role through its trope of the hand:

> *From the stump of the arm, the amputated hand,*
> *I undo the clotted lint, remove the slough, wash off the matter and blood,*
> *. . . These and more I dress with impassive hand . . .*
> *The hurt and wounded I pacify with soothing hand.* (44–45, 58, 61)

The poet's clinical, "impassive," "soothing" hand now holds dominion over the soldier's failed "stump" and the severed hand that fired the rifle or tapped the drum.[23] Similarly and with solemnity, Whitman's wartime role changes in the poem, from rallying drummer-boy to restrained nurse.

The poet's duties as nurse closely parallel the tasks that Civil War bandsmen performed as their regiments battled. Musicians on both sides were trained to transport and care for the wounded, were taught basic first aid skills, and "were ex officio members of the hospital detail."[24] Bandsmen frequently had to abandon their instruments to bear stretchers to hospitals and assist surgeons with amputations. At the Battle of the Wilderness, the members of Stewart's Band of the Fourth Brigade, Second Division, Sixth Army corps, served as surgeon's assistants, helping to dress wounds and nurse patients; drummer-boys of the Eighth Maine were ordered to work with surgeons performing amputations in the field hospital; and the 148th Pennsylvania Infantry Company D band devised an elaborate system for nursing the wounded and was also responsible for burying amputated limbs.[25] "I often thought that no one could place his finger on any part of the human body, but what I could say, 'I saw a man wounded there'," said J. B. Holloway, drummer in Co. D, of his nursing duties. His comment could readily have come from the vigilant Whitman of "The Wound-Dresser" who tends to "a wound in the side . . . / . . . the perforated shoulder, the foot with the bullet-wound, / . . . The fractur'd thigh, the knee, the wound in the abdomen" (50, 53, 57).[26] As the bandsmen left their instruments behind, so Whitman abandons his enthusiastic drumbeating to confront the disastrous toll in wartime casualties. The loss of inspiring music is perhaps best expressed in a comment made by the band director Frank Flinn at the siege of Port Hudson: "The ambulance corps is made up largely of the musicians; but music, we never hear it now, not even the drum and fife. It is too stern a time for that."[27]

Indeed, when not tending to the wounded, the bandsmen were often called on to perform at military burials: "Civil War musicians were kept very busy both in camp and at the front, playing dirges at the funerals of their comrades who fell victim to disease or enemy bullets."[28] Similarly, in "Dirge for Two Veterans," Whitman turns away from the inspiring sounds of the earlier poems, and of the war itself, to a slow death march. Instruments that previously sounded the call to battle now somberly accompany a father and son to their double grave.[29] The poem's division into short stanzas conveys its dirge-like rhythm:

> *I see a sad procession,*
> *And I hear the sound of coming full-key'd bugles,*
> *All the channels of the city streets they're flooding,*
>     *As with voices and with tears.*
>
>     *I hear the great drums pounding,*
> *And the small drums steady whirring,*
> *And every blow of the great convulsive drums,*
>     *Strikes me through and through.* (9–16)

The quatrain pattern of two longer lines flanked by single shorter lines suggests the central placement of the two coffins in the procession, and more specifically, the formal, deliberate steps of the march. As "nearer blow the bugles, / And the drums strike more convulsive," the musical dirge overcomes the poet: "And the strong dead-march enwraps me" (21–22, 24). The "Dirge" represents Whitman's attempt to mingle poetry with the funereal music that has so wholly absorbed him: "What I have I also give you," he remarks (32). Whitman adds himself to the scene as another instrument playing elegiacally, as a musician offering his own contribution to the dirge, with a difference but not apart: "And the bugles and the drums give you music, / And my heart, O my soldiers, my veterans, / My heart gives you love" (34–36). The more potent bond in "Dirge for Two Veterans" is shared not, as one might assume, by the father and son who are jointly buried, but, as the title more subtly suggests, by the two performers of the dirge, Whitman and the bandsmen-soldiers. They not only give the scene its gravity but create its lasting impressions, both immediately, on the poet himself, and enduringly, on his readers.

Surely one gauge of Whitman's successful attempt to invest "Dirge for Two Veterans" with, in the words of one critic, "the idea of music"—as opposed to the literal correlation between musical and literary form—is the poem's unique position in the history of Whitman settings.[30] In 1880 the "Dirge" became the first Whitman poem set to music in the United States, as a recitation with piano accompaniment by Frederick Louis Ritter. Although formally quite dated, this "antique curiosity" nevertheless demonstrates that even during Whitman's lifetime the poem possessed a certain ready appeal to composers, a point corroborated by the fact that the "Dirge" rivals "Beat! Beat! Drums!" for the largest number of settings for any *Drum-Taps* poem.[31] A sense of impending conflict permeates the well-known Vaughan Williams setting (written 1911, though it would appear later in *Dona Nobis Pacem*) as well as that of Gustav Holst (1914), written immediately before *The Planets*. Holst's piece is remarkable both for its tonal restraint and its trumpet fanfares prescient of "Mars the Bringer of War."[32] As a later example, and in a quite different vein, Weill's 1942 setting undercuts the sobriety of the lyrics with characteristic cabaret-inflected flourishes, dissentient counterparts to the poet's mournful pathos.[33]

Whitman passes from the solemn sounds of the "Dirge" to those of "The Artilleryman's Vision," where the only music heard is the chaotic noise on a nightmarish battlefield.[34] In the veteran's apocalyptic vision, random shell fire replaces the unified march and dirge:

> *The skirmishers begin, they crawl cautiously ahead, I hear the irregular snap! snap!*
> *I hear the sounds of the different missiles, the short* t-h-t! t-h-t! *of the rifle-balls,*
> *I see the shells exploding leaving small white clouds, I hear the great shells shrieking as they pass,*
> *The grape like the hum and whirr of wind through the trees* . . . . (6–9)

Amid "the crashing and smoking," "the cry of a regiment," and "eager calls and orders of officers," one cannot hear drums, fifes, or bands, but merely rounds of ammunition: "the patter of small arms, the warning *ss-t* of the rifles" (11, 14, 18, 24). Whitman's beloved martial music, the drum-tap of the band itself, dissolves underneath "the chaos louder than ever . . . / And ever the sound of the cannon far or near" (18, 20). The poem's final line is a travesty of a line from "The Star Spangled Banner," the song that more than any other symbolizes the Union: "And bombs bursting in air, and at night the varicolor'd rockets."[35] Ironically, "the rockets' red glare" and "the bombs bursting in air" that once heralded American nationalism now announce civil discord. In "The Artilleryman's Vision," Whitman implies that the Civil War breaks both melody and the unity of the band, just as it does the nation, into fragments.

The musical representations in the concluding poems of *Drum-Taps* recall in sobering ways those in the opening "First O Songs" and "Beat! Beat! Drums!" The confrontational tone of "To a Certain Civilian" reasserts Whitman's love of the drum and march, but such a statement now comes couched in parentheses and intrinsically linked to a wartime burial scene:

> *(I have been born of the same as the war was born,*
> *The drum-corps' rattle is ever to me sweet music, I love well the martial*
> *    dirge,*
> *With slow wail and convulsive throb leading the officer's funeral). (5–7)*

Born from the same source as the war, Whitman emphatically and musically speaks for its inhumanity and incomprehensibility, as both it and his poetic cycle end: "For I lull nobody, and you will never understand me" (10). His book closes as the now solemn "Spirit" that brought war and inspired him departs with hollow echoes of its earlier eagerness for battle:

> *Spirit of many a solemn day and many a savage scene—electric spirit,*
> *That with muttering voice through the war now closed, like a tireless*
> *    phantom flitted,*
> *Rousing the land with breath of flame, while you beat and beat the drum.*
> ("Spirit Whose Work Is Done," 4–6)

But that drum, once energetically sounded by the spirit-possessed poet, has now lost its substance and persists only in jarring echoes: "the sound of the drum, hollow and harsh to the last, reverberates round me" (7). The beats that replace these are not military but corporeal, pulses of postwar frustration and anger, in a strikingly violent passage:

> *Leave me your pulses of rage—bequeath them to me—fill me with currents*
> *    convulsive,*
> *Let them scorch and blister out of my chants when you are gone,*
> *Let them identify you to the future in these songs. (16–18)*

In this way, *Drum-Taps* moves from its rousing opening call to a mournful march and beyond, to the dissonance of the battlefield and the pulse of the poet himself. Whitman uses the medium of his text to express the war, with its range of moods from glorious to chaotic, as a musical phenomenon, with his own role divided between performer and audience. As one of the poet's recent biographers, David Reynolds, puts it, Whitman saw "music as a prime agent for unity and uplift in a nation [tending toward] fragmentation and political corruption," an explanation that goes some way toward justifying the central role music plays in *Drum-Taps*.[36] The volume's invocations of martial strains, its persistent echoes of wartime drums and brass, however, suggest not only Whitman's belief in the healing qualities of music, but more specifically his affinity with instrumental performance. "The Wound-Dresser"—the poem that fortifies the connection between the poet and the army musicians in their mutual hospital work—goes far toward spelling out the subtext of Whitman's fascination with the sound of the military band. It also is helpful to consider Stone's claim that "music during wartime gives an air of normality to what is essentially an abnormal social condition."[37] The musicality of *Drum-Taps* makes more approachable and further aestheticizes images that would other-wise be overly painful to face, in ways that resonate for both nineteenth- and twentieth-century readers all too familiar with war and its shadows. Giving his Civil War poetry a musical dimension, then, Whitman endows *Drum-Taps* with auditory immediacy and permanence.

## Music in *Army Life*

Like *Drum-Taps,* Thomas Wentworth Higginson's *Army Life in a Black Regi-ment* represents a unique, enduring record of the Civil War. Published in 1869, the book is both a detailed account of Higginson's military activities during the conflict and a pivotal document in the history of African American music. Higginson's instinctive curiosity and eye for detail enable him to record what many white Northerners in his day knew of only vaguely: the dramatic and mysterious spiritual life of the African American soldiers in his regiment. This life is captured most thoroughly in the chapter entitled "Negro Spirituals," which, along with incidents recounted throughout the book, pro-vides vital information about the musical atmosphere in camp. In transcribing the words of his soldiers' music, however, Higginson acts in characteristic opposition to the Whitman of *Drum-Taps*. Whereas the poet produces writ-ings notable for their striking musicality, the colonel transforms the sounds he hears into written language, constructing a printed text to represent an audi-tory phenomenon that seems to him enchanting but undisciplined, and at least partially inscrutable.

The text's musicological significance lies in its publication history. Al-though included in the first edition of *Army Life,* "Negro Spirituals" appeared originally as an article in June 1867 (the text is identical in both versions).[38] Higginson's work represented a watershed in literature, music, and sociology, as the first substantial published collection of African American "slave spiri-tuals." Its influence on the pioneering book-length anthology of this music,

*Slave Songs of the United States* (published five months later), can be gathered from this passage from the editors' introduction:

> To Col. T. W. Higginson, above all others, they [the editors] are indebted for friendly encouragement and for direct and indirect contributions to their original stock of songs. From first to last he has manifested the kindest interest in their undertakings. . . . It is but little to say that without his cooperation this *Lyra Africana* would have lacked greatly of its present completeness and worth.[39]

As the editors themselves admit, had Higginson not provided them interest and assistance, the monumental *Slave Songs* would have been a far less thorough work. Furthermore, as Dena Epstein notes, the prospectus for *Slave Songs* even included a section, planned but later abandoned, of "Words Without Music" taken primarily from Higginson's article. In a period when, as Higginson biographer Howard Meyer indicates, "no one knew what folk music was," the colonel clearly played a pivotal role, undertaking a conflicted challenge to transcribe the spirituals.[40]

For this was at once an aesthetically generous and a reductive task, one underscored by what Eric Lott, discussing blackface minstrelsy, describes as the "mixed economies of celebration and exploitation."[41] That is to say, while white Northerners such as Higginson clearly felt attracted to the songs as sublime examples of religious feeling, their need to represent the songs in text could and often did result in distortions and oversimplifications. Recent criticism of *Slave Songs* and other early documents relating to the spirituals expands this claim into a more potent allegation:

> Without reducing reform efforts to a callous solipsism, we can recognize the white claim to give voice to the slave as an act of ventriloquism, whose motivations were necessarily complicated and ambivalent. By embracing the ideals of romantic perfectibility associated with folklore and the spirituals, these reformers described qualities felt to be missing in themselves, to which they could only gesture in a series of rather desperate, imitative acts.[42]

As an articulation of the complex motives of writers such as Higginson, this conclusion seems in essence accurate. Writing down African American song indeed becomes a principal means for whites to move toward self-awareness, to discover in the voice of the other "the alter-ego of the white self," or to achieve "white self-completion."[43] Criticism such as this, however, often downplays the fact that the project of recording spirituals takes on greater significance precisely against the backdrop of the Civil War, when the issue of identity in crisis becomes not only personal or racial, but also national. If

Higginson uses transcription to achieve some degree of psychological and cultural stability in part to resolve his own questions of identity, he also, more profoundly, uses that same transcription to compensate for the fragmentation of identity experienced by his regionally and racially divided nation.

In recording his first encounter with the soldiers' "shout," the religious call-and-response ritual that takes its name from the Wolof word *saut,* meaning "to dance before the tabernacle," Higginson searches for words to describe accurately what he sees.[44] His entry for 3 December 1862 reads: "This hut is now crammed with men, singing at the top of their voices, in one of their quaint, monotonous, endless, negro-Methodist chants, with obscure syllables recurring constantly, and slight variations interwoven, all accompanied with a regular drumming of the feet and clapping of the hands, like castanets."[45] What makes this passage so curious is that it allows readers to watch Higginson as he struggles to classify something he cannot comprehend. The "shout" seems to him a locus of ambiguity that he must try to pin down. It is at once "quaint" and "regular," but also "endless" and "obscure." Such a description shows Higginson gesturing toward accurate preservation in print, yet not quite achieving it.[46] Confronted with an undocumented and unanalyzed experience, Higginson reveals his frustrated desire to clarify the "shout," to read (and write) it as he would a text.

In the "Negro Spirituals" chapter, Higginson turns this desire on the songs themselves, even as he draws attention to the problems that result from considering the spirituals as texts. He claims in the chapter's opening passage to be inspired by those like Walter Scott who transcribed Scottish ballads "from the lips of aged crones," and he delights in his access to "a kindred world of unwritten songs" (187). His word choice is particularly eye-opening here. Since many of the spirituals he hears have, of course, already circulated and developed over decades, Higginson means "unwritten" in its strictest sense. He implies that a song is "unwritten" if it is not physically represented on paper. In a later instance, after transcribing a children's "shouting" performance of "Hold Your Light," a spiritual that makes reference to Satan, he includes a metaphorical postscript in which he likens the performers to writing instruments: "It seems pathetic that these little innocents (straight and black as so many short lead pencils) should thus early appreciate the peripatetic habits of the Evil One."[47] The singing children here are likened to the means of inscription, in a parallel that resonates with Higginson's persistent attempts throughout the chapter to pencil in the "unwritten songs." For Higginson, writing a work down appears to be the most crucial part of the process of musical composition, and, as the "Negro Spirituals" chapter shows, it is this aspect in which he excels and moreover, for which he is necessary—the African American children may be *like* pencils, but apparently they cannot wield them.

Higginson emphasizes a classifying approach throughout the chapter by metaphorically linking the spirituals to horticultural specimens. "I could now gather on their own soil these strange plants, which I had before seen in museums alone," he tells readers (187). Like a scientist trying to snare a rare species, he cautiously seeks out his target and closes in. He recounts how he "silently approached some glimmering fire. . . . Writing down in the darkness, as best I could,—perhaps with my hand in the safe covert of my pocket,—the words of the song, I have afterwards carried it to my tent, like some captured bird or insect, and then, after examination, put it by" (188). Discussing the relationship between exotic and erotic impulses in *Army Life,* Christopher Looby observes that this memoir "is a text full of flowers, a textual bouquet."[48] Indeed, the organic musical experience of a spiritual also becomes for Higginson a "specimen" that must be pinned down and analyzed (188). While Whitman's war poetry might assume musical force as in "Beat! Beat! Drums!" and leap off the page, overcoming everything in its path, Higginson's actions ensnare the music he hears such that he quite literally captures the spirituals in words.

This process represents not just a quest for song texts but a means for Higginson to express his own anxieties about the limits of identity. In a revealing moment, he apologizes for inconsistencies in his dialect spellings of the lyrics: "It is because I could get no nearer," he explains (188). This phrase resonates with an important secondary meaning. Not only can Higginson get no nearer to spelling out a dialect, but he also can get no nearer, in the everyday reality of the camp, to the inner lives of his troops. His status as outsider recurs throughout *Army Life.* At one point, he attempts to enter his own camp and a border guard prevents him. "I could not pass in," he remarks, suggesting his inability to pass *through* the gate, as well as to pass *for* an insider (68). The same unconscious anxiety returns in Higginson's revelation that he "could get no nearer." As his comment here suggests, recording the spirituals demonstrates not only the limitations of Higginson's abilities with written language but also the extent to which he will go to try to "pass in." Of slavery, Ronald Radano writes that "white Northerners merely observed it, remaining conspicuously outside the circle." For Higginson, excluded in complex ways from the most intimate circle of his own regiment, transcribing spirituals partly becomes an ardent attempt to write his way back in.[49]

One of his principal concerns in the chapter is how to create stable texts for a medium that is inherently fluid and combinative. He frequently observes the unfixed characteristics of the spirituals. For instance, he writes that "one of their best choruses, without any fixed words, was 'De bell done ringing'"; that the spiritual "Ride in, Kind Savior" is a "conglomerate" of Northern and Southern lyrics; that "In the Morning" contains "one of those odd transformations of proper names"; and finally, he lists "three wholly distinct versions" of "The Ship of Zion" (191, 203–204). Higginson is thus particularly interested in the challenge of constructing texts from songs that by definition constantly undergo transformations, of codifying what is naturally variable. He seeks, in Foucauldian terms, "to discipline and constrain" the songs, to fix them in a particular language and context, in essence to impose the settled qualities of print on transformative specimens of orality.[50]

As part of his desire to clarify what seems ambiguous in the spirituals, Higginson attempts rudimentary textual analyses in which he tries to decipher lyrics or explain the origins of words. But his analyses are often tinged with doubt. "I fancied that the original reading might have been 'soul' instead of 'soldier,'—with some other syllable inserted to fill out the metre," he comments about the words to "Hail Mary"; and of "Bound To Go" he writes, "Sometimes it was 'tink 'em' (think them) 'fare ye well.' The ye was so detached that I thought at first it was 'very' or 'vary well'" (191, 189). Indeed, Higginson twice voices his frustration at not clarifying the lyrics enough, using the same phrase in both instances: "I could get no explanation of the 'mighty Myo'," he admits after "My Army Cross Over," and concerning "One More River," he writes, "I could get no explanation of this last riddle" (191, 194). Higginson's desire to organize and discipline the spirituals works at cross-purposes with his inability to resolve their ambiguities, creating a predominant source of anxiety within the text.

This anxiety becomes most evident toward the end of the chapter, when the colonel inserts a curious digression. He notes that he has heard two songs that do not fall into the genre of the spiritual. One of these consists of the "endless repetition . . . of the mysterious line,—'Rain fall and wet Becky Lawton'." Here he comments: "But who Becky Lawton was, and why she should or should not be wet, and whether the dryness was a reward or penalty, none could say. I got the impression that, in either case, the event was posthumous, and that there was some tradition of grass not growing over the grave of a sinner; but even this was vague, and all else vaguer" (211). In this passage, Higginson ultimately subverts his own attempts at analysis. After suggesting what seems like an intriguing interpretation of the line, he concludes ambivalently, "but even this was vague, and all else vaguer." Using phrases such as "none could say" and "all else vaguer" to emphasize the "mysterious" elements surrounding the transcription of what is after all a fragmentary text, Higginson in effect celebrates the troops' exclusionary circle at its widest.

At the same time, Higginson also is aware of the severe limitations of his transcription process. In one sense, it enables him to bring to a large audience lyrics that he finds sincerely moving, including "I Know Moon Rise," which he calls, in horticultural fashion, a "flower of poetry" (199). Yet his close attention to the texts of the songs means that he relegates the music to the sidelines, a fact that he addresses with a resigned awareness of the inadequacies of language.[51] About "Go in the Wilderness," he writes, "There was a kind of spring and *lilt* to it, quite indescribable by words"; and for the third version of

"The Ship of Zion," he tells us, "This abbreviated chorus is given with un-speakable unction" (202, 206). The sonic skill that Whitman displays in *Drum-Taps* seems less important to Higginson, whose primary ability here lies in relaying not so much sounds as text.

A scene early in *Army Life* specifically addresses this issue. Higginson relates an incident after presenting the lyrics to the spiritual "Can't Stay Be-hind": "I have heard this very song dimly droning on near midnight, and, trac-ing it into the recesses of a cook-house, have found an old fellow coiled away among the pots and provisions, chanting away with his 'Can't stay behind, sinner,' till I made him leave his song behind" (45). With a seemingly in-significant anecdote, Higginson provides a subtle commentary on his own scholarly project. In the most immediate sense, he orders the man to "leave his song behind" so as to keep the camp quiet in the middle of the night. But the old man also, consciously or not, "leave[s] his song behind" with Higgin-son himself, to be transcribed and eventually published. Finally, the colonel will leave the song behind as well, within his memoir and with his readers. The reception of the spiritual in this case becomes a form not of sharing be-tween colleagues but of surrender from subordinate to commander. The ac-quisition of the lyrics reinforces the colonel's regimental authority even as it demonstrates his forceful encroachment on the musical and spiritual culture that excludes him.

Higginson's desire for order and discipline not only motivates him to copy down the spirituals. It also influences his attitude toward the rest of the camp's musical life, specifically, toward the drummer boys. In his description of the "route step," he comments on the unruliness of the drummers: "Grave little boys, blacker than ink, shook hands with our laughing and utterly un-manageable drummers" (135). Ironically, throughout *Army Life,* the very fig-ures who are responsible for giving music its rhythm and order behave in the most disorderly way. In "The Baby of the Regiment," Higginson makes clear his intolerance of their behavior: "Her especial favorites were the drummer-boys, who were not my favorites by any means, for they were a roguish set of scamps, and gave me more trouble than all the grown men in the regiment" (179). As he clarifies and makes presentable the spirituals, so he would like to, but frustratingly cannot, refine the drummer-boys' roles. Higginson pre-sents the drummers as occupying a wild, unconquerable terrain of uncertain rhythm, beyond the boundaries of verbal communication and aloof from the linguistic containment of transcription.

When music historians observe that the initial scholarly interest in African American spirituals, led by Higginson and his colleagues, coincided with the Civil War, they suggest that the spirituals received this attention both because Northern whites came into contact with large numbers of former slaves for the first time during this period, and because nineteenth-century European nationalism exerted its influence on white Americans who were searching for a uniquely American music.[52] An equally valid explanation, however, can be found in the psychological significance of the spiritual itself. Eileen Southern identifies five significant recurring themes of the spiritual songs: faith, optimism, patience, weariness, and fighting.[53] While all of these themes have particular relevance to slavery, they also are concepts that readily apply to those in a nation plagued by war, who, though worn down by rising death tolls, poverty, and blockades, nonetheless aspire toward and await a better future. Spirituals enabled African American communities to endure enslavement and yet survive; since the songs provided such strength and reassurance for African Americans, it is no wonder that white Americans also were attracted to them during a time of national crisis.

Perhaps more than any other type of folk music, African American spirituals are capable of uniting groups against the challenges of instability and discord. One critic writes about the songs, "They are a premier corpus of documents commenting on the nature of chaos and they constitute the first major antidote for avoiding, and countering, chaos."[54] These characteristics would surely resonate with Americans witnessing the chaotic atmosphere of civil war. In particular, these qualities help considerably to explain Higginson's attraction to the songs. Facing the unprecedented disarray and devastation of the conflict at hand, yet so firmly believing in discipline, restraint, and regimen, Higginson finds a haven in the strength and stability of the spirituals. The songs represent a psychological stronghold against the national disintegration occurring all around him. Within them persists the virtue of sublime endurance that he, and the Union, so much desire.

## Music and Memory

The Civil War writings *Drum-Taps* and *Army Life* contain a prominent and perpetually relevant intermingling of music and text. In his excellent book on representation and the Civil War, Timothy Sweet suggests that the war put the nation's "adhesive function" into question, and that Whitman "invokes adhesiveness, in the form of the love of comrades, as the only healing power that might hold together . . . his poetics and the Union."[55] Although Sweet makes a valid claim, I would add to his argument that both Higginson *and* Whitman imply adhesiveness in the ways that they bring war music and war writing together. They not only indicate that rhythm and melody are ubiquitous during the conflict. More important, both authors suggest that the nation must give serious attention to its music in the effort to recuperate from, and come to terms with, its experience of civil discord.

Whitman invested his war volume with powerful forms of martial music. The poems of *Drum-Taps,* with their movement from march to dirge and their thematization of the band and its music as emblems of Whitman's own war experience, show the development of a kindred relationship between the poet and the band, a relationship that continued to grow after the war ended. Whitman first heard the Marine Corps Band in the capital as early as 1865, and for approximately six years beginning in 1866 he reviewed their concerts for the Washington *Sunday Herald,* an activity in which he delighted. At one point he even went so far as to publish a plea for federal funds to establish a "President's Band."[56] Toward the end of his life, Whitman looked back fondly on these experiences, confirming the lasting effect that such performances had on him. His interest in bandsmen and their music transformed his war poetry even as it persisted beyond the confines of the war.

Whitman's attempt to express the war musically, moreover, did not end with the *Drum-Taps* poetry itself. The collection has long been a favorite source for composers, who have published an estimated seventy or more settings of its poems, beginning with Ritter and his 1880 "Dirge" and extending up to the present day.[57] In what is certainly one the most significant of the settings, John Adams emphasizes the contemporary relevance of "The Wound-Dresser" in his 1989 piece of the same title. Incorporating "sensitive writing for the strings, spacious harmonies, and a warm lyricism," Adams uses the 1865 poem to make an extended, moving commentary on the AIDS crisis of the present day.[58] The poem, says Adams, "is a statement about human compassion that is acted out on a daily basis, quietly and unobtrusively and unselfishly and unfailingly."[59] As a counterpart to *The Wound Dresser,* Thomas Hampson's remarkable recording *To The Soul* testifies to the breadth of Whitman's influence and to "the musicality of the poetry itself," particularly of *Drum-Taps,* which provides settings for four of the songs in the selection: Weill's "Dirge," Charles Naginski's and Ned Rorem's equally impressive versions of "Look Down Fair Moon," and Henry Thacker Burleigh's "Ethiopia Saluting the Colors."[60] Adams's and Hampson's works, though different in kind and degree, demonstrate how Whitman's Civil War volume continues to have musical significance and cultural resonance for contemporary artists and audiences.

Higginson's *Army Life* remains musically relevant as well, but primarily in an archival rather than an aural sense. The editors of the monumental *Norton Anthology of African American Literature* consider Higginson "one of the first to pay respectful attention to the spirituals" and reprint a number of the song texts he transcribed. Attesting to the historical significance of Higginson's work, Southern includes all of "Negro Spirituals" and selections from the "Camp Diary" in her *Readings in Black American Music.* Sherrill Martin claims that Higginson "wrote one of the most valuable sourcebooks about the musical activities of black soldiers during the war," and in the introduction to his comprehensive spiritual collection *Lyrics of the Afro-American Spiritual,* Erskine Peters writes: "The first substantial group of Afro-American spiritual lyrics was published in June of 1867 in the *Atlantic Monthly* by Thomas Wentworth Higginson. . . . He sought in his article to introduce lyrics (without music) by discussing their musical and poetic nature, their themes, origin, performance context, frequency, and utility."[61] As Higginson desired to solidify the fluid songs in printed texts, so his work is remembered and honored as a formative text in anthologies and criticism of African American spirituals. And at the present juncture, as questions about social constructions of racial identities have become paramount, scholars have begun to consider Higginson's work less a transparent lens through which to discover the songs, and more a subjective performance, one motivated by pressures of a particular time, place, and culture.

Although Whitman and Higginson diverge in their musical and textual goals, then, they share the sense that music has a profound significance both for themselves and for the war. Two passages, one from Higginson's letters, the other from Whitman's memoranda, at once show their musical affinities and their stylistic differences. On 30 May 1863, after observing the funeral of Lieutenant Gaston in Beaufort, South Carolina, Higginson writes: "As I sat in the empty church the doves cooed into the window and the mocking-bird trilled, and then the cavalry bugles rang through with their shriller sound; and then I walked out again among the luxurious Southern growths, and thought there could not be in a strange land a sweeter resting-place for a discarded body."[62] This scene seems reminiscent of the bittersweet mood Whitman captures in his "Dirge for Two Veterans," yet Higginson's extract is marked by more jarring language. The bugles ring out with a "shriller sound" over a "strange land," which serves as a repository for a "discarded body." With this writing, juxtapose Whitman's, one night in March 1865, as he steps outdoors to admire the starry Washington sky:

> Then I heard, slow and clear, the deliberate notes of a bugle come up out of the silence, sounding so good through the night's mystery, no hurry, but firm and faithful, floating along, rising, falling leisurely, with here and there a long-drawn note; the bugle, well play'd, sounding tattoo, in one of the army hospitals near here, where the wounded (some of them personally so dear to me) are lying in their cots, and many a sick boy come down to the war from Illinois, Michigan, Wisconsin, Iowa, and the rest.[63]

This sentence, which leisurely flows like the bugle tones it conveys, makes apparent the characteristic restraint and limitations of Higginson's account. Whitman's description progresses from the solitary notes of the bugle out to the hospital, to the bedridden wounded, farther out still to the midwestern states, and, with a final bit of wordplay, comes to rest with "the rest," a phrase that encompasses the greater Union. Such intertwined expansiveness of language and form facilitates Whitman's musicality not only in this moment of resonant prose, but throughout the lyrical, "well-play'd" poems of *Drum-Taps*.

## Notes

Part of an earlier version of this essay appeared in the *Walt Whitman Quarterly Review* 12 (Spring 1995). I wish to thank the editors for granting permission to reprint the relevant sections.

1. Thomas Wentworth Higginson, *Part of a Man's Life* (Boston: Houghton Mifflin, 1905), p. 164.

2. Higginson, *Contemporaries* (Boston: Houghton, Mifflin, 1899), p. 80; [Higginson], "Recent Poetry," *Nation* 33 (1881), 476–77, rpt. in *Walt Whitman: The Contemporary Reviews,* ed. Kenneth M. Price (Cambridge: Cambridge University Press, 1996), p. 239.

3. Tilden G. Edelstein, *Strange Enthusiasm: A Life of Thomas Wentworth Higginson* (New Haven: Yale University Press, 1968), p. 354; Higginson, *Contemporaries,* p. 78.

4. Edelstein, *Strange Enthusiasm,* p. 353; Higginson, *Contemporaries,* p. 83. Higginson admitted to finding a small number of Whitman's poems appealing, especially (and predictably, given its relatively strict observance of meter and rhyme) "O Captain! My Captain!," which he considered "one of the few among his compositions which will live." See Higginson, *The New World and the New Book* (Boston: Lee and Shepard, 1892), p. 67.

5. [Higginson], "Recent Poetry," p. 240.

6. Higginson, *Cheerful Yesterdays* (1898; rpt. New York: Arno Press, 1968), p. 231.

7. Justin Kaplan, *Walt Whitman: A Life* (New York: Simon and Schuster, 1980), p. 24.

8. Conversation with Horace Traubel, 24 September 1888, quoted in Scott Giantvalley, "'Strict, Straight Notions of Literary Propriety': Thomas Wentworth Higginson's Gradual Unbending to Walt Whitman," *Walt Whitman Quarterly Review* 4 (1987), 17.

9. Conversation with Horace Traubel, 15 April 1890, in Horace Traubel, *With Walt Whitman in Camden,* ed. Gertrude Traubel and William White (Carbondale: Southern Illinois University Press, 1982), VI, 362.

10. Scott Giantvalley has argued that Higginson reconsidered his opinions in his later years and changed his mind about Whitman's poetry. Giantvalley's evidence, however, is questionable. He bases his argument on the third revised version of Higginson's Whitman chapter from *Contemporaries,* which appears in *A Reader's History of American Literature* from 1903. But Higginson coauthored this version with Henry Walcott Boynton, who may have made the changes himself. Although Higginson's active dislike of Whitman may have subsided, I do not think it reversed itself to the extent that Giantvalley claims; as late as 1905, Higginson still identified Whitman's poetry with feelings of "nausea." See Giantvalley, "'Strict, Straight Notions of Literary Propriety'," pp. 18–22.

11. Conversations with Horace Traubel, 10 November 1890, in Traubel, *With*

*Walt Whitman in Camden,* ed. Jeanne Chapman and Robert Macisaac (Carbondale: Southern Illinois University Press, 1992) VII, 264; 12 October 1889, VI, 62; 28 October 1889, VI, 95; 6 November. 1890, VII, 253.

12. I am indebted here to Kaplan's argument for the way the title reflects the shift in poetic mood (*Walt Whitman,* p. 299).

13. See Michael Moon, *Disseminating Whitman: Revision and Corporeality in Leaves of Grass* (Cambridge, Mass.: Harvard University Press, 1991), pp. 171–73.

14. James Stone, "War Music and War Psychology during the Civil War," *Journal of Abnormal and Social Psychology* 36 (1941), 554. Similarly, Harry Hall states that "music, as a military adjuvant, might well be regarded as the oil which makes the wheels of war machines run smoother." Harry H. Hall, *A Johnny Reb Band from Salem* (New York: Da Capo Press, 1980), p. 1.

15. All references to *Drum-Taps* are taken from Walt Whitman, *Leaves of Grass: Comprehensive Reader's Edition,* ed. Harold W. Blodgett and Scully Bradley (New York: New York University Press, 1965), and will be cited in text by poem and line number.

16. Stone, "War Music and War Psychology," p. 555; Catherine Moseley, "Irrepressible Conflict: Differences between Northern and Southern Songs of the Civil War," *Journal of Popular Culture* 25 (1991), 50.

17. The poetry of *Drum-Taps* is rich in sound symbolism, as "First O Songs" makes clear. There are a number of studies on sound symbolism that attempt to set forth a systematic method accounting for the ways particular poets employ verbal sounds. These include Walter Nash, "Sound and the Pattern of Poetic Meaning," in *Linguistics and the Study of Literature,* ed. Theo D'haen (Amsterdam: Rodopi, 1986), pp. 128–51; Marie Borroff, "Sound Symbolism as Drama in the Poetry of Robert Frost," *Publications of the Modern Language Association* 107 (1992), 131–44; and Reuven Tsur, *What Makes Sound Patterns Expressive? The Poetic Mode of Speech Perception* (Durham, N.C.: Duke University Press, 1992).

18. Robert Leigh Davis claims that in *Drum-Taps* Whitman champions the "possibility of intermingled states" over the "binary deadlock" of the Civil War; Davis provides a compelling discussion of how Whitman's use of the "tympanum" (eardrum) denies closure, since the eardrum is perpetually open and therefore allows the poet to "enact the defeat . . . of social and linguistic fixidity." See Robert Leigh Davis, "Whitman's Tympanum: A Reading of Drum-Taps," *American Transcendental Quarterly* 6 (1992), 163–64, 166–67.

19. Some critics consider "Beat! Beat! Drums!" "fundamentally anti-democratic" and even imperialist. See two political analyses of *Drum-Taps:* Katherine Kinney, "Whitman's 'Word of the Modern' and the First Modern War," *Walt Whitman Quarterly Review* 7 (1989), 4; and M. Wynn Thomas, "Whitman and the American Identity Before and during the Civil War," *Journal of American Studies* 15 (1981), 86.

20. John Carlos Rowe, "Whitman's Body Politic," in *America's Modernisms: Revaluing the Canon,* ed. Kathryne V. Lindberg and Joseph G. Kronick (Baton Rouge, La.: Louisiana State University Press, 1996), pp. 172–73.

21. *Musical Settings of American Poetry,* comp. Michael Hovland (New York: Greenwood Press, 1986), pp. 377–78.

22. Kenneth Olson, *Music and Musket* (Westport, Conn.: Greenwood Press, 1981), p. 67.

23. For more on the significance of amputation in Whitman's work, see Robert Leigh Davis, "Wound-Dressers and House Calls: Medical Representations in Whitman and Williams," *Walt Whitman Quarterly Review* 6 (1989), 133–39.

24. Robert Garofalo and Mark Elrod, *A Pictorial History of Civil War Era Musical Instruments and Military Bands* (Charleston, W.V.: Pictorial Histories Publishing, 1985), p. 69; George Worthington Adams, *Doctors in Blue: The Medical History of the Union Army in the Civil War* (1952; Baton Rouge, La.: Louisiana State University Press, 1996), p. 68.

25. These and similar incidents are recounted in Francis A. Lord and Arthur Wise, *Bands and Drummer Boys of the Civil War* (New York: Thomas Youseloff, 1966), pp. 50, 80–81, 111, 206–08.

26. Holloway quoted in Olson, *Music and Musket,* p. 119.

27. Quoted in Olson, *Music and Musket,* p. 184.

28. Lord and Wise, *Bands and Drummer Boys,* p. 170.

29. Robert Faner, *Walt Whitman and Opera* (Philadelphia: University of Pennsylvania Press, 1951), p. 108.

30. See William F. Mayhan, "The Idea of Music in 'Out of the Cradle Endlessly Rocking'," *Walt Whitman Quarterly Review* 13 (1996), 113–28.

31. John Samuel Wannamaker, *The Musical Settings of the Poetry of Walt Whitman: A Study of Theme, Structure, and Prosody* (Ph.D. diss., University of Minnesota, 1972), p. 27.

32. Michael Short, *Gustav Holst: The Man and His Music* (Oxford: Oxford University Press, 1990), p. 120; liner notes, Gustav Holst, *Choral Works,* Chandos 9437 (1996).

33. To this can be added a contemporary setting of the "Dirge" that was brought to my attention shortly after I wrote this. Lawrence Kramer's version, the second part of his "'That Music Always Round Me': Three Poems by Walt Whitman" (1984), forms a powerfully evocative and pensive centerpiece for the song cycle, which also features "I Hear America Singing" and "That Music Always Round Me" (my thanks to the composer for supplying me with a recording of this).

34. Kinney makes the musical connection here as well: "the sounds of the guns call like the beat of the drums in the earlier poems" ("Whitman's 'Word of the Modern'," p. 7).

35. Though "The Star Spangled Banner" was not adopted as the national anthem until the twentieth century, it had achieved widespread popularity long before this as a patriotic song. Whitman was quite familiar with it early on in his career. In 1846 the *Brooklyn Daily Eagle* published his own adaptation of it under the title "Ode.—By Walter Whitman.—To be sung on Fort Greene, 4th of July, 1846. Tune 'The Star Spangled Banner'." For the text, see Walt Whitman, *The Early Poems and*

*the Fiction,* ed. Thomas L. Brasher (New York: New York University Press, 1963), pp. 34–35.

36. David S. Reynolds, *Walt Whitman's America: A Cultural Biography* (New York: Alfred A. Knopf, 1995), p. 176. Reynolds makes a good argument for Whitman's poetry "enact[ing a] permeability of modes" of popular song and opera (p. 193). But while Reynolds discusses similar examples of this blending of the high and the low within vocal musical modes of the period (singing families, minstrelsy, Stephen Foster), he provides only a momentary sense of how this phenomenon manifested itself in instrumental music (a brief mention of Dodsworth's Band [p. 177]), and even less on how such bands and modes might specifically have influenced Whitman himself.

37. Stone, "War Music and War Psychology," p. 553.

38. Higginson, "Negro Spirituals," *Atlantic Monthly,* June 1867, pp. 685–94.

39. *Slave Songs of the United States,* ed. William Francis Allen, Charles Pickard Ware, and Lucy McKim Garrison (1867; rpt. New York: Dover, 1995), quoted in *Readings in Black American Music,* ed. and comp. Eileen Southern (2nd edn. New York: Norton, 1983), pp. 161–62. *Slave Songs* contains the words and music of 136 songs.

40. Dena J. Epstein, *Sinful Tunes and Spirituals: Black Folk Music to the Civil War* (Urbana, Ill.: University of Illinois Press, 1981), p. 326, n. 11; Howard N. Meyer, *Colonel of the Black Regiment: The Life of Thomas Wentworth Higginson* (New York: Norton, 1967), p. 231. Music history textbooks often include discussions of Higginson's article and its importance: see, for example, Eileen Southern, *The Music of Black Americans: A History* (3rd edn. New York: Norton, 1997), pp. 207–11; and Charles Hamm, *Music in the New World* (New York: Norton, 1983), p. 136.

41. Eric Lott, *Love and Theft: Blackface Minstrelsy and the American Working Class* (New York: Oxford University Press, 1993), p. 641.

42. Ronald Radano, "Denoting Difference: The Writing of the Slave Spirituals," *Critical Inquiry* 22 (1996), 511.

43. Radano, "Denoting Difference," pp. 522–23.

44. For more on the "shout," see John Storm Roberts, *Black Music of Two Worlds* (Tivoli, N.Y.: Original Music, 1972), pp. 162–69; and Southern, *Music of Black Americans,* pp. 181–83.

45. Higginson, *Army Life in a Black Regiment* (New York: Norton, 1984), p. 45. Further references to this edition will be cited in parentheses.

46. See Radano, "Denoting Difference," p. 524.

47. Higginson, in a letter dated 21 April 1864, *Letters and Journals of Thomas Wentworth Higginson 1846–1906,* ed. Mary Thatcher Higginson (Boston: Houghton, Mifflin, 1921), p. 219.

48. Christopher Looby, "Flowers of Manhood: Race, Sex and Floriculture from Thomas Wentworth Higginson to Robert Mapplethorpe," *Criticism* 37 (1995), 130. Looby examines related questions in his "'As Thoroughly Black as the Most Faithful Philanthropist Could Desire': Erotics of Race in Higginson's *Army Life in a Black*

*Regiment," Race and the Subject of Masculinities,* ed. Harry Stecopoulos and Michael Uebel (Durham, N.C.: Duke University Press, 1997), pp. 71–115.

49. Radano, "Denoting Difference," p. 544. Radano derives the image of the circle from Frederick Douglass, who in his *Narrative* reminisces about being "within the circle" of spiritual singers (p. 507). Spirituals often have represented an autonomous space in which African Americans can construct and protect a group identity; Higginson can get "no nearer" in part because he begins to intrude on this highly personal and powerful territory. For more on spirituals and identity formations, see *Lyrics of the Afro-American Spiritual,* ed. Erskine Peters (Westport, Conn.: Greenwood Press, 1993), p. xv.

50. Radano, "Denoting Difference," p. 508.

51. As Hamm notes, Higginson "was not a musician and was incapable of writing down the music of these spirituals" (*Music in the New World,* p. 136). The music, full of bent notes, would have resisted standard notation in any case.

52. See, for example, Southern, *Music of Black Americans,* p. 153; and Meyer, *Colonel of the Black Regiment,* p. 231.

53. Southern, *Music of Black Americans,* pp. 200–01.

54. Peters, *Lyrics of the Afro-American Spiritual,* p. xv.

55. Timothy Sweet, *Traces of War: Poetry, Photography, and the Crisis of the Union* (Baltimore: Johns Hopkins University Press, 1990), p. 42.

56. See Hans Nathan, "Walt Whitman and the Marine Band," *More Books* 18 (1943), 47–56; and Emory Holloway, "Whitman and Band Music," *Walt Whitman Review* 6 (1960), 51–52.

57. Wannamaker lists fifty-five settings as of 1972 (*Musical Settings of the Poetry of Walt Whitman,* p. 135). My estimate is conservatively adjusted to account for the additional years' worth of work.

58. Ben Arnold, *Music and War: A Research and Information Guide* (New York: Garland, 1993), p. 117.

59. John Adams, quoted in jacket notes by Sarah Cahill, *The Wound Dresser* and *Fearful Symmetries,* Elektra Nonesuch 79218-2 (1989).

60. Thomas Hampson and Carla Maria Verdina-Süllwold, liner notes, *To the Soul: Thomas Hampson Sings the Poetry of Walt Whitman,* EMI CDC 7243-5-55028-2-7 (1997). *Drum-Taps* is second only to *Calamus* for representation among Hampson's twenty-two selections.

61. *The Norton Anthology of African American Literature,* ed. Henry Louis Gates, Jr. and Nellie Y. McKay (New York: Norton, 1997), p. 7; Southern, *Readings,* pp. 175–202; Sherrill V. Martin, "Music of Black Americans during the War Years, 1861–1865," in *Feel the Spirit: Studies in Nineteenth-Century Afro-American Music,* ed. George R. Keck and Sherrill V. Martin (New York: Greenwood Press, 1988), p. 3; Peters, *Lyrics of the Afro-American Spiritual,* pp. xvi–xvii.

62. Higginson, *Letters and Journals,* p. 206.

63. Walt Whitman, *Prose Works 1892,* vol. I, *Specimen Days,* ed. Floyd Stovall (New York: New York University Press, 1963), p. 95.

# CHAPTER 2

# "No Armpits, Please, We're British"
## Whitman and English Music, 1884–1936

*Byron Adams*

*For Mitchell Morris*

"Too fond of the smell of his own armpits." Thus did Ralph Vaughan Williams (1872–1958) bluntly express to his wife Ursula, herself an ambitious poet, his chief reservation concerning Walt Whitman's poetry.[1] At the same time, near the end of his long life Vaughan Williams confided to Michael Kennedy his ongoing love of Whitman: "I've never got over him, I'm glad to say."[2] Vaughan Williams, who was introduced to Whitman's verse at Cambridge in 1892, carried a pocket edition of *Leaves of Grass* with him throughout his period of active service in World War I. As demonstrated by the skill with which he ransacked Whitman's poetry for texts, Vaughan Williams knew *Leaves of Grass* thoroughly. Even the apparently dismissive remark to his wife testifies to the composer's retentive memory for Whitman's work. Vaughan Williams was surely recalling these lines from "Song of Myself": "Divine I am inside and out, and I make holy whatever I touch or am touch'd from, / The scent of these arm-pits aroma finer than prayer, / This head more than churches, bibles and all the creeds" (524–26).

Although ambivalence was a hallmark of Vaughan Williams's personality, his attitude toward Whitman provides a clue to the ambiguous way that many of the English composers of his era received the American poet. From 1884 to 1936, English composers repeatedly turned to Whitman for texts and inspiration. But these composers were highly selective, embracing only certain aspects of the American poet's work while ignoring others. What British composers found fascinating about Whitman, and which aspects of his life and poetry they elected to minimize, show patterns that yield insights into the relationship between societal stresses and English musical aesthetics during this period.

Notice, for instance, that Vaughan Williams, himself no adherent of churches, bibles, or creeds, recalled only the armpits—those aromatic and highly physical entities. What received no mention was the Transcendentalist disdain for institutional religion, one of the central ideas expressed by the passage from "Song of Myself" that contains the reference. In general, this English and Victorian discomfort (and Vaughan Williams, for all of his longevity, spent the first thirty years of his life as a Victorian) with Whitman's arrant and shameless homoerotic exhibitionism conditioned the response of English composers to his poetry. For Vaughan Williams and his English contemporaries, the poet's fragrant armpits are merely a metonym for other embarrassing parts of his extravagantly sexualized body that they chose to ignore.

The ambivalence with which Vaughan Williams and other composers viewed Whitman was conditioned in part by the American poet's literary reception in Britain. Whitman came to the attention of the English literary avant-garde with remarkable swiftness. Published in 1855, *Leaves of Grass* was read by the Pre-Raphaelites as early as 1856. William Michael Rossetti, the brother of both Christina and Dante Gabriel, published a sympathetic article on Whitman in 1867. In the following year, Rossetti further demonstrated his practical support by editing—and fastidiously expurgating—a collection drawn from the fourth edition of *Leaves of Grass*. As Harold Blodgett drolly notes, "Rossetti even deleted the words 'womb' and 'prostitute' from Whitman's preface . . . as if he feared that the mention of 'prostitute' might bring one to the British Isles."[3] Rossetti crafted his bowdlerization with Whitman's wary acquiescence. The American poet was understandably weary of the continual disrespect shown to his work at home and hoped that a British edition would boost both his prestige and sales. Whitman later regretted his decision, exclaiming to his faithful interlocutor Horace Traubel: "Damn the expurgated books! I say damn'em. . . . In a day and month and year of weakness I yielded to the idea that the English reader could not stand a dose of Walt Whitman. It was an evil decision growing out of the best intentions."[4] The Rossetti editions were in fact popular, going through several editions, including one in 1892, the year that Bertrand Russell recommended Whitman's verse to Vaughan Williams. (Alas, Whitman made no money from those expurgated editions; to receive the three author's copies sent by his English publisher he had to pay a customs duty.)

Whitman's work struck deep chords with several leading Victorian poets. Tennyson, who may have discerned an echo of his own *In Memoriam* in Whitman's professions of homoerotic desire, was generally enthusiastic about *Leaves of Grass*. Algernon Charles Swinburne initially hailed Whitman as a liberator; later he turned on the American poet, showing the characteristic timidity that was born of artistic envy united with homosexual panic.[5] Gerard Manley Hopkins wrote that "first I may well say what I should not otherwise have said, that I always knew in my heart Walt Whitman's mind to be more like my own than any other man's living."[6] The highly repressed Hopkins rejected Whitman as "a very great scoundrel," however, for Whitman dared, as Richard Dellamora suggests in his volume *Masculine Desire,* to transgress Hopkins's "prohibition of genital contact between men."[7]

The two Victorian literary figures who read Whitman with the greatest understanding and fiercest devotion were John Addington Symonds and Edward Carpenter. Both Carpenter and Symonds recognized in Whitman's poetry reflections of their democratic ideals and also their erotic attraction to young, hardy working-class men. Indeed, for Symonds, Carpenter, and other English literary figures of the period (both homosexual and heterosexual), the very name "Whitman" became a signifier of both male corporeality and sexual desire between men.[8] Carpenter modeled his own poetry after Whitman's style and practice and traveled to America in the spring of 1877 to meet his idol. A pioneering sexologist as well as an author, Carpenter found in Whitman a wellspring for his courageous crusade to gain social and legal recognition for what he termed "homogenic love."

Symonds was introduced to Whitman in the autumn of 1865, when he first encountered *Leaves of Grass* in the rooms of a friend, Frederic Myers, at Trinity College, Cambridge.[9] Symonds corresponded with Whitman for years, insistently questioning him on the nature of "adhesive" relations between comrades as found in the *Calamus* section of *Leaves of Grass.* In the face of Symonds's persistent queries, Whitman himself panicked, lost his nerve, and sent the English author a letter full of preposterous biographical lies attesting to his robust procreative manliness.[10] Although discouraged and confused by this truculent (and utterly dishonest) reaction from his hero, Symonds was undeterred in his admiration for Whitman's poetic achievement, publishing his insightful *Walt Whitman: A Study* in 1893. Symonds analyzes Whitman's message into four distinct themes: "First come religion or the concept of the universe; then personality or sense of self and sex; then love, diverging into amative and comradely emotions; then democracy, or the theory of human equality and brotherhood."[11] While Symonds's study represents only one strain of Whitman criticism arising during this period, all of the various Victorian commentators, including Rossetti, stress the liberal, democratic, and (in both Spenserian and Darwinian terms) "evolutionary" aspects of Whitman's message.

Like certain reviewers in America, British commentators were powerfully disturbed by Whitman's celebration of the "adhesive love" between comrades and raised their voices in protest. Dellamora offers one such case: "The Rev. St. John Tyrwhitt, in his attack on Symonds in *The Contemporary Review* of March 1877, cites Whitman repeatedly as a code word for illicit desire. In a paragraph following one in which Tyrwhitt points out that 'Greek love of nature and beauty went frequently against nature,' he snorts at Symonds's 'concluding exhortation to follow Walt Whitman as far as our Hebraistic training and imperfect nature will enable us'." While this criticism is particularly strong in its homophobic tenor, even poets such as Swinburne and Hopkins were troubled by Whitman's frank portrayals of desire between men. As Dellamora writes, "Whitman's practice clarifies by contrast the hesitations, compromises, at times the panic of English male writers."[12]

Whitman himself was prey to the pressures of late nineteenth-century British and American homophobia. After the 1860 edition of *Leaves of Grass,* which of all the editions is the most uninhibited in its celebration of desire between male comrades, Whitman began his own process of expurgation and obfuscation. Beginning with the 1867 edition, he gradually edited out the more overt expressions of "adhesive love" between men and softened the frank eroticism of some passages.[13] As his own body aged after the Civil War, Whitman's emphasis on the corporeal began to lessen. In an essay from 1920, Emory Holloway eloquently writes: "Battered in body and bruised in his affections, poor and generally rejected of critics, Whitman henceforth has less to say in praise of untrammeled natural impulses, but more and more to sing of democracy, of immortality, and of the soul."[14] If in later years Whitman came to feel uncomfortable with some of his earlier rhapsodic and homoerotic effusions and omitted them from his work, it is not surprising that Victorian composers would display a similar caution in making their selections from *Leaves of Grass.* In company with the older Whitman, they chose "to sing of democracy, of immortality and of the soul," thereby selecting those portions of his poetry that were the most palatable to Victorian and Edwardian tastes and mores.

With the possible exception of the cosmopolitan outsider Frederick Delius (1862–1934), English male composers who used Whitman's poetry either as texts or as inspiration were prey to the same hesitations, compromises and, indeed, panic as were their literary counterparts. This meant that the use of Whitman's poetry by British composers was conditioned and circumscribed by a series of social and aesthetic boundaries that kept them from exploring it fully. And with certain composers, the very idiom they chose for setting the verse acted as a kind of aesthetic deodorant, putting a safe distance between themselves and the fragrant corporeality of the poet's ever-present armpits. As a consequence of this unease, those British composers who set Whitman, from Stanford to Vaughan Williams, returned repeatedly to a very limited selection of themes. Indeed, they tended to set the same poems again and again. (For example, Stanford, Vaughan Williams, and Delius set "Joy, Shipmate, Joy," while Stanford, Wood, Holst, and Vaughan Williams made settings of "Darest Thou Now, O Soul." Vaughan Williams set it twice: once as a "song" for chorus and orchestra in 1907 and once as a unison song for voice and piano in 1925.)

The earliest settings of Whitman by British composers characterized those that followed. Consider how Charles Villiers Stanford (1852–1924) set verses drawn from "When Lilacs Last in the Dooryard Bloom'd" in his *Elegiac Ode* (1884). Stanford selected the text for this work for soprano, baritone, chorus, and orchestra from the climactic central section of the poem, beginning with the line "Come lovely and soothing death" (135). Never less (and rarely more) than a complete professional, Stanford sets the verse to music characterized by immaculate part writing, deft orchestration, and elegant formal proportions. Unfortunately, however, the smooth assurance of the music turns Whitman's ecstatic hymn to death into an exercise in genteel post-Mendelssohnian choral composition. The effect of Stanford's technical assurance is to expurgate all the life and urgency from the poetry with music just as surely as Rossetti's bowdlerized editions of *Leaves of Grass* vitiated Whitman's verbal power.

Stanford's younger contemporary, the Cambridge composer Charles Wood (1866–1926), approached Whitman with greater insight. Wood's songs with Whitman texts, such as his songs "Darest Now Thou, O Soul" and "Æthiopia Saluting the Colours,"[15] are in general more forceful and individual than Stanford's efforts. Wood's fine choral work *A Dirge for Two Veterans* was written for the Leeds Festival of 1901, in the midst of the waste, tactical blundering, and bloodshed of the Second Anglo-Boer War. By using Whitman's Civil War poetry to comment, however indirectly, on a British military entanglement, Wood set an important precedent for his pupil Vaughan Williams and others. Whitman became the "war poet" for a generation of composers who lived in a period of growing conflict and who lacked a relevant tradition of war poetry. (That, sadly, would be supplied for later composers by the national experience of the Great War.)

Stanford and Wood influenced the younger generation of English composers by selecting a canon of acceptable Whitman texts. To return to Symonds's useful classification of Whitman's poetry, both composers emphasized "religion or the concept of the universe." Thus Wood's *Dirge for Two Veterans* touches on "comradely emotions" only in the context of war and death. The "concept of the universe" that attracted Stanford and Wood the most was the ability of the soul to transcend death, and it was this promise of release that would speak also to Vaughan Williams, Gustav Holst (1874–1934), and their colleagues.

As Whitman sang convincingly of the soul, he gave voice to what Symonds calls the "religious impulse." During the crises of faith that beset the Victorian and Edwardian thinkers,[16] composers searched for alternatives to biblical texts that yet would express both the spiritual restlessness and "evolutionary" optimism of their times. Vaughan Williams and Holst, both political radicals and agnostics,[17] were looking for symbolic and mystical poetry that was resonant and new, free from the taint of a Christianity that seemed outmoded and intellectually compromised. In Whitman they found a poet at once democratic, mystical, and "evolutionary." (Charles Darwin was Vaughan Williams's great uncle, and Hubert Parry [1848–1918], one of Vaughan Williams's most influential teachers at the Royal College of Music,

wrote a book entitled *The Evolution of the Art of Music*.) These composers
pounced on those passages in Whitman's work that celebrate a pantheistic,
transcendentalist deity, another version of Emerson's numinous and vague
"Oversoul." Whitman's long lines and persistent use of parallelism echo the
psalms, making his verses ideal for the sort of music these English composers
were longing to compose. To the aspiring young Vaughan Williams, *Leaves of
Grass* was "full of fresh thoughts" that suggested to him "the idea of a big
choral work about the sea—the sea itself and the sea of time, infinity and
mankind."[18] In all this vertiginous exultation there is not the merest hint of
that other, irritating Whitman, the one with the smelly armpits: "hankering,
gross, mystical, nude."[19] By limiting their view, Vaughan Williams and colleagues sought to transform Whitman into a disembodied visionary, tran-
scending Time and Death, shuttling off that nasty, stinking mortal coil to sail
blissfully around the Kosmos. (The peroration of the finale of Vaughan
Williams's *A Sea Symphony* begins with the two soloists ecstatically singing
the words "O Thou Transcendent.")

Despite their best efforts, however, Whitman's body keeps interfering
with this program in some unexpected ways. Whitman's masculinity, allied to
his patently homoerotic gaze at young "roughs," creates an insistent problem
that compositional strategies could not conjure away. Even Rossetti's exci-
sions could not purge the homoerotic content from "Song of Myself" and the
*Calamus* poems; homophobic English reviewers such as Tyrwhitt were well
aware of the subversive nature of Whitman's adoration of male beauty and
desire. Meanwhile, English composers had good reasons of their own to di-
vest Whitman of his insistently homoerotic and corporeal self.

Vaughan Williams was clearly elated at having found such a masculine
poet as Whitman. Of all of the composers of his generation, Vaughan
Williams was the most deeply affected by Whitman's poetry. He especially
admired Whitman for the sturdy, out-of-doors quality that seemed to connote
radiant, democratic masculinity. But Vaughan Williams's interest in Whitman
was also related to his repudiation of the "aesthetic" Pre-Raphaelite verse of
Dante Gabriel Rossetti and Algernon Charles Swinburne that he had found
attractive during the 1890s. The reasons for such repudiation can be found in
the repressive social environment of Victorian and Edwardian society.

Throughout the Victorian and Edwardian periods, English musicians
were viewed with suspicion by the dominant culture. Musicians were considered effeminate at best and at worst prone to "unnatural" vice. The composer
Lord Berners (1883–1950) commented in his memoirs on the environment of
his Victorian childhood and on accepted ideals of masculinity and the in-
grained distrust of musicians in that area: "Manliness was a virtue in which
one had to be laboriously instructed. Like so many other virtues, it did not
seem to correspond with the natural instincts of the human being. I came to
the conclusion that 'manliness' was a very complicated ideal. . . . Why were

music and painting held to be effeminate when all the greatest painters and composers had been men?"[20] The sexologist Havelock Ellis reflected the darker assumptions held by the society of his day when he wrote: "It has been extravagantly said that all musicians are inverts . . . the musical disposition is marked by great emotional instability, and this instability is a disposition to nervousness." Ellis then goes on to assert that "the musician has not been rendered nervous by his music, but he owes his nervousness (as also, it may be added, his disposition to homosexuality) to the same disposition to which he owes his musical aptitude."[21] Given the censorious outlook of Victorian and Edwardian society toward effeminacy, it is unsurprising that composers opted to create public personas that emphasized their hearty masculinity. Hubert Parry hid his highly strung and intellectual disposition beneath a public mask that stressed both his athletic prowess as a yachtsman and his backslapping bonhomie. In a similar strategy, Edward Elgar (1857–1934) acted the "English gentleman" almost to the point of caricature. Elgar's shame at being a musician was manifested in sad incidents during which he would deny his unfashionable musical profession altogether; he even forced his wife to sell his violin so that he could purchase that ultimate symbol of Edwardian masculinity, a billiard table.

In this climate, the social insecurity of all English male artists, both homosexual and heterosexual, was exacerbated by the disastrous trials that sent Oscar Wilde to Reading Gaol in 1895. The Wilde trials had a deep and inhibiting effect on British art after 1895, for the conviction of Wilde on charges of "gross indecency" confirmed the worst suspicions held by popular moralists concerning the degenerate character of the artistic temperament. Furthermore, one particularly inhibiting effect of the Wilde trials was the false conflation of effeminacy with homosexuality in the public mind;[22] for decades afterward Englishmen would, in Quentin Crisp's coruscating phrase, search themselves "for vestiges of effeminacy as though for lice."[23]

The effect of the Wilde trials on artists was reflected in a rapid change in aesthetics on the part of poets, painters, playwrights, and composers. The "aestheticism" of both the heterosexual Pre-Raphaelites and the homosexual Wilde was now banished, and a new, more self-consciously "masculine" aesthetic took its place. As the British art historian William Gaunt wrote in 1945: "The trial and conviction of Oscar Wilde had seemingly brought the aesthetic movement in Britain to a halt. It caused a wholesale literary and social fumigation. An exaggerated robustness was one of the consequences. Poets, no longer velvet-collared, absinthe-sipping, were now a hearty and virile race, tweed-clad, pipe-smoking, beer-drinking, Sussex-Downs-tramping. . . . The subject of sex was buried beneath fresh layers of discretion, beneath cryptic phrases and obscure turns of speech which might or might not conceal some romantic or extraordinary secret."[24]

Vaughan Williams was an impressionable young composer of twenty-

three in 1895, the year of the Wilde trials. As he was living in London, studying at the Royal College of Music, it is inconceivable that he was able to escape either news of the trials or the chill wind that blew through his artistic
community in its wake. Vaughan Williams, who was a most assured and passionate heterosexual, was never homophobic;[25] he numbered Edward Dent,
Arthur Benjamin, E. M. Forster, and Sylvia Townsend Warner among his
many homosexual friends and acquaintances. Nor was he unaware of homosexuality in history and myth. In her biography of her husband, Ursula
Vaughan Williams relates the following anecdote from 1951: "Rehearsals
[for the revival of Vaughan Williams's operatic 'morality' *The Pilgrim's
Progress*] started again, so he spent a good deal of time at Covent Garden. At
one rehearsal someone in the chorus, hearing Lord Lechery's new song,
asked who on earth Hylas was. 'Hercules' boy friend,' Ralph replied with firm
unconcern and the chorus all seemed surprised and amused that he should
know about such things."[26]

With all of his broadmindedness concerning homosexuality, Vaughan
Williams was still acutely uncomfortable with effeminacy. This aversion occasionally crops up in Vaughan Williams's writings on music, as when he sar-
castically cites the "young exquisite" who says to him "I don't like Bach, he
is so bourgeois." The lisp of the "young exquisite" fairly leaps off the page,
and one can well imagine the elongated "so" that Vaughan Williams clearly
had in his mind's ear. The composer's forthright, manly, British reply is "that
being bourgeois myself I considered Bach the greatest of all composers."[27]
Oddly enough, Vaughan Williams's dislike of effeminacy was shared by
Whitman, but for vastly different reasons. In a letter to Emerson, Whitman
pours scorn on the "helpless dandies" who can be seen "smirking and skip-
ping along . . . no one behaving . . . out of any natural and manly tastes of his
own." Where Vaughan Williams displays a socially inculcated unease with effeminacy, Whitman, as Byrne Fone observes, "poses against his manly young
men whose language he hopes to infuse with terms descriptive of passionate
friendship a detailed rendering of the cliché of the effeminate homosexual."[28]
In other words, Vaughan Williams feels uncomfortable around sissies because he knows that musicians, to their cost, are accused of being such; Whitman, on the other hand, likes his boys rough.

The question naturally arises: What exactly did Vaughan Williams know
about Whitman's sexual inclinations? Although there is no way to answer this
question with any certainty, it is equally true that, as his wife Ursula once remarked, "Ralph was never innocent."[29] Vaughan Williams was introduced to
Whitman's poetry by Bertrand Russell, who, as a member of the sexually obsessed secret society at Cambridge known as the "Apostles," was scarcely
reticent about sharing with his university friends his varied knowledge of
sexual arcana. Unsympathetic critics in England had repeatedly alluded in
print to Whitman's expression of desire between men. And, finally, Vaughan

Williams, as an insightful reader, may have found out the import of Whitman's comradely adhesiveness through repeated readings of *Leaves of Grass* itself, of which he owned several copies and editions.[30] One has always to approach the subject of sexual knowledge in British society during this era with caution, however; as late as the 1920s, the homosexual author J. R. Ackerley, of all people, had to have the question "Are you homo or hetero?" explained to him.[31]

It is very likely that, as a young composer in Cambridge and London, Vaughan Williams was affected by social prejudice against musicians, in particular the conflation of musicality and effeminacy that pervaded his society. The viciousness of the Wilde trials and the public's confusion of effeminacy and homosexuality must have given heterosexual musicians like Vaughan Williams an acute case of homosexual panic. Vaughan Williams's instinctive solution was to create for himself a public face that was self-consciously "masculine" just as his admired teacher Parry had done a generation earlier. The Vaughan Williams who was a fashionably dressed, almost willowy, undergraduate at Cambridge turned himself into a tweed-clad, pipe-smoking, beer-drinking, Downs-tramping, folk-song-collecting composer highly reminiscent of the hearty poet sketched so deftly by William Gaunt. The journalist and music critic Charles Kenyon, writing under the pseudonym "Gerald Cumberland," draws a convincing portrait of the "public" Vaughan Williams in his 1919 volume *Set Down in Malice*. Of this encounter between the two, which took place sometime between 1908 and 1914, Kenyon writes:

> I am unable to recall the name of that very attractive hotel in Birmingham where, early one evening, Dr Vaughan Williams, travel-stained and brown with sun, walked into the lounge and began a conversation with me. He had walked an incredible distance.... He told me that he had studied with Ravel.... To me he, with his British downrightness, his love of space, his freedom from all mannerisms and tricks of style, seemed Ravel's very antithesis.[32]

Most of Vaughan Williams later biographers, most notably Percy Young, Hubert Foss, and Frank Howes, colluded with the composer to make "British downrightness" the keynote of his public persona, thereby protecting an ambivalent, intellectual, and complex personality from public scrutiny.

Vaughan Williams's search for a masculine but visionary poet landed him, metaphorically speaking, in the arms of Walt Whitman. That the composer would have used Whitman's poetry for texts was a logical, if ultimately ironic, result of Vaughan Williams's search for a new, more "masculine," aesthetic. During the first seven years of the twentieth century, Vaughan Williams moved away from such hothouse poets as Dante Gabriel Rossetti, whose sonnets provided the texts for the composer's song cycle, *The House of*

*Life.* In his search Vaughan Williams first tried the bracing out-of-doors verse
of Robert Louis Stevenson, setting it in *Songs of Travel,* but ultimately he
would settle on verse with more symbolic depth.

As Vaughan Williams felt that he had the right to cut all parts of a text
that did not consort with his aesthetic purpose, he did not hesitate to discard
erotically charged passages from any poem that he was setting to music. Thus
he earned the bitter enmity of A. E. Housman by excising the stanza that contains the wildly phallic lines "The goal stands up, the keeper / Stands up to
keep the goal" when he set "Is my team ploughing" (15–16) in the song cycle
*On Wenlock Edge.* Vaughan Williams was uncomfortable with any kind of
overt display of eroticism, whether heterosexual or homosexual. Given the
way he set biblical texts, it is very likely that he planned to set verses from the
*Song of Songs* in his sensuous *Flos Campi* for viola, chorus, and small orchestra.[33] Although *Flos Campi* remains one of Vaughan Williams's most
overtly voluptuous scores, the final version has no lyrics: The chorus sings
wordless melismas, while mottoes from the *Song of Songs* are only printed in
Latin above each movement. The "voice of the turtle" may sing, it seems, but
it is denied the embarrassing specificity of words.[34]

Vaughan Williams did set a Whitman poem word for word: "Darest Thou
Now, O Soul" in his 1907 "song" for chorus and orchestra, *Toward the Unknown Region,* but like Stanford, he vitiates the poetry with the music. The
setting utterly misses Whitman's conception of death as a "bursting forth," a
delirious species of cosmic orgasm:

> *All waits undream'd of in that region, that inacessible land.*
>
> *Till when the ties loosen,*
> *All but the ties eternal, Time and Space,*
> *Nor darkness, gravitation, sense, nor any bounds bounding us,*
>
> *Then we burst forth, we float,*
> *In Time and Space, O Soul, prepared for them,*
> *Equal, equipt at last, (O joy! O fruit of all!) them to fulfill O soul.* (9–15)

There is invariably a sexual connotation when Whitman invokes the idea of
bursting forth; here it is doubled by the poetic gasp "(O joy! O fruit of all!)."
The peroration of *Toward the Unknown Region,* a dignified and touching tribute to Parry, hardly suggests the ecstatic ejaculation of the soul into the universe. (Vaughan Williams's *Three Poems by Walt Whitman* for voice and
piano of 1925, are, like *Toward the Unknown Region,* touching and dignified,
but the poems chosen from *Leaves of Grass* are also more muted than "Darest
Thou Now, O Soul.")

In his next choral work, the massive *A Sea Symphony* for soprano and
baritone soloists, chorus, and orchestra (1910), Vaughan Williams builds a
text out of lines from five of Whitman's poems, all but one dating from after

1870. (The exception is "On the Beach at Night Alone," which was first published in 1855 under the title "Clef Poem.")[35] Vaughan Williams arranges his selections from *Leaves of Grass* so that the sea stands, rather predictably, for the evolution of the individual soul and, by extension, all humanity, toward a transcendent unity. One might ponder why the second and third movements, where the poetic texts suffered the least tampering,[36] are the most successful formally; the first and last movements, where Vaughan Williams anthologizes, are formally far more diffuse. And the score has a curious conclusion: Despite the strenuous hopes for spiritual and evolutionary progress expressed throughout the protracted finale, *A Sea Symphony* ends with tonal and expressive ambivalence. By concluding his vast choral and orchestral fresco on a note of musical interrogation, Vaughan Williams undercuts the movement's soulful, climactic exhortations to the "brave Soul" to sail forth on the "seas of God." The music reflects the composer's deepseated and profoundly reflective agnosticism, not the unalloyed exultation expressed in Whitman's lines.

Certain passages that Vaughan Williams *doesn't* cut from Whitman for *A Sea Symphony* are worth noting. In the first movement the composer retains lines that celebrate in no uncertain terms the physical glamour of Whitman's sexy sea captains, mates, and sailors, as well as "the few, very choice, taciturn, whom fate can never surprise nor death dismay." The physicality of Whitman's sailors begins to pervade the musical fabric, by some mysterious alchemy infusing the music with a previously unwonted intensity, poignancy, and virility. Later in the same movement, the grandiose apostrophe to Whitman's flaunting and phallic "pennant universal, subtly waving all time, o'er all brave sailors" sung by the soprano is all the more enthralling after the descriptions of those taciturn sailors "whom fate can never surprise." Vaughan Williams, quite unconsciously, sets sail for deep waters irresistibly beckoned forward by the warmth of Whitman's homoerotic rapture.

The last of Vaughan Williams's large-scale works with a text by Whitman is the searing antiwar cantata *Dona Nobis Pacem* of 1936. Like *A Sea Symphony,* this cantata is scored for soprano and baritone soloists, chorus, and orchestra. The text of *Dona Nobis Pacem* contains three of Whitman's Civil War poems as well as passages from the Roman Catholic liturgy, selections from the Bible, and an excerpt from John Bright's famous "Angel of Death" speech, delivered in Parliament during the Crimean War. The third movement, a setting for chorus and orchestra of "A Dirge for Two Veterans," dates from 1911, thus preceding the composition of the rest of the cantata by some twenty-five years. As he composed this score, Vaughan Williams may well have had in mind the one composed by his Cambridge teacher Charles Wood in 1902. Perhaps memories of the anguish of the Second Anglo-Boer War also played some part in the younger composer's choice of text. Vaughan Williams returned to his musical version of "A Dirge for Two Veterans" only after having seen active service during World War I and after his extensive work during the 1920s and 1930s for the Federal Union, an organization that promoted peace through the creation of a federated Europe.[37]

The second movement of *Dona Nobis Pacem,* a setting of one of Whitman's finest Civil War poems, "Reconciliation," also contains one of the few overtly homoerotic references in Whitman's poetry to be used by an English composer. In the middle of this movement, accompanied by an orchestral fabric of the utmost tenderness and intimacy, the baritone sings "For my enemy is dead, a man divine as myself is dead, / I look where he lies white-faced and still in the coffin—I draw near, / Bend down and touch lightly with my lips the white face in the coffin" ("Reconciliation," 4–6). This poignant but necrophiliac kiss is yet another example of how Whitman's erotic vision is inextricably intertwined with his fascination with death, which he personifies tellingly earlier in the poem: "The hands of the sisters Death and Night incessantly softly wash again and ever again this soiled world" (3). This kiss reflects Whitman's own experience as a volunteer in the wards of Washington hospitals during the Civil War; he was constantly planting kisses on soldiers, both Union and Confederate, whether they were healthy, wounded, dying, or dead. At the conclusion of his supremely moving poem "The Wound-Dresser," Whitman parenthetically confesses that "(Many a soldier's loving arms about this neck have cross'd and rested, / Many a soldier's kiss dwells on these bearded lips.)" (64–65).

Why, then, did Vaughan Williams, who did not hesitate to cut or modify a text to suit his purpose, retain these homoerotic lines from "Reconciliation" in his cantata? He may have chosen to ignore their homoerotic import, deciding to concentrate instead on the message of the human waste and tragedy of war that they portray so powerfully. But is it also possible that Vaughan Williams may have observed during his years on active service during World War I how strong and heartrending the bonds of comradely affection could become in wartime? Such questions are impossible to answer with any certainty; perhaps the best one can do is to cite the final stanza of "A Dirge for Two Veterans":

> *The moon gives you light,*
> *And the bugles and the drums give you music,*
> *And my heart, O my soldiers, my veterans,*
> *My heart gives you love. (33–36)*

Vaughan Williams's friend and colleague Gustav Holst was also fascinated by Whitman's poetry, although the musical response of the two composers could not have been more different. Early in his career Holst composed a *Whitman Overture* for orchestra (1890);[38] later he used Whitman's verse for three mature works: *The Mystic Trumpeter* for soprano and orchestra, op. 18 (1904); *A Dirge for Two Veterans* for male chorus, brass, and percussion (1914); and the *Ode to Death* for chorus and orchestra, op. 38 (1919). Holst dealt with the social pressures that impinged on composers in his period by developing a Zen-like detachment, ignoring society as much as possible. Unlike Vaughan Williams, who once counseled his friend to have a love affair, Holst gradually cut himself off from anything remotely resembling eroticism. A persistent and plausible story relates that when one of the pupils of St. Paul's Girl's School, where Holst worked as a music master, attempted to seduce him, he looked at the unfortunate girl as if he didn't know what she was talking about. Thus Holst's compositions to Whitman texts, such as the eerily prescient setting of *A Dirge for Two Veterans,*[39] which was completed just before the start of the Great War, possess a certain expressive tension generated by the contrast between the warmth of the American poet's verse and the austerity of the English composer's music.

Among the most ambitious and successful works in which Holst set passages from *Leaves of Grass* is his *Ode to Death.* For this elegy mourning the dead of World War I, Holst selected the same section of "When Lilacs Last in the Dooryard Bloom'd" that his teacher Stanford had set in his *Elegiac Ode* thirty-five years earlier. Any similarity between the two scores stops with their words, however. Unlike Stanford's suave but conventional score, Holst's powerful *Ode* shows the composer at his best: It is filled with daring bitonal passages, varied textures, startlingly brilliant orchestration and unusual chord structures. Unlike his teacher, whose music weakens the power of Whitman's sentiments, Holst strengthens the impact of the poem by his imaginative daring.

Frederick Delius was English only by accident of birth, for in all other ways he was a deeply cosmopolitan composer, personally and musically influenced by his sojourns to Florida, Scandinavia, and France. Delius did not consult the views of Victorian society concerning the supposed effeminacy of musicians: He simply disregarded them as irrelevant to his personality or experience. Vaughan Williams, with whom he shared little but an admiration for *Leaves of Grass,* loathed both Delius and his luscious post-Wagnerian, highly chromatic, cosmopolitan, and overtly erotic music.[40] In contrast to Vaughan Williams, Holst, or any other English-born composer, Delius responded to Whitman's verse with music of palpitating sensuality. Delius was not an earnest agnostic but rather a pantheistic atheist, who would never see Whitman's poetry as an up-to-date replacement for the Bible. In Whitman, Delius found the perfect poet of sensuous nostalgia and voluptuous loss. Although he was nothing if not sexually experienced, especially during the years he spent assiduously exploring the sexual underground of Paris,[41] no composer has ever been less prone to an interest in homoeroticism, either consciously or unconsciously, than Frederick Delius.

Delius's most perfectly realized large work is *Sea Drift,* a setting for baritone, chorus, and orchestra (1903–04) of an expert redaction of Whitman's haunting "Out of the Cradle Endlessly Rocking."[42] The chief expressive focus of *Sea Drift* is the protracted operatic lament of the anguished he-bird bereft of his mate. Delius's own passionate and thwarted love affair with a beautiful young African American woman during the 1880s when he was ostensibly managing a citrus grove in Florida explains both his initial attraction to the poem and his method of reducing it. Interestingly enough, Delius does not entirely delete the erotically charged relationship between the he-bird, mourning for his disappeared companion, and the boy who listens, learns from the plaint of the sorrowful bird, and narrates the poem.

This characteristic mood of sensuous longing and regret, so particular to this composer as to merit the adjective "Delian," is also found in his *Idyll* for soprano, baritone, and orchestra (1932). The text for this score is based largely on Whitman's "Once I Pass'd Through a Populous City," which Delius's librettist, the poet Robert Nichols, extended by adding shards of various poems from *Leaves of Grass*. Neither Delius nor his literary collaborator could have known at the time that "Once I Pass'd Through a Populous City" originally described a romantic encounter between the poet and another man; Whitman's notebooks reveal that he switched the pronouns from masculine to feminine sometime before publication. That Delius adapted music from his unsuccessful 1902 opera about an unlucky Parisian prostitute, *Margot la Rouge,* for the *Idyll* only deepens the unintentional irony.

The final lines of the *Idyll* compound the irony, for Nichols based the conclusion of his text on the following patently homoerotic passage from Whitman's Civil War threnody "Ashes of Soldiers":

> *Sweet are the blooming cheeks of the living—sweet are the musical voices*
> *    sounding,*
> *But sweet, ah sweet, are the dead with their silent eyes.*
> *Dearest comrades, all is over and long gone,*
> *But love is not over—and what love, O Comrades!*
> *Perfume from the battle-fields rising, up from the fœtor arising.* (29–33)

Whitman's conception intertwines the themes of war, death, and love with the same necrophiliac homoeroticism expressed in "Reconciliation." Nichols, who behaved more like a *bricoleur* than a poet in this instance, significantly distorts the meaning of these haunting lines as he wrenches them from their original homoerotic context ("ah my brave horsemen! / My handsome tan-faced horsemen!" [13–14]) and intersperses them with fragments from other poems by Whitman. Thus he provides a fitting conclusion for Delius's musical exercise in heterosexual nostalgia.

Delius's final major score, the *Songs of Farewell* for double chorus and orchestra (1929–30), also represents the last time that the composer set poetry by Whitman. Dictated note by note by the blind and paralyzed composer to his amanuensis Eric Fenby, the *Songs of Farewell* possess something of the luxuriant nostalgia of *Sea Drift* without its disturbing undercurrent of violence, passion, and despair. The text comes from the final, valedictory sections of *Leaves of Grass,* and the setting of autumnal words to reflective music expresses an affecting combination of pantheistic rapture and contemplative resignation in the face of death.

After the 1930s, the musical fashion for Whitman waned in England. After *Dona Nobis Pacem,* Vaughan Williams never again completed a score that included poetry by the American poet. Perhaps the despair and disillusionment that Vaughan Williams felt at the outbreak of World War II—responses vividly captured in such works as the anguished Sixth Symphony of 1948—made him less attuned to Whitman's unquenchable optimism. Younger composers such as Britten were not attracted to Whitman for much the same reasons that Vaughan Williams came to see, in Oliver Neighbour's trenchant phrase, "how one might get over him."[43] For the anxious homosexual Britten, Whitman may have been too obvious a homosexual signifier to approach with impunity. In addition, Whitman's poetry belonged to the generation of composers who had preceded Britten and against whom he reacted decisively. And it is hard to imagine Britten, the classic ephebephile, being inspired by Whitman's barrel-chested roughs and soldiers. For whatever reasons, Whitman's part was played out.

In his magisterial study *The Works of Ralph Vaughan Williams,* Michael Kennedy rightly declares that "Walt Whitman's poetry played a major rôle in the renascence of British music in the early twentieth century."[44] For fifty years, English composers found in Whitman a bracing aesthetic alternative to the "decadence" and introspection of much late Victorian poetry. Composers such as Vaughan Williams and Holst were invigorated by the "fresh thoughts" suggested by reading Whitman: his democratic idealism; his freedom from religious or political dogma; and his extroverted hope for the future of humanity. Finally, whether or not these composers invariably approved of his roistering style or homoerotic corporeality, Whitman's subversive celebration of his own individuality, both transcendent soul and fragrant armpits, helped liberate them from the conformity and parlorbound propriety of most Victorian music and inspired them to compose some exalted and, indeed, imperishable music.

### Notes

1. Oliver Neighbour, "The Place of the Eighth among Vaughan Williams's Symphonies," in *Vaughan Williams Studies,* ed. Alain Frogley (Cambridge: Cambridge University Press, 1996), p. 216.

2. Michael Kennedy, *The Works of Ralph Vaughan Williams* (London: Oxford University Press, 1980), p. 100.

3. See Harold Blodgett, *Walt Whitman in England* (Ithaca, N.Y.: Cornell University Press, 1934), p. 30.

4. Blodgett, *Whitman in England,* p. 24.

5. "Homosexual panic" can be defined as the fear of being identified as a homosexual as distinct from "homophobia," which is an irrational fear of homosexuals. See Eve Kosofsky Sedgwick, *Between Men: English Literature and Male Homosocial Desire* (New York: Columbia University Press, 1985), pp. 83–96.

6. Quoted in Richard Dellamora, *Masculine Desire: The Sexual Politics of Victorian Aestheticism* (Chapel Hill: University of North Carolina Press, 1990), pp. 87–88.

7. Dellamora, *Masculine Desire,* p. 88.

8. Ibid., pp. 86–88.

9. Blodgett, *Whitman in England,* p. 59.

10. Gary Schmidgall, *Walt Whitman: A Gay Life* (New York: Penguin Putnam, 1997), p. 74.

11. John Addington Symonds, *Walt Whitman: A Study* (London: John C. Nimmo, 1893), p. 34.

12. Dellamora, *Masculine Desire,* p. 87.

13. Schmidgall, *Walt Whitman,* pp. 143–52. Also see Byrne R. S. Fone, *Masculine Landscapes: Walt Whitman and the Homoerotic Text* (Carbondale: Southern Illinois University Press, 1992), p. 54.

14. Quoted in Schmidgall, *Whitman,* p. 144.

15. Vaughan Williams also loved this poem and made two sets of sketches for a setting of it: the first around 1908, and the second in 1957–58. See Michael Kennedy, *A Catalogue of the Works of Ralph Vaughan Williams* (2nd edn. Oxford: Oxford University Press, 1996), p. 42.

16. I have dealt at length with the origins of this crisis of belief in my essay "Scripture, Church and Culture: Biblical Texts in the Works of Ralph Vaughan Williams," in *Vaughan Williams Studies.* See esp. pp. 101–08.

17. See Paul Harrington, "Holst and Vaughan Williams: Radical Pastoral," in *Music and the Politics of Culture,* ed. Christopher Norris (London: Lawrence and Wishart, 1989), pp. 106–27.

18. Ursula Vaughan Williams, *R. V. W.: A Biography of Ralph Vaughan Williams* (Oxford: Oxford University Press, 1964), p. 65.

19. From "Song of Myself," section 20.

20. Lord Berners, *First Childhood* (Chappaqua, N.Y.: Turtle Point Press, 1998), p. 82.

21. Havelock Ellis, *The Psychology of Sex: Sexual Inversion,* vol. II (New York, 1910), p. 295. On the relationship of "musicality" and homosexuality, see Philip Brett, "Musicality, Essentialism, and the Closet," in *Queering the Pitch: The New Gay and Lesbian Musicology,* ed. Philip Brett, Elizabeth Wood, and Gary C. Thomas (New York: Routledge, 1994), pp. 9–26.

22. Joseph Bristow, *Effeminate England: Homoerotic Writing after 1885* (New York: Columbia University Press, 1995), p. 2.

23. Quentin Crisp, *The Naked Civil Servant* (New York: Penguin Books, 1983), p. 21.

24. William Gaunt, *The Aesthetic Adventure* (New York: Harcourt, Brace and Company, 1945), pp. 214–15.

25. Ursula Vaughan Williams, in conversation with the author.

26. Ursula Vaughan Williams, *A Biography of Vaughan Williams,* p. 313.

27. Ralph Vaughan Williams, "Bach, the Great Bourgeois," in *National Music and Other Essays* (Oxford: Oxford University Press, 1987), p. 171.

28. Quoted in Fone, *Masculine Landscapes,* p. 21.

29. Ursula Vaughan Williams, in conversation with the author.

30. Ursula Vaughan Williams, *A Biography of Vaughan Williams,* p. 65.

31. Joseph Bristow, *Effeminate England,* p. 151.

32. Gerald Cumberland, *Set Down in Malice* (London: Grant Richards, 1918), p. 255.

33. A study of Vaughan Williams's Bible, now in the British Library, strongly suggests that he originally planned a sung text for *Flos Campi*.

34. An undated letter from Ursula Vaughan Williams to Michael Kennedy throws light on the unusual circumstances surrounding the genesis of *Flos Campi:* "He behaved rather badly, I think, to a woman who was obviously rather in love with him, as he used to go & see her rather a lot then, to work himself up into the terrific state he needed to be in to be able to write it—but never went far enough to get actually involved—rather a tight-rope performance. He was much surprised when I said I thought it was very immoral to go so far & no further!" (KEN/3/1/7, no. 29, The Michael Kennedy Collection, John Rylands Library, Manchester).

35. Kennedy, *Catalogue,* p. 48.

36. Although Vaughan Williams excises four lines from "On the Beach at Night Alone," he does not otherwise alter Whitman's basic import.

37. Perhaps as part of his own peace effort, Vaughan Williams conducted a performance of *Dona Nobis Pacem* with the BBC Orchestra and Chorus, broadcast by the BBC in November 1936. A recording of this performance (with Renee Flynn, soprano, and Roy Henderson, baritone) has been issued on a Pearl compact disc, GEMM CD 9342.

38. Another orchestral score from roughly the same period inspired by the American poet is W. H. Bell's *Whitman Symphony* of 1900.

39. Holst probably knew Vaughan Williams's then unpublished setting of the same poem and may have known that of Wood as well.

40. Vaughan Williams once approached Delius's amanuensis Eric Fenby and demanded to know how much Delius's royalties had brought in that year. After listening to Fenby's reply, Vaughan Williams said "You tell Delius I made twice that much" (Eric Fenby, in conversation with the author).

41. Delius died as what Whitman termed a "venerealee."

42. Vaughan Williams set lines from "Out of the Cradle Endlessly Rocking" as the second of his early, unpublished Whitman settings, *Two Vocal Duets* for soprano,

baritone, piano, and string quartet ad lib from 1893. See Michael Kennedy, *Catalogue of the Works of Ralph Vaughan Williams,* pp. 23–24. An earlier unpublished example of a setting of Whitman's verse by Vaughan Williams is the ambitious *Three Nocturnes* for baritone, semichorus, and orchestra of 1908. See pp. 41–42.

43.  Oliver Neighbour, *Vaughan Williams Studies,* p. 216, n. 10.

44.  Kennedy, *Works,* p. 82.

CHAPTER 3

# Eros, Expressionism, and Exile
## Whitman in German Music

*Werner Grünzweig and Walter Grünzweig*

## Whitman's German-Language Reception:
## Themes and Translations

The story of Walt Whitman's reception in the German-speaking countries is one of radicalism and revolution. From 1868 on, when Ferdinand Freiligrath came out with the first small translation, Whitman excited some of the finest and most unorthodox minds in Germany, Austria, and Switzerland. *Leaves of Grass* was an important factor in the modernist revolution in German-language poetry, literature, and the arts starting in the first decade of the twentieth century. Whitman's poetry provided great formal and thematic inspiration for both German naturalism and turn-of-the-century artistic and literary movements and is also directly connected with the emergence of Expressionism.

But its significance is not limited to literature. The history of Whitman's multifaceted German reception includes politics, youth movements, sexuality, various subcultures such as the nudist movement, the arts and—significantly—music. Although Germans traditionally differentiate meticulously between highbrow and popular culture, the reception of Whitman frequently obliterates this distinction—proof of the American's democratizing force even in a foreign culture.

The nonliterary varieties of reception help bring out the general cultural impact of Whitman in the German-speaking world. Important issues to which Whitman's reception was relevant include the democratization of society and art in Prussian-dominated Germany and in Austria-Hungary; the initial German debate over gay emancipation (the first occasion on which this now prominent topic was discussed publicly, and therefore the origin of gay literary discourse relating to Whitman); and the cultural politics of the left. Whitman also helped shape Nazi poetry, but was nonetheless very influential among exiled Germans and Austrians. In the postwar years, Whitman's poetry contributed to the construction of new transatlantic bridges between the German-speaking countries and the United States.

The many German, Austrian, and Swiss literary, cultural, and social reactions to Whitman amount to new constructions of the author. Taken together, they make up an idealized mythical "German" Whit*mann*. In studying Whitman's cultural constructions in the German-speaking countries, one traces processes of exchange between Central European and American cultures.[1]

Interest in Whitman in the German-speaking countries has been intense from the very start. Since 1889, fifteen different book-length translations of Whitman's works have appeared, eight of which include major and representative selections from the *œuvre,* making Whitman's works available to large audiences. In many cases, the translators are significant literary personalities (albeit mostly on the countercultural side) whose commitment to the American poet proved favorable for Whitman's reception.[2]

Given the stifling authoritarianism in German and Austrian politics in the second half of the nineteenth century, it is not surprising that the initial impetus for Whitman's German reception came from abroad. As noted above, in 1868 Ferdinand Freiligrath, a prominent revolutionary German poet and former friend of Karl Marx, who, like Marx, lived in exile in England, translated and published the first selection of Whitman's poems in German. Overwhelmed by the poetry's formal innovations and by its American and democratic message, Freiligrath predicted that it would be a measure of things to come in international literature. This translation was the beginning of an intense love relationship between the German left and Walt Whitman.

The first book-length translation of Whitman's poetry appeared in 1889, the year in which the poet celebrated his well-publicized seventieth birthday. Again, the impetus came from outside Germany. The translated volume was a joint project of a German-American literary scholar and educator, Karl Knortz, and Thomas William Rolleston, an Irish philologist who greatly admired the Germans *and* Whitman. This translation of Whitman's poetry shocked the German bourgeoisie with their petrified aesthetic standards and renewed both German art and German literature. The volume was published by a radical Swiss publisher and made Whitman well known among the naturalist group of German and Austrian writers that included Gerhart Hauptmann.

One member of the naturalist group, Johannes Schlaf, became Whitman's most important spokesman in the German-speaking countries. A correspondent of Whitman's main propagandist in the United States, Horace Traubel, Schlaf became Whitman's "prophet" in Germany. He was responsible for Whitman's cultic reception there between the 1890s and the 1920s. His 1907 translation of selections of *Leaves of Grass* was published in an inexpensive mass-market literary series that made Whitman immensely popular. Schlaf's translation, anticipating the messianic mode of German Expressionism, further intensified Whitman's already oratorical style.

Two less influential book-length translations by Karl Federn and Wilhelm Schölermann appeared three years prior to Schlaf's edition. Federn's translation attempted to do justice to the musical quality of Whitman's poetry, whereas Schölermann, a German nationalist, recreated many of Whitman's poems in the spirit of German military marches.

A further series of translations appeared after Germany's defeat in World War I. The majority of the translators were allied to the left, which helped to confirm Whitman's place in the German and Central European workers movement. The most important personality among these translators was Gustav Landauer, an important figure in the history of the German left and of German letters. The variety of his occupations and vocations rivals Whitman's: critic, translator, journalist, writer, and, for a brief time, member of the short-lived revolutionary Bavarian government after the breakdown of the German Empire in 1918. Landauer was a Jewish anarchist, a visionary mystic, and an ardent admirer of Whitman who read the American author in a spiritual and radically pacifist mode.

If there is a "classic" translation of Whitman's poetry and prose, it is by Hans Reisiger, a first-rate translator and a friend of Thomas Mann. Mann, himself a Whitman devotee, endorsed the translation, calling it a "great, important, indeed holy gift . . . [for which] the German public [ . . . ] can not be grateful enough [ . . . ]."[3] Although the two-volume edition with gold-lettered spines forms the most comprehensive selection from Whitman's prose and poetry to date, it also has a specific focus. Reisiger's selection highlights the (homo)erotic tendencies of Whitman's poetry, for the first time including the "Children of Adam" and "Calamus" poems almost in their entirety. Its "classic" quality is expressed more through its diction, which is stylistically reminiscent of German authors such as Goethe and Rilke.

Several translations, all quite different, emerged after World War II. One brief volume, a very subjective and "artistic" translation by Georg Goyert, appeared in 1948. The largest and most ambitious project is that of Erich Arendt, published in the German Democratic Republic in 1966. Emphasizing Whitman's social(ist) and in this sense revolutionary dimension, Arendt is faced with the twin task of escaping a *pathos* that had been discredited by the rhetoric of German national-socialist propaganda and of presenting Whitman as a positive force in the construction of socialism. In this endeavor, he makes successful use of his experience during the Nazi regime as an exile in South America, where he was introduced to Whitman's poetry by friends, including Pablo Neruda.

The interest taken in Whitman in the German Democratic Republic was a special case. After the immediate postwar years were over, he lost his massive creative appeal for both German poets and the reading public at large. Although he is by no means forgotten, Whitman's influence is far from being as pervasive as it was in the first half of the twentieth century.

## German Composers and Whitman

Unlike their literary counterparts, German composers were mostly fascinated by Whitman as a political poet. We have found no attempts to translate literary forms into musical ones; Whitman's musical reception was shaped by his language and themes. As a result of his innovations in these areas, almost no "minor" composers seem to have tried their hands at Whitman's texts. His poetry did not lend itself to the epigonous production of strophic songs that had become negligible in the history of German music after Hugo Wolf. Rather, it opened up possibilities for the elaboration of modern "musical prose."

At the same time there were no Whitman composers who decisively influenced the history of music in the German-speaking countries. Othmar Schoeck, Franz Schreker, and Johanna Müller-Hermann were much more a part of late Romanticism than of the avant-garde, in spite of the latter two composers' relationship with Arnold Schoenberg's Second Viennese School. The situation is similar with Hans Werner Henze, Karl Amadeus Hartmann, Friedrich Wildgans, and Ernst Toch, whose Whitman compositions all premiered after 1945. They took up a middle position between twelve-tone music and neoclassicism and largely rejected later developments.

There also are a number of special cases among German-language Whitman composers. Eduard Zuckmayer belongs to a species of "pedagogical" composers whom we subsume under the term *Jugendmusikbewegung* (youth music movement). Their initial antibourgeois impetus soon gave way to a petit bourgeois notion of music as entertainment, even though Zuckmayer's specific choice of text may suggest a subtle oppositional stance against the threat of a Nazi regime. Paul Hindemith, hailed as an alternative to the Viennese School in the interwar years, had become altogether conservative by the time he wrote his *Flieder-Requiem* based on Whitman's "When Lilacs Last on the Dooryard Bloom'd." Kurt Weill made a conscious decision to become an American composer and accordingly set Whitman in English.

Musical settings of Whitman in the German-speaking countries usually take the form of songs with orchestral or instrumental accompaniment, even though they are often designated differently. It is therefore necessary to consider the status of German song genres in the twentieth century.

The choice of texts was critical for those composers who were not engaged in standardized mass production. The *Lied* was raised from the eminently private context of *Hausmusik,* a repertoire of Classical and Romantic music adopted by the bourgeoisie to be played in concerts in private homes, to a highly respected status in concert life.[4] The artistic prestige of the *Lied* in the chamber music of the early decades of this century can be compared only to that of the string quartet, which took over the "paradigm of the idea of absolute music"[5] from the symphony starting in 1870. Both genres, the string quartet and the *Lied,* became important experimental grounds for the progressive composers of the Second Viennese School (Schoenberg's Second Quartet is a critical instance in which the genres fuse), although there was quite a bit of flexibility in the transitional period. The tradition of the Romantic *Lied* was still unbroken, but its significance had changed. Never before in the history of music, not even in the case of Schubert, the *Lied* composer *par excellence,* had the genre played such an important role.

There was a surprising degree of agreement regarding the significance of the *Lied.* Both Brahms and his self-declared mortal enemy Hugo Wolf wrote songs and song cycles. But Wolf early on exhibited a new attitude toward the text. He called his song cycles "Poems . . . for voice and piano" as if wanting to stress the primary significance of the text. To him, the task of music was to provide a detailed interpretation of the text, which the vocalist would treat *as* a text, not as verbal music. Wolf's artistry was grounded in his ability to balance these innovations with the traditional patterns of the *Lied.* But the *Lied* had already lost many of its traditional characteristics, such as melodic formation in periodic musical syntax and simplicity of construction. The fact that Wolf, unlike Brahms, only used first-rate authors for his settings is of great interest for an understanding of German Whitman music.

In addition to the *Lied,* German song includes the genre of the *Gesang.* Although this differentiation derives from literary criticism, it was applied to music by composers themselves and not by theoreticians. There is a difference between the simplicity of the *Lied* and the complexity of the *Gesang.* The *Lied* tends to be stanzaic, the *Gesang* through-composed. The increased prestige of the *Lied* around 1910 encouraged interest in the *Gesang*—a development that favorably influenced the reception of Whitman's "free" verse. Many translators render Whitman's *Song of Myself* as "Gesang von mir selbst."

The majority of German Whitman settings do not call for accompaniment by piano, but by orchestra or instrumental ensemble, suggesting that Whitman's poetry was read "politically" in the sense that it required a large audience. Whereas a simple *Lied,* based on a lyrical poem, has a natural place in a private context, a concert ensemble and especially an orchestra always have a larger and public appeal.

It is difficult to ascertain how German-speaking composers came to know Whitman. If there is one composer who acted as a mediator, however, it is Frederick Delius, an Englishman whose life and career connected him with both the United States and Germany. Delius was born of German parents in Bradford in 1865. In 1884 he settled in Florida to become an orange farmer but then moved to Leipzig in 1886 in order to study music. In 1903/04 Delius wrote a piece for solo baritone, mixed choir, and large orchestra based on a poem by Walt Whitman. Considered to be one of Delius's most important compositions, *Im Meerestreiben/Sea Drift* was published in Berlin in 1906 in a bilingual edition; the translation was by Delius's wife, Jelka Rosen. On

12 December 1912, *Im Meerestreiben* was performed in Vienna by the Philharmonic Choir directed by Franz Schreker. Some twelve years later, Schreker himself would set Whitman to music. Thus, Whitman compositions appeared early on in the musical life of the German-speaking countries.

## An Overview

What follows is a chronological survey of the various Whitman compositions by German composers. The titles as well as the information on genre and instrumentation are in the original German.

1.  Othmar Schoeck, *Trommelschläge*. Gedicht von Walt Whitman, für gemischten Chor und großes Orchester, 1915, trans. Johannes Schlaf ("Beat! Beat! Drums!").
2.  Paul Hindemith, *Drei Hymnen von Walt Whitman,* für Bariton und Klavier, op. 14, 1919, trans. Johannes Schlaf (1. "Der ich, in Zwischenräumen" ["Ages and Ages Returning at Intervals"]; 2. "O, nun heb du an, dort in deinem Moor" ["Sing on there in the Swamp" from "When Lilacs . . ."]; 3. "Schlagt! Schlagt! Trommeln!" ["Beat! Beat! Drums!"]).
3.  Franz Salmhofer, *Der Geheimnisvolle Trompeter,* Melodram mit Orchester, premiered 1924, no published music found.
4.  Franz Schreker, *Vom ewigen Leben*. Zwei lyrische Gesänge nach Dichtungen von Walt Whitman (aus den "Grashalmen"), 1924 (orchestral version 1929), trans. Hans Reisiger (1. "Wurzeln und Halme sind dies nur" ["Roots and Leaves Themselves Alone"]; 2. "Ein Kind sagte: 'Was ist das Gras?' " ["A child said *What is the grass?*"]).
5.  Paul Hindemith, *Eine lichte Mitternacht,* Chor a cappella, trans. Johannes Schlaf, 1929 ("A Clear Midnight").
6.  Johanna Müller-Hermann, *Lied der Erinnerung. In memoriam*. Dichtung von Walt Whitman aus dem Zyklus "Zum Gedächtnis des Präsidenten Lincoln," Lyrische Kantate für vier Solostimmen, Chor, Orchester und Orgel, op. 30, 1930, original text and translation by Johannes Schlaf ("When Lilacs Last in the Dooryard Bloom'd").
7.  Eduard Zuckmayer, *Kameradschaft*. Kantate nach Worten aus den "Grashalmen" von Walt Whitman für einstimmigen Chor (oder eine Einzelstimme) und Streichinstrumente (Bläser nach Belieben), 1932 (Neue Schulkantaten zur Pflege des gemeinsamen Musizierens von Schulchören und Schulorchestern hg. von Fritz Jöde, Nr.1). Translation not identified ("For You O Democracy").
8.  Kurt Weill, *Four Walt Whitman Songs,* for voice and piano, No. 1–3: 1942, No. 4: 1947 (1–3 auch in Orchesterfassung, Datum unklar),

original text (1. "Oh Captain! My Captain!"; 2. "Beat! Beat! Drums!"; 3. "Dirge for Two Veterans"; 4. "Come Up from the Fields Father").

9. Paul Hindemith, *Nine English Songs,* original text, 1943. (Songs based on poems from different poets, including Whitman's "Sing on there in the Swamp" from "When Lilacs"; this version later included in the *Flieder-Requiem*).

10. Paul Hindemith, *When Lilacs Last In The Door-yard Bloom'd: A Requiem "For Those We Love"/Als Flieder jüngst mir im Garten blüht. Ein Requiem "Für die, die wir lieben,"* nach der Dichtung von Walt Whitman, Mezzo-Sopran und Bariton-Solo, Chor und Orchester, 1946, trans. Paul Hindemith.

11. Ernst Hermann Meyer, *Nun Steuermann fahr hin.* Ode für Bariton (oder Mezzosopran) und Streichquartett (oder Streichorchester) nach Worten von Walt Whitman, 1946, trans. Susan Jacobs (combination of several Whitman poems).

12. Karl Amadeus Hartmann, *1. Symphonie (Versuch eines Requiems),* nach Worten von Walt Whitman für eine Altstimme und Orchester, 1947–48 (Frühfassung 1935–36), probably Reisiger, adapted by the composer. (1. "Introduktion" ["I Sit and Look Out"]; 2. "Frühling" ["When Lilacs Last in the Dooryard Bloom'd"]; 3. "Tränen" ["Tears"]; 4. "Epilog: Bitte" ["Pensive on Her Dead Gazing"]).

13. Hans Werner Henze, *Whispers of Heavenly Death.* Kantate auf das gleichnamige Gedicht von Walt Whitman für hohe Singstimme (Sopran oder Tenor) und Klavier oder acht Solo-Instrumente, 1948, original text and trans. by Georg Goyert ("Darest Thou Now O Soul").

14. Friedrich Wildgans, *Der mystische Trompeter,* op. 52. Ein Zyklus nach sechs Gedichten von Walt Whitman. Hohe Stimme, Trompete in C und Klavier, fünfziger Jahre (early version op. 47, 1946?), trans. Gustav Landauer ("The Mystic Trumpeter").

15. Ernst Toch, from "Leaves of Grass" (*Song of Myself,* section 32) by Walt Whitman for mixed Chorus a cappella, unpublished 1961, original.

16. Gerd Kühr, *Walt Whitman for President.* Music on three poems by Walt Whitman for Soprano and Seven Players, 1984, original. (1. "When I Peruse the Conquer'd Fame," 2. "Lo, Victress on the Peaks," 3. "Long, Too Long America").

The large majority of German settings of Whitman poems deal with the theme of war. Schoeck's *Trommelschläge* are a direct reaction to World War I. The Nazi regime and World War II are significant contexts for Weill's Whitman songs, Hindemith's *Flieder-Requiem,* Hartmann's symphony, and the cycle by Wildgans. Zuckmayer's cantata presents a special case. Composed in 1932, it amounts to a warning against antidemocratic developments in German politics. Seven of the sixteen compositions or cycles were created within a period of only a few years prior to and after 1945. Compared to the creative reception in German literature, especially by German-language authors of the naturalist period around 1890 and the Expressionist period between 1910 and 1920, there is a lag of several decades. A second set of themes, intersecting with the first, is that of remembrance, grief, and death. The works by Müller-Hermann, Weill, Hindemith (the Requiem), Hartmann (*Versuch eines Requiems*), Meyer, and Henze would have to be included here. A third thematic group includes depictions of natural settings with transcendentalist and utopian undertones such as those in the compositions by Schreker, Zuckmayer, Wildgans, and Toch.

There are individual poems and whole sections of *Leaves of Grass* that are repeatedly used by composers. Schoeck, Hindemith, and Weill selected poems from *Drum-Taps*. Hindemith initially set parts of "When Lilacs Last in the Dooryard Bloom'd" to music. Later, Müller-Hermann used the whole poem, and eventually Hindemith did so himself. Hartmann used the beginning for one movement of his symphony. "The Mystic Trumpeter" was set by Wildgans and Salmhofer.

Whether the various composers inspired each other in the use of particular texts and whether Whitman's reception was significantly furthered by the composers remains uncertain. Only one such case is documented, namely that of Henze, who became acquainted with Whitman through Hartmann's symphony. It remains a distinct possibility that there is a special Viennese reception of Whitman (Schreker, Müller-Hermann). Schoeck became acquainted with Whitman through the Swiss author and Whitmanite Gustav Gamper.

The various composers had no preferred translator; possibly, it was more the availability than the quality of the translation that counted. Only Schlaf and Reisiger appear several times; translations by Goyert, Landauer, and Susan Jacobs are used once each. Weill and Toch, who had been exiled to the United States, used the original texts. Only one composer, Hindemith, produced a translation of his own in order to ensure that the number of syllables would correspond precisely to the original text. Henze and Müller-Hermann, in whose works the translation also appears next to the original version, did not use this approach.

The following brief analyses are designed to provide a synoptic understanding of the individual German composers' musical constructions of Whitman. The bases of the analyses include the historical context of the works—always a factor even with the most abstract-seeming music; the works' specific musical languages; and, in some cases, events in the composer's life.

## Othmar Schoeck

The Swiss-born composer Othmar Schoeck (1886–1957) was deeply immersed in the Romantic tradition of the *Lied*. The authors he had set to music earlier included Eichendorff, Uhland, Lenau, Mörike, and Keller, the "classical" canon of German poetry. His *Trommelschläge,* composed in 1915, therefore has a strategic place in his *œuvre.* Under the influence of World War I, his aesthetic standards changed radically, and he moved closer to the expressionist variant of German Modernist art. His Whitman composition is his personal political statement against the war. It premiered in a concert by the renowned Tonhalle Orchestra in Zürich in March 1916 and was designed to carry the horrors of war right into the heart of the life of the Swiss bourgeoisie, the concert hall.

At that time, Schoeck had a solid and respected position as director of the *Lehrergesangsverein* (teachers' choral association) in Zürich. He knew that the performance of this musical invitation to carnage would threaten his employment: "This piece may break my neck in Zürich," he wrote to Hermann Hesse on 24 August 1915.[6] The concert hall scandals of Vienna and Paris had occurred only two years previously. Extreme aesthetic innovation could result in very real physical threats to an artist. According to the majority view of the audience, a concert hall was a nonpolitical area, and by introducing a topic related to current international politics, Schoeck clearly broke the rules.

In his composition, Schoeck commented on the war indirectly. The point was not to draw forth pity and sympathy from the public by producing a text in the pacifist-humanist vein. Such sympathy can easily be obtained and usually involves regret merely over the seemingly unchangeable *condition humaine,* the—supposedly—eternal destiny of humankind. Rather, Schoeck wanted to shock the audience by deliberately breaking aesthetic taboos. Whitman's text enthusiastically calls for the drums to beat, to destroy bourgeois life and all of its values. In those places where the drums flatten everyday urban life, Schoeck's music is often bitonal: One layer covers the next and finally buries it. The whole composition is distorted by dissonances. Although traditional musical elements are still present, they lose their significance or remain isolated, lacking their original syntactical context. Many dimensions of this music are enormously exaggerated. In addition to a very large brass section, there is a huge drum section adequate to the title, containing no less than six tenor drums marking the all-flattening drum tap that is kept up throughout the composition. In an Expressionist manner, the whole orchestra functions as one single drum supporting this central rhythm. Without saying so explicitly, this exaggerated music amounts to an "épater le bourgeois"—an attempt to provoke contradiction.[7]

### Kurt Weill

Almost three decades later, Kurt Weill (1900–50) also used "Beat! Beat! Drums!" in his *Whitman-Songs*. In doing so, he arranged the irregular lines rhythmically so that they make up three stanzas of roughly the same length, whereas Schoeck derived his expressiveness directly from the special nature of the text and its linguistic rhythm. David Drew wrote about the origin of Weill's compositions:

> The [1942] set was intended for Paul Robeson . . . and was offered to the Fight for Freedom organization. . . . In the aftermath of Pearl Harbor, Fight for Freedom had necessarily changed its programme, and was now involved in the new national task of morale-boosting. That purpose, with its essentially popular implications, is reflected in the very nature of Weill's settings, which are clearly not intended as "art songs" in the European sense.[8]

Compared to Schoeck's, Weill's means are relatively simple. Using the conventions of the propaganda song, Weill, a German-Jewish composer who not only identified with his country of exile but decidedly *wanted* to identify with it, created his own political statement. In 1942 Weill well understood the ambiguity of "Beat! Beat! Drums!" as an at least partially positive statement on war. With the actress Helen Hayes, he recorded the poem as an accompanied recitation, along with *The Star Spangled Banner* and *The Battle Hymn of the Republic*. In compiling his Whitman songs, however, he complemented this purely patriotic gesture by framing the fully composed "Beat! Beat! Drums!" with two poems of sorrow and grief. A third such poem was added in 1947. The first deals with the death of Lincoln, the leader fighting the forces of slavery (during World War II, Lincoln was frequently seen as an antecedent of Roosevelt, especially by exiles from Europe). The second poem, "Dirge for Two Veterans," conjures up two soldiers, son and father, who "dropt" and are buried together; the third, "Come Up from the Fields Father" shows a family's reaction to the news of the death of their only son. These compositions create a cycle that both issues a call to war and expresses grief over the necessity of such a call.[9]

### Requiems: Hindemith and Hartmann

Following the end of World War II, two German Whitman compositions were written under the designation "Requiem." This generic designation relates these compositions to the great requiems of music history as well as to a requiem's traditional text. The most famous German example is Johannes Brahms's *Ein deutsches Requiem,* which departs from the original (Latin) text of the requiem Mass.[10] The specific use of the text was probably a central issue in these compositions.

Paul Hindemith (1895–1963) originally had not planned to set the whole of "When Lilacs Last in the Dooryard Bloom'd" to music.[11] He had composed parts of it earlier. When he decided to round out the whole work, he faced the problem of structuring the text. Accordingly, he did not write a sequence of orchestrated songs for one single voice but a type of oratorio for baritone, mezzo-soprano, and chorus. The distribution is plainly symbolic— two individuals of different sex and a group of people united in grief form an image of humankind. In the solo voices, songlike passages alternate with passages resembling recitative.

Hindemith contracts the sixteen sections of Whitman's text to eleven. While he mostly respects the original structure and rarely separates individual stanzas, the first three sections are synthesized in a baritone solo with a middle section sung by the chorus (no. 2 of the original text). The baritone opens the narrative; the symbols of life and death are introduced. Then the chorus enters and grief leads to indictment. While the chorus sustains its last note, the baritone once more takes up the lyrical narrative. The conclusion, *recitativo*-style, involves the breaking of the "sprig of lilac" summarizing the sad news of the first section, which now also points to the subsequent narrative.

Hindemith's second section corresponds to Whitman's fourth stanza. Its aria for female voice corresponds to the song of the solitary thrush that is one of the poem's primary symbols. (By means of orchestration, Whitman's stanzas 9 and 13 are subsequently connected with stanza 4 and marked as inserts in the narrative.) If the baritone voice is identified as that of the narrator, the mezzo-soprano may identify yet another level, a superordinated voice allegorically requesting the narrator to continue his song.

The chorus expresses collective experiences by referring to nature or to the country as a whole. Its sections include the laments, the "Hymnus für den Tod" (Hindemith's designation for "Come lovely and soothing death"), the visualization of the coffin's travel through the country, and especially the central section 7 (the second part of Whitman's eleventh and the twelfth stanza), which evokes the grandeur of the country in a choral fugue.

The way that Hindemith divides Whitman's poem does justice to it. Although there are definitely topical explanations for the assignment of certain passages to solo voice or chorus, the distribution of voices is not exclusively thematic. Although the baritone takes up the major part of the narrative, he is not sharply separated from the chorus. Thus his solo voice mingles with the chorus, reflecting both the integration of the individual in the social whole and the claim of the author, not merely to sing with one single voice, but to represent a multiplicity of voices.

Hindemith's musical language and his forms are conventional throughout the requiem. In spite of many harmonic alterations, the music is not truly chromatic. Rather, its harmonic structure involves modality. The work as a

whole is neither through-composed nor does it consist of a sequence of autonomous songs. The different parts are connected through motifs, some of
which could be called *Leitmotivs*. Because Hindemith places much emphasis
on the "correct" rhythm of language, the vocal line is constructed freely and
does not fit into any one scheme. The composer, however, draws no radical
conclusions from either the text or its form. He provides solid workman-
ship—no more, but also no less.[12]

The first impression gained from the Whitman composition of Karl
Amadeus Hartmann (1905–63), especially compared to Hindemith's Requiem, is the high degree of expressivity, the subjective musical interpretation of the text. Hartmann places the language in the foreground much more
prominently than Hindemith. In many places, the voice recites more than it
sings, so that the expressive language can fully unfold. Where the vocal part
separates from the recital, its expressivity is extremely heightened. Initially,
the voice alternates between two reciting tones. Suddenly, at the words "Mär-
tyrer und Gefangene" (martyrs and prisoners), it ascends melodically. Hartmann's orchestra is not "objective" like Hindemith's; rather, it is colorful and
highly expressive.

Unlike Hindemith, Hartmann did not set Whitman's elegy as a whole; he
simply included a passage from it in a textual composite drawn from several
poems. The resulting cycle at times seems more well rounded and complete
than some of Whitman's own. Hartmann probably used Hans Reisiger's
translation, which he freely adapted and shortened.

The symphony has a symmetrical structure. An introduction and epilogue enclose two movements, which in turn enclose a theme and four variations. This central variation movement forms a compact image of the
symphony itself; the four variations are like variations on grief. The outer
movements, an introduction and epilogue subtitled "Elend" (distress) and
"Bitte" (plea), seem to be connected thematically. The alto voice of the
"Elend," which could be identified with the "Mother of All" of the final
movement, sings: "Ich sitze und schaue aus auf alle Plagen der Welt . . ." (I
sit and look out upon all the sorrows of the world . . . ). As she seems to see
everything, one is reminded of the all-knowing Erda from Wagner's *Ring
des Nibelungen*. In the "Bitte" we hear: "Ich hörte die Allmutter, als sie
gedankenvoll auf all ihre Toten schaute" (Pensive on her dead gazing I
heard the Mother of All). The ensuing plea to the earth not to lose the dead
provides consolation only in a pantheistic frame of mind. Textually—
though not musically—Hartmann returns to the beginning of the symphony
at its very end as if he wanted to prove the impossibility of change, to express a fatalistic view of history. This philosophical position is in marked
contrast to Hartmann's political thinking, which was close to the ideals of
socialism.

The second movement, entitled "Frühling" (Spring), is based on a modified version of the first section of "When Lilacs Last in the Dooryard Bloom'd":

> *Als jüngst der Flieder blühte vor der Tür*
> *Und der Stern am Himmel früh in die Nacht sank,*
> *trauerte ich, und werde trauern mit jedem Frühling neu.*
> *Sooft du, Frühling, ach Frühling, wiederkehrst,*
> *Dreiheit immer wirst uns bringen:*
> *Flieder blühend jedes Jahr,*
> *Elend ach, gibst du uns all'.*
> *Und Gedanken an den Tod, der uns nah'.*

Hartmann's final two lines, "Distress you give to all of us / And thoughts of death, which is so close," depart from Whitman's poem and support the pessimistic character of the symphony. The blooming lilac, a symbol of spring and thereby of vitality and hope for a better life, is here connected with misery and death. In the final line of Whitman's section 1, "And thought of him I love," the word "love" assumes great expressive weight because it is located at the very end of both the line and of the stanza. The memory of a beloved person is an image of consolation. Even if the person is dead, he lives on in our memory—a notion important to many mythologies and to the elegiac tradition. Hartmann might have used a different line, for example, "Gedanken an die, die uns nah" (Memories of those we love), which would have been closer to the original and would have ensured the coherence of the stanza. Instead, he replaced the consolatory image by the painful and unmitigated thought of death.

The poem "Tears," on which the third movement is based, is part of the "Sea Drift" section of *Leaves of Grass*. With an ostinato in the orchestra, extreme variations in the vocal part, which reaches to very low ranges, and instruments such as the double bass in very high ranges, Hartmann produces a musical image of tension and nervousness. This image is in stark contrast to the resigned character of the recitation.

At the beginning of the epilogue, the effect of the text is further sharpened. The female voice now speaks in the *Sprechstimme* style of Schoenberg's melodramas accompanied only by the orchestra's drums. Further reinforcing the power of the text, the military connotations of the drums assume a programmatic function.

A requiem eventually must express consolation and signal peace, salvation, and victory over death, but Hartmann's symphony declines to do this. Unlike Hindemith, Hartmann found that a requiem with a consolatory message was no longer possible. Grief becomes meaningless when mere survival engenders guilt because so many others have been killed. Consequently, Hartmann calls his symphony only "Versuch eines Requiems" (Attempt at a Requiem). But does not the round and symmetrical structure and the life-affirming

future-directed designation "1st [!] Symphony" contradict this negative attitude? Is not "the dark dirge a song nevertheless and therefore [something
that] keeps up our hope," as Dieter Schnebel once put it?

### Friedrich Wildgans

At one point the Whitman composition of Friedrich Wildgans (1913–65), *Der
mystiche Trompeter,* is reminiscent of the Introduction to Hartmann's symphony, which paraphrases lines from "I Sit and Look Out":

> Ich beobachte die Geringschätzung und Erniedrigung, die die Armen von
> Hochmütigen zu erleiden haben; auf alle Gemeinheit und Qual ohne Ende.
>
> (I observe the slights and degradations cast by arrogant persons upon the
> poor—all the meanness and agony without end.)

In *Der mystiche Trompeter,* a line in the fifth part ("Empörung," corresponding to the seventh stanza in Whitman's poem) reads:

> Ich sehe die Getret'nen, Unterjochten, Leidenden, Gedrückten des ganzen
> Erdenrunds.
>
> (I see the enslaved, the overthrown, the hurt, the opprest of the whole earth.)

In every other respect, however, Wildgans's piece lies at the opposite end
of the spectrum from Hartmann's, which was written at about the same time.
*Der mystiche Trompeter* also deals with repression and war but it ends with a
Utopian hymn. The text has a key feature in common with "When Lilacs Last
in the Dooryard Bloom'd"; in both, redemptive memory is connected with a
musical vision, a solitary sound heard from afar in the night. That the sound
here belongs to a trumpet allows Wildgans to realize it directly, as Hindemith,
for example, could not do in his "Lilacs" requiem, where the sound of the
bird is symbolized by both an English horn and the voice of the mezzo-
soprano. Wildgans's trumpeter does not require a representative: he himself
plays his own part.

The eight stanzas of Whitman's original poem can be roughly divided
into an introduction, a main section, and a conclusion. The introduction
would comprise stanzas 1–3, the main section 4–7, and the conclusion 8. In
the introduction, the lyrical persona addresses the trumpeter "that I may thee
translate." The "imbonded spirit" is to be liberated by the force of life, probably from the limitations of place and time.

The main section then deals with the following themes in one stanza
each: the distant past, love ("pulse of all"), war, and humiliation ending in resistance. The conclusion presents the utopian vision of a new society based

on joy (or, as Wildgans has it in Landauer's translation, in "Lust"). Wildgans has eliminated stanzas 4 and 5 (the past and love). Whitman's topical presentation of life and his illustration of the history of humankind in several incompatible examples seem to have given way to a more conclusive sequence. The series love—the past—war—humiliation / resistance—utopia is rendered more concrete and linear by the elimination of its first two terms. From a damaged present, a potentially better future (the utopian conclusion) is predicted as a result of resistance.

Musically, *Der mystische Trompeter* suggests a somewhat distanced neoclassicism. It seems as though the starting point of Wildgans's composition were the initial line "Horch, welch wilder Musikant" (Hark, some wild trumpeter). "Musikant" is an important term in the anti-intellectual youth movement of the period and is in ideological contrast to the neutral term "Musiker." It implies the task of the musician to bridge class differences in the name of an idealized intact community and the hope to be able to ignore the challenges of modernity. The similarity to Hindemith's *Drei Hymnen* written some thirty years earlier is conspicuous. Wildgans seems consciously to have selected a bygone, possibly obsolete musical language.

### Eduard Zuckmayer

Zuckmayer (1890–1972), brother of the author Carl Zuckmayer, was a representative of the "Jugendmusikbewegung." The youth movement in Germany and Austria started around 1900 and lasted well into the 1920s. It called for the liberation of young people from the constrictions of home and parents, school and teachers, and the urban environment at large. It cultivated outdoor feelings through hiking trips and tours. In principle, these activities were to be self-managed by young people—with individuals in their late teens or twenties as leaders of groups of younger people.

The main success of the musical wing of the youth movement was that members of the petit bourgeoisie were won over to active music making. Whereas the original goal was to ground music firmly in everyday life, this concept soon became tainted with ideology. The notion of "Gemeinschaft" (community), which was central to the youth movement, became an ideological weapon in the hands of a politically and economically powerless petit bourgeoisie against the emancipation of the working classes and against a democratic society at large. The "communities" of the youth movement based on the "Führer" principle thus anticipated—and paralleled—the development of society toward National Socialism. It was not difficult for the Nazis to incorporate this movement into their own ranks. Of course, this does not mean that all representatives of this movement became Nazis or that this incorporation automatically compromised the movement as a whole (after all, Handel, Beethoven, Bruckner, and Wagner also were claimed by the

Nazis as their own). Many members of the movement in fact became staunch anti-Nazis.

Musically, the main representatives of the movement strove for aesthetic simplicity in order to include those who had not benefited from educational privileges. By singing together, the social division of labor was to be obliterated. Furthermore, old musical material and old musical forms were revived. Zuckmayer's "Schulkantante" (school cantata) *Kameradschaft* is an example of this strategy. The musical process is determined by pedal points, fuguelike entrances, and melodic lines that have no specific harmonic functions but come together coincidentally. Rather than dissolving tonality, whole-tone sections are employed to avoid leading tones.

The text is an abbreviated and significantly adapted version of Whitman's "For You O Democracy" from the "Calamus" series. The title is omitted, the first person singular is replaced by the first person plural, and the famous last lines in which democracy is addressed as "ma femme" are eliminated. The themes thus emphasized—the latent homosexuality of male bonding, the notion of a new beginning, and the suspension of social classes—all became part of the mandatory ideology in Nazi Germany shortly after the composition of the cantata in 1932. Nevertheless, there are indications that the use of this poem in the composition expresses a criticism of Nazi ideology. In spite of the omission of the original title, which praises democracy, the selection of this particular poem implies a protest against the antidemocratic and authoritarian developments in Germany that loomed on the horizon. In 1934 Zuckmayer lost his job as a teacher in an alternative school and joined the large group of exiles who turned their back on Germany.

### Johanna Müller-Hermann

The most extensive of Germanic Whitman compositions was created by the Viennese composer Johanna Müller-Hermann (1878–1941). As a student of Alexander Zemlinsky, she must have had at least some contact with the Second Viennese School. There is hardly any literature on Müller-Hermann, even though she was obviously a well-known composer and educator whose works were printed in respectable editions and also performed, for example, by the Philharmonic Choir directed by Franz Schreker. A letter she wrote to Schoenberg in 1911 suggests a direct acquaintance with the leader of Viennese modernism.

Müller-Hermann's "lyrische Kantate" *Lied der Erinnerung: In Memoriam* (1930) is a monumental work with a large orchestra, divided chorus, and solo voices. The work is a late representative in the tradition of Schoenberg's *Gurre-Lieder,* which had been written around 1900. Following nineteenth-century modes, the highly Romantic musical language presents and attempts to interpret every detail of the text. The stanzas of the original poem ("When

Lilacs Last in the Dooryard Bloom'd" again) remain, but the distribution of the individual voices is complex. There is no clear division as in Hindemith's work; the voices frequently come together in one single song, and the chorus plays a much more important role.

The motivation for such a large composition cannot be ascertained based on the biographical data available. The choice of Whitman's text seems to be connected with the composer's interest in Native American music. At the beginning of part II/6, Müller-Hermann includes a musical quotation from the "Love Song of the Bella-Coola Indians." The "Final Song of the Warrior, 'Wa-Wan' Iroquois Melody" emerges from the epilogue. This shows that the composer-musicologist, who had access to ethnological research in music, consciously chose an author from a foreign culture and that she organized her work accordingly. Rather than appealing to fashionable exoticism, she included these melodies in her music like a quotation from a foreign text.

### Schreker, Toch, and Meyer

Franz Schreker (1878–1934), who had published a piano version of his Whitman Gesänge *Vom ewigen Leben* six years prior to Müller-Hermann's composition, had probably read the American author earlier in his life. Schreker, who wrote his own opera libretti, may have felt an artistic kinship with Whitman. In any case, he seems to have known the poet well as the two texts from "Song of Myself" and "Calamus" that he selected are central to Whitman's confessional nature poetry. Schreker used two strategies in setting Whitman's texts to music. The earlier, shorter song ("A child said *What is the grass?*") is in strict counterpoint in spite of its irregular structure and through-composition. Many musical variations of individual motifs run through the composition. The second poem ("Roots and Leaves Themselves Alone") is composed as a recitative; the text is recited rather than sung.

Hermann Danuser has produced a comprehensive musicological analysis of Schreker's Whitman songs, and his findings do not need to be repeated here.[13] Schreker selected Whitman's texts following a period of classicist stabilization; together with several other works, the Whitman *Gesänge* are central to the "subjective expressionism" in which he approached the positions of the Second Viennese School.[14] At the same time, the genre of the orchestral song, which celebrated its greatest success around the turn of the century, had become somewhat anachronistic in the context of new objectivity and neo-classicism.

Ernst Toch (1887–1964) approached Whitman in 1961, long after being exiled to the United States. A slightly abbreviated version of the first three stanzas of section 32 of "Song of Myself" became a small *a cappella* choral composition. Although Toch, like Schreker, conjures up an image of nature, his theme is not a grandiose victory over death but a profession of faith in life as it is. Although his small composition may seem harmless enough and entirely nonpolitical, it amounts to an unequivocal philosophical statement on the part of the aging composer. Whitman's identification with the animals ("They do not make me sick discussing their duty to God . . . / Not one kneels to another, nor to his kind that lived thousands of years ago" ["Song of Myself," 688, 690]) has a strongly antireligious quality. In conclusion, Toch has the chorus fall silent, and one single solo tenor poses the question whether there is not something in the nature of animals that human beings have lost: "I wonder where they get those tokens, / Did I pass that way huge times ago and negligently drop them?" ("Song of Myself," 694–95).

Ernst Hermann Meyer (1905–88) was a German exile in Great Britain when he wrote his Whitman composition. The text, which he patched together from several Whitman poems, was printed in the original by an English publisher. In the 1950s, it was published by Edition Peters, Leipzig, in a translation by Meyer's sister, Susan Jacobs.[15] The composition was commissioned by the Rationalist Press Association, London, on the occasion of the death of its president, Charles Watts. Meyer, who would later become one of the leading musicologists, composers, and cultural politicians of the German Democratic Republic, was active in various antifascist groups in England; for a time, he was president of the *Freie Deutsche Kulturbund* in London. Prior to the war, he had already collaborated with Hanns Eisler. In 1930 he joined the Communist Party of Germany; from that time on, vocal compositions and agitprop works became constituent parts of his *œuvre*.

Meyer himself stated that his Whitman composition was his first contribution to the composition of cantatas. *Nun Steuermann, fahr hin* (Now Voyager, depart) fits well in the series of requiems as it expresses grief but also consolation. The consolation arises from the political work that is to have a permanent effect on humankind (the following lines are adapted from "Song of the Redwood-Tree"; the translation follows the German adaptation):

> Doch beugt uns Trübsal nicht, erhab'ne Brüder, uns, deren Tage herrlich ausgefüllt in weihevoll hohem Glück, im Kampf für Fried' und Licht, die sehend, die tätig wir gelebt und streitend für der Menschheit Sieg.

> (But grief does not bow us down, noble brothers, us, whose days are splendidly filled with solemn lofty fortune, battling for our vision of peace and light, living an active life and striving for humankind's victory.)

### Hans Werner Henze

Henze (b. 1926) created his Whitman composition under the influence of Hartmann's symphony. Its title, *Whispers of Heavenly Death*, is misleading because the cantata is not based "on the poem of the same title" as he indicates, but on the first poem in this cycle of Whitman's poetry, "Darest Thou Now O Soul." The work is significant because it represents an experiment with twelve-tone composition. Henze was originally influenced by Hindemith, but as a result of his training with René Leibowitz, the French propagator of the Second Viennese School, he became interested in the new music.

The influence of Alban Berg's Concerto for Violin on Henze's early twelve-tone composition is well known. There are several characteristic intervals (e.g., in the voice part of Henze's first section) that, as in the Berg Concerto, do not rupture their connection to tonal music in spite of a rigid twelve-tone organization. As a consequence, we get a melody *molto cantabile,* especially in the vocal music that would later become the composer's special strength. The "unknown region" the soul addresses in this poem is thus also an unknown aesthetic region. The special aesthetic status of this composition is also reflected in the instrumentation. Certain instruments with fixed tuning, such as xylophone, vibraphone, carillon, drums, celesta, and harp, are central to the work. They are identical in their sound-pattern. Their tones cannot be held but slowly fade, which gives them a filigreed, tender, and soulful quality. Traditionally, the sound of the harp has been an image for the harmony of the soul, its ethereal resonance.

Against this group of instruments, which can play single tones but not *espressivo* melodic lines, the singing voice stands out. At any time the voice can arbitrarily change its tone. Its "volume" activates the sound of the other instruments, the symbols of the soul. Also prominent are two other instruments, a trumpet in C and a violoncello, one rather high- and one rather low-pitched. These two instruments do not so much accompany the voice as fill out the vocal pauses. Voice always remains dominant. Given this musical environment and the new possibilities for composition that opened up to the young composer in 1948, one can fathom the special meaning the following Whitman lines from "Darest Thou Now O Soul" must have had for Henze:

> *Till when the ties loosen . . .*
> *Nor darkness, gravitation sense, nor any bounds bounding us.*
> *Then we burst forth, we float. . . .* (10, 12–13)

## Gerd Kühr

The most recent example of a musical Whitman setting by a German-speaking composer again points to the themes of war and peace and may hint at the future of the musical reception of Walt Whitman. In 1984 the Austrian composer Gerd Kühr (b. 1952) was commissioned to write a composition on the topic of peace. Kühr had studied with Hans Werner Henze, but it was not his teacher who inspired him to select a Whitman text. Kühr encountered Whitman in an anthology with the title *Gedichte gegen den Krieg* (Poems against War), which contains several Whitman poems in German translation. Kühr then turned to the original version of *Leaves of Grass* in order to search for suitable poems and used three short poems for his brief cycle, namely "When I Peruse the Conquer'd Fame" (from "Calamus"), "Lo, Victress on the Peak" and "Long, Too Long America" (both from "Drum Taps").

The title of the composition, *Walt Whitman for President,* alludes to the United States presidential elections of 1984. Kühr wanted to contrast the policy of the Reagan administration with what he perceived as America's long humanist and pacifist tradition. The flashiness of the title is an ironical stylistic critique of the hollow strategies of the American public relations industry; the work itself excludes any such gaudy effects. *Walt Whitman for President* is a very delicate work. Seven "individualistic" instruments (flute, clarinet, drums, guitar, piano, viola, and violoncello) accompany a soprano voice. The female voice, singing the line "I do not envy the generals," is decidedly symbolic, excluding propagandistic realism of any kind.

Like many other Germanic Whitman composers, Kühr has brought nothing *Lied*-like into this song. Rather, it is through-composed and the melodious element is replaced by expression and tension. But, in contrast to the earlier compositions, everything is subtle and restrained. No simple solution is offered to the world; the tone of the poems, as well as that of the music, is not triumphant; there is no certainty, but doubt and pain. The final lines of "Lo, Victress on the Peak" also seem to reflect the innermost meaning of the composition:

> *No poem proud, I chanting bring to thee, nor mastery's rapturous verse,*
> *But a cluster containing night's darkness and blood-dripping wounds,*
> *And psalms of the dead.*

**Notes**

This essay is an updated version of our German-language section on this subject, which appeared in Walter Grünzweig, *Walt Whitmann: Die deutschsprachige Rezeption als interkulturelles Phänomen* (Munich: Fink, 1991), pp. 224–37.

1. For a detailed study of the German constructions of Whitman, see Walter Grünzweig, *Constructing the German Walt Whitman* (Iowa City: Iowa University Press, 1995).

2. A brief survey of the different translations and their cultural contexts can be found in Walter Grünzweig, "Whitman in the German-Speaking Countries," in *Walt Whitman and the World,* ed. Gay Wilson Allen and Ed Folsom (Iowa City: Iowa University Press, 1995), pp. 160–230.

3. Thomas Mann, "Letter to Hans Reisiger," in *Walt Whitman and the World,* p. 201.

4. See Hermann Danuser, "Der Orchestergesang des Fin de siècle: Eine historische und ästhetische Skizze," *Die Musikforschung* 3O (1977), 427.

5. Carl Dahlhaus, *Die Idee der absoluten Musik* (Kassel: Bärenreiter, 1978), p. 23 ("Paradigma der Idee der absoluten Musik").

6. Quoted from Werner Vogel, *Othmar Schoeck: Leben und Schaffen im Spiegel von Selbstzeugnissen und Zeitgenossenberichten* (Zurich: Atlantis, 1976), p. 98.

7. See Werner Grünzweig, "Music in the Rhythm of War: Othmar Schoeck and the Beginning of Whitman Music in the German Speaking Countries," *Walt Whitman Quarterly Review* 8 (1990), 29–40.

8. David Drew, *Kurt Weill: A Handbook* (Berkeley and Los Angeles: University of California Press, 1987), pp. 320–21.

9. See Werner Grünzweig, "Propaganda der Trauer: Kurt Weills Whitman-Songs," in *A Stranger Here Myself: Kurt Weill Studien,* ed. Kim H. Kowalke and Horst Edler (Hildesheim: Olms, 1993), pp. 297–313.

10. It is entirely possible that composers well versed in Whitman, such as Hindemith and Hartmann, alluded to a famous, almost Whitmanesque passage from the *Deutsches Requiem:* "Denn alles Fleisch ist wie das Gras und alle Herrlichkeit des Menschen wie des Grases Blumen." This line goes back to 1 Peter 1:24 ("For all flesh is as grass, and all the glory of man as the flower of grass"); the imagery of this passage is actually anticipated by passages in the Old Testament, e.g., Psalms 90:5–6.

11. See Charles Jacobs, introduction, *Paul Hindemith: Sämtliche Werke,* ed. Kurt von Fischer and Ludwig Finscher, vol. VII/2, *"When Lilacs Last in the Dooryard Bloom'd: A Requiem 'For Those We Love',"* ed. Charles Jacobs (Mainz: Schott, 1986), p. ix.

12. Hindemith himself valued the "Flieder-Requiem" much more highly. In 1956 he wrote in a letter: "I even wrote the piece [the *Requiem*] that in due time and after the waning of that musical ignorance may well become one of the few musical treasures of the nation [the United States . . . ]" (quoted from Jacobs, introduction, *Paul Hindemith,* p. x).

13. See Hermann Danuser, "Über Franz Schrekers Whitman-Gesänge," in *Franz Schreker-Symposion,* ed. Elmar Budde and Rudolf Stephan (Berlin: Colloquium, 1980), pp. 49–73 (Schriftenreihe der Hochschule der Künste Berlin, vol. 1).

14. See Gösta Neuwirth, "Der späte Schreker," in *Franz Schreker: Am Beginn der Neuen Musik* (Graz/Vienna: Universal-Edition, 1978), pp. 107*ff. (Studien zur Wertungsforschung,* vol. 11).

15. See Ernst Hermann Meyer, *Kontraste, Konflikte: Erinnerungen, Gespräche, Kommentare,* ed. Dietrich Brennecke and Mathias Hansen (Berlin: Verlag Neue Musik, 1979), p. 187.

# CHAPTER 4

# Reclaiming Walt
## Marc Blitzstein's Whitman Settings

*David Metzer*

In the intimate space of a diary entry, first names are sometimes all that are needed. Even the famous and deceased can be on familiar, perhaps sexual, terms with the diarist. For Jeb Alexander, a young office clerk struggling to be a writer, his recorded musings of 5 July 1923 placed him in an embrace with "Walt"—Whitman, that is: "Often I yearn toward Walt as toward a father, look up at his picture, then close my eyes and feel him beside me, rugged and strong with his gentle hands caressing and comforting me."[1] Alexander's entry captures the way many homosexual readers have approached Whitman's poetry. The casually dropped "Walt" attests to the intimate relationships they have established with the poet—bonds that, given Whitman's efforts to create an erotic connection with his readers, often turn sexual. Later

**Table 4.1**

| Blitzstein's Whitman Settings |
| --- |
| "As If a Phantom Caress'd Me" (1925, Philadelphia) |
| "After the Dazzle of Day" (1925, Philadelphia) |
| "Joy, Shipmate, Joy" (1925, Philadelphia) |
| "What Weeping Face" (1925, Philadelphia) |
| "Gods" (1927, Paris) |
| "O Hymen! O Hymenee!" (1927, Paris) |
| "As Adam" (1927, Berlin) |
| "I Am He" (1928, Philadelphia) |
| "Ages and Ages" (1928, Philadelphia) |

*Note:* Manuscripts of the songs can be found in the Marc Blitzstein Papers, Archives Division, The State Historical Society of Wisconsin in Madison, Wisconsin.

in that decade, Hart Crane formed such a relationship with Whitman, calling out to "Walt" and clutching his hand in *The Bridge.*

To this group of 1920s "comrades" can be added Marc Blitzstein, who composed nine songs to texts by Whitman between 1925 and 1928 (see Table 1). This act of composition sprang from and strengthened a sexual bond of discipleship between reader and poet, for Blitzstein responded here to several texts that reject prejudices surrounding male-male eroticism and voice Whitman's plea for erotic companionship. Forgotten and left unpublished, Blitzstein's songs represent significant works not only in the tradition of Whitman settings, particularly those by gay composers, but also in the broader reception of the poet. They belong to a group of early twentieth-century artistic and scholarly works that embrace and promote Whitman's homosexuality. By illuminating the homoerotic thematics in Whitman's verse, Blitzstein abetted a reclaiming of the poet by homosexual readers such as Alexander and Crane, an effort that challenged the dominant homophobic views of his verse. Blitzstein's assault on those views was forceful: His songs represent one of the boldest celebrations of Whitman's homoeroticism by an American artist, a remarkable distinction given the oppressive environment in which they were written.

Blitzstein composed his Whitman songs during a period that marked the end of his student years and his initial steps as an independent composer.[2] The first four works—"As If a Phantom Caress'd Me," "After the Dazzle of Day," "Joy, Shipmate, Joy," and "What Weeping Face"—were written in 1925, during his years at the Curtis Institute. In 1926 Blitzstein followed the growing contingent of young American composers traveling to Paris to study with Nadia Boulanger. Under her eye, he set two more Whitman texts: "Gods" and "O Hymen! O Hymenee!" Soon after completing those songs, he left Paris against Boulanger's wishes to study with Arnold Schoenberg in Berlin. "As Adam," his next setting, was one of the few works completed during Blitzstein's frustrating studies with Schoenberg. Having abruptly ended that relationship, Blitzstein left for the United States. "I Am He" and "Ages and Ages," incorporating elements of jazz, represent a musical home-coming.[3]

Blitzstein's settings jarred with dominant views of the poet. These repressive notions were largely shaped by literary critics, who regarded Whitman's sexuality as a threat to his legacy.[4] Their intolerance often resulted in such blunt denials as Bliss Perry's in his 1906 biography: "As far as I know there has never been the slightest evidence that Whitman practised homosexuality."[5] Denial may have helped stamp out biographical fires, but it barely doused Whitman's "flaming" verse. Nevertheless, what could not be obliterated could be obscured. Scholars clouded Whitman's homoeroticism, which he had already carefully shrouded, by promoting his works in universalist, normalized readings. In this light, Whitman's male-male erotics were often diffused into abstract, genderless discussions of mystical unions.[6] In addition, nationalist promotions of Whitman eclipsed the poet's sexual thematics.

These strategies of obfuscation and denial were employed in Emory Holloway's writings on Whitman. Contemporary with Blitzstein's settings, his studies reveal the deep prejudices that the composer confronted. In an article published in 1920, Holloway unearthed an earlier unpublished version of Whitman's "Once I Pass'd Through a Populous City," which describes the poet's affair with "one rude and ignorant man" instead of the romance with a woman mentioned in the published version.[7] The latter version was upheld by many as proof of Whitman's heterosexuality.[8] This discovery, with its clear homoeroticism and demand for biographical revision, troubled Holloway, who then went to great lengths to downplay it. Noting that the original version of the poem belonged to the "Calamus" cluster, he reduced the vibrant homoeroticism of that section to an "intimate friendship of man for man" that "Whitman preached as a sort of sentimental-religious democracy." Further, he sought to reinforce the cultural "charge of effeminacy" and vague threats of "danger" that men of "such a nature as [Whitman's]" face. The only remaining step was to erase Whitman's homosexuality. In a 1926 book, he omitted the original version of "Once I Pass'd Through a Populous City" and accepted the heterosexual romance story surrounding the published one, which he had earlier questioned, albeit superficially.[9]

The interpretations of Holloway and like-minded literary scholars contaminated discussions of Whitman in other aesthetic fields, including music. The musical press propagated such diluted, universalist views. In an article in *Musical America,* T. Carl Whitmer exhorted composers to set Whitman: "Whitman sung will give to audiences broad, sweeping gestures of love and life that will make the concert room the birthplace of a noble art instead of an enfeebled one, the latter pretty surely indicated in recent years by the great number of effeminate compositions used in recitals."[10] Whitmer not only subsumed Whitman's homoeroticism within a "broad, sweeping" love, but also dispelled any charges of "effeminacy" (a potent code word) raised by Holloway and other homophobic readers of the poet. For their part, composers generally shunned Whitman's homoerotic and corporeal verse, concentrating instead on poems emphasizing nature or patriotism. The most frequently set Whitman texts from the early decades of the century include "When Lilacs Last in the Dooryard Bloom'd," "The Mystic Trumpeter," and "O Captain! My Captain!" It is not surprising then that Blitzstein was one of the first, if not *the* first, to set many of his texts.[11]

Transgressing this dominant asexual view of Whitman, Blitzstein was among a group of readers, homo- and heterosexual, who responded to the poet's celebration of the male body and began to scrape away the encrusted prejudices surrounding his poetry. This counterinterpretation sprouted vigorously in England, where homosexual readers led by John Addington Symonds and Edward Carpenter praised the poet for reigniting the homoeroticism of the ancient Greeks in modern verse.[12] In the United States, Whitman similarly became a mentor to a devout following of homosexual men, which included the writers Charles Warren Stoddard and Bayard Taylor.

During the period that Blitzstein composed his Whitman settings, Crane also explored and promoted the poet's homoerotic verse.[13] Besides his exaltation of the "love of comrades," Whitman's nationalism, views of democracy, and spirituality attracted Crane. In his poetry, Crane blended these different thematics, presenting Whitman as "a valid poetic, spiritual, and homosexual precursor."[14] This manifold Whitman presides over Crane's early poem "Episode of Hands," which ratifies, through the encounter between a worker and a factory owner's son, the "Calamus" tenet that erotic bonds between men can advance social and political unity. In the "Cape Hatteras" section of *The Bridge,* Crane again evokes Whitman. On the lonely beach where Whitman strolls, Crane grabs the poet's hand and becomes his "comrade."

> *yes, Walt,*
> *Afoot again, and onward without halt,—*
> *Not soon, nor suddenly,—no, never let go*
>    *My hand*
>      *in yours,*
>        *Walt Whitman—*
>          *so—*

In "As If a Phantom Caress'd Me" (CD track 1) Blitzstein stages a similar shoreline scene of "comradeship." Of the four 1925 settings, this song has the deepest homoerotic resonances and most strongly establishes the composer's erotic bond with Whitman. Blitzstein presents a resolution to the text that suggests not only the reunion of the two poetic lovers but also the grasping of hands between himself and Whitman. This declaration of "comradeship" both heightens the forbidden caress in the poem and bolsters Whitman's condemnation of social hostility toward homosexuals.[15]

> *As if a Phantom caress'd me,*
> *I thought I was not alone walking here by the shore;*
> *But the one I thought was with me as now I walk by the shore, the one*
>    *I loved that caress'd me,*
> *As I lean and look through the glimmering light, that one has utterly*
>    *disappear'd,*
> *And those appear that are hateful to me and mock me.*

Whitman's text seethes with the reticence dictated by the closet.[16] The poet shades his erotic interest by refusing to clarify gender, referring to his lover only as a "phantom"; nevertheless, the surrounding poems in the "Whispers of Heavenly Death" cluster of *Leaves of Grass,* notably "Of Him I

Love Day and Night," strongly suggest that the lover is male. Although Whitman may capitulate to the pressures of the closet, he also surveys the anguished terrain of that space, particularly the rift between the public and the private. In "As If a Phantom Caress'd Me," Whitman delineates the private, a realm of darkness and ghosts where physical love between men can be expressed, with the public, an arena of "glimmering light" in which such love succumbs to social scorn. Blitzstein heightens that opposition by framing the setting of the last two lines, those presenting the public realm, with isolated fermata chords, anxious pauses that convey the hesitant movement from the shadowy private sphere into the cruel light of public contempt.

The tension between public and private reverberates throughout the musical language and is heard in the unstable tonal syntax and vacillating vocal style. During the course of the song, the tonic C♯ minor attempts to assert itself, but it is obscured within an agitated mix of triadic and nontriadic sonorities that provides little tonal clarification. The vocal idiom, trembling between lyrical melodic writing and *recitativo*-like declamation, also suggests the protagonist's anxiety. Blitzstein, though, heightens this tension by eradicating those conventional borders of song. At the moment when the protagonist initially realizes his lover's disappearance, the vocal part suddenly disintegrates into speech, just like the evanescent phantom. Blitzstein notates this metamorphosis in a manner similar to Schoenberg's *Sprechstimme,* indicating approximate pitch and duration. Given its associations with intense emotion, Blitzstein's evocation of *Sprechstimme* enhances the anguish expressed by the protagonist.

Blitzstein also enhances the corporeal elements in the text, illustrating the physical gestures by various means. A steady, repeated eighth-note pattern in the bass depicts the protagonist's "walking by the shore." Blitzstein suggests the fleeting caress of the lover by means of a mysterious wisp figure in the accompaniment. The spectral lover also is evoked in the overall tonal ambiguity. Like the phantom, the C♯-minor tonic maintains a shadowy presence, alluded to frequently by unresolved dominants but never strongly defined until the final cadence.

Blitzstein's presence in the work emerges most clearly in his annotations of and departures from Whitman's text. The composer, for instance, prefaces the last line of the poem with an untransposed statement of the "Tristan chord" (F–B–D♯–G♯). To this an extra G♯ is added in the bass, and there is an enharmonic change from F♮ to E♯, which moves to F♯. Despite these alterations, the sound of the chord, especially in its original transposition, is striking.[17] Blitzstein's appropriation of Wagner's sensuous harmony releases a variety of associations. It may suggest that, like the relationship between Tristan and Isolde, this one too will be crushed by the misunderstanding of others. Further, the quotation seems to connect heterosexuality with the anguish expressed in Whitman's "those that appear are hateful to me and mock me."

In the postlude following that painful line, Blitzstein reorients Whitman's poem, suggesting a more hopeful resolution. Rather than ending with an emphatic statement of Whitman's condemnation of social prejudices, Blitzstein returns to the original erotic scene. The "walking music" heard previously in the introduction and in the setting of the line "as now I walk by the shore" is here echoed in the piano postlude. The protagonist (and the listener) again treads in darkness and, as implied by the return of the wisp figure, feels the phantom caress. Unlike the earlier statement of that figure, this one is followed with a cadence in the tonic, the only strong cadence in the song. Responding to the caress with harmonic surety, this resolution suggests either the fulfillment of erotic desire or the comfort found in solitude. The postlude also evokes a scene similar to that at the end of Crane's "Cape Hatteras." Like Crane, Blitzstein concludes his work beside the shore and with a physical embrace. In the postlude, a musical space created around and separate from Whitman's text, that caress can be heard as an offering to the poet: Blitzstein, having coupled his music with Whitman's words throughout the song, extends his musical hand to the now silent poet, declaring his "comradeship" and offering him refuge from the "glimmering light" of hate.

In his four last settings, Blitzstein more fervently cultivated corporeal and erotic thematics, while simultaneously developing a leaner, more dissonant idiom. He labeled these works "Songs for a Coon Shouter." This subtitle evoked the "coon song," a genre infested with black stereotypes that was popular from 1880 to around 1910.[18] Created by white composers and lyricists as well as a few black artists taking advantage of the popularity of the genre, these songs incorporated ragtime elements and explored a variety of racist topics, including the aspiration of blacks to be white, the sexual and physical violence of black men, and the dietary preferences of blacks. "Coon shouters," most of whom were white women, performed their works in a raucous, vociferous manner, which was supposed to imitate both African American singing and speech. Donning black "musicality" instead of, or sometimes in addition to, paint, these singers worked within the tradition of racial impersonation inaugurated by blackface minstrelsy. In evoking the "coon song," Blitzstein most likely aimed to capture the masquerade elements and raw vocal style associated with it. Apart from performance gestures, his revival of the by-then outdated and offensive term provided the shock value that he and many modernists sought. This penchant for controversy led him to consider a performance of the settings a "success" for earning him "especial vituperation" from the critics.[19] In "I Am He" and "Ages and Ages," Blitzstein dipped further into popular repertoires, infusing these pieces with jazz elements. He defended this unusual pairing of jazz and Whitman: "Several people have questioned my use of a jazz idiom with the Whitman words; it seems to me perfectly natural to couple two media whose implications are alike universal, and whose methods are alike primitive, both jazz and Whitman contain a primal and all-pervading sex-urge."[20]

In Blitzstein's songs, the cultural forces of Whitman and jazz collide, an impact producing racial, cultural, and sexual sparks.[21] His comments notwithstanding, the two forces could not be more incompatible within the contemporary attitudes of the dominant white culture. Whitman was viewed as an icon of American culture, whereas jazz was considered primitive, exotic music. Moreover, the two had disparate sexual associations. In Whitman's works, those associations were in conflict: The potent eroticism of his verse was generally denied and obscured, even as it was celebrated by Blitzstein and other sympathetic readers. The eroticism of jazz, on the other hand, was both inflated and distorted by white audiences. The clash of these discordant sexual, racial, and aesthetic views invokes oppositions between the "civilized" and the "primitive," and between high and low art.[22] As is typical of racial borrowing, Blitzstein's incorporation of jazz idioms and his allusions to the "coon song" produce ambivalent effects, which, in the case of his songs, are the tensions between undermining and reinforcing the above dualisms.[23]

Fixing jazz as "primitive," Blitzstein reveals his investment in the opposition that dominated contemporary discourses of race, particularly the associations of sexual potency embedded in that atavistic view. The crux of his "coon shout" settings is that African American music, be it jazz or the faux "coon song," can erotically ignite Whitman's texts. Claiming Whitman as "primitive," Blitzstein complicates the division of whites and blacks along the lines of the opposition between "civilized" and "primitive." This assertion not only draws attention to Whitman's eroticism, thus bolstering Blitzstein's reclaiming of the poet, but also destabilizes that dualism by contending that a "civilized" poet embodies "primitive" sexuality. Despite this rattling, the discursive structure remains intact. Blitzstein's defense ultimately realigns sex, primitivism, and blackness, as an obsession with "primitive" sexuality thwarts his attempts to establish an erotic parity between Whitman and African American music. It is, after all, the "primal sex urge" of jazz that is being used to coax out the socially suppressed eroticism in Whitman's poetry, and not the other way around.

Although Blitzstein's settings do little to upset contemporary views of the "primitive," they more effectively decenter the opposition between low and high art, a dichotomy that the composer, inspired by leftist politics, would continue to subvert throughout his career. In his defense, Blitzstein describes both Whitman and jazz as "universal," an approbation that helps to erase the racial and aesthetic boundaries sequestering African American music. Moreover, the adjoining of black styles and Whitman's words in the small confines of an "art" song exposed to white audiences the fragility of those lines. Blitzstein's breaching of these borders antagonized some critics, who, drawing on the rhetoric of corruption and inferiority often used to assail jazz, accused him of sullying Whitman. The critic-composer Marion Bauer found the union of jazz ("interesting rhythms") and the national bard to be "incongruous and debasing."[24] Olin Downes added that the settings were "of a singularly repellant puerility."[25] By dismissing Blitzstein's songs with language employed to denigrate African American music, these critics sought to equate the two and to push the settings onto the "Other" side of the racial/aesthetic divide, clearing the concert hall and, above all, the revered Whitman from such contamination.

The "coon shout" settings, though, fail to topple this opposition of low and high art. African American styles remain the "low" element, imported into the "art" song, where, on arrival, they need to be "refined," molded into Blitzstein's modernist idiom. Only in such a transformed state could those styles reside within that "high" genre and carry Whitman's words. This "necessary" alteration contradicts Blitzstein's assertion of parity between Whitman and African American idioms. For if they were as equal as he claims, then why not, in addition to his own settings, offer Whitman's poems to Bessie Smith or Duke Ellington? Such a gesture, though, would rob him of the racial and aesthetic privileges that he enjoys in the appropriation of black styles.[26]

An opposition implicit in Blitzstein's defense that comes visibly to the fore in the performance of his settings is the tension between white and black bodies. The few performances of these songs have featured singers of both races. On 13 March 1928, Nelson Eddy performed "As Adam" and "O Hymen! O Hymenee!" at a concert sponsored by the Society of Contemporary Music in Philadelphia. (Eddy, as a singer whose career included both Hollywood movie musicals and opera, virtually personified the high/low question.) Later that same year (30 December 1928), the African American baritone Benjohn Ragsdale, a member of the Hall Johnson Choir of New York, sang all four settings at a concert in the series organized by Aaron Copland and Roger Sessions.[27]

In her account of a party after the Copland-Sessions performance, Eva Goldbeck, Blitzstein's future wife, provides an apt analogy for the relationships between both white and black bodies and Whitman and black styles in the "coon shout" settings.[28] She describes the tension between the African American guests and the white party-goers: "Ragsdale and other Negroes were there, but the 'mixing' didn't work as it should naturally have; everybody too self-centered. . . . Marc was white, tired, intense and charming—a bad combination, but in him very nice."[29] The black guests occupy a space analogous to that of African American idioms in Blitzstein's settings: foreign elements placed, largely for the sake of exoticism, against a white backdrop. With the exception of her telling offhand description of Blitzstein as "white," Goldbeck significantly fails to mention the race of the other guests, an omission that both reveals and reinforces the invisible hegemony of whiteness, that is, the ability of whiteness to maintain its racial dominance by appearing to be nonapparent.[30] Contrary to Goldbeck's expectations, it is only "natural" that in such a racially unbalanced space, be it social or musical, the " 'mixing' didn't work."[31] Despite this marginalization of black musicians and music, however, it is important not to dismiss, as is so often done in theoretical discussions of racial representation, the significance of their inclusion. African American performers rarely had access to the "official" white concert hall, and, notwithstanding reductive racial motivations, Blitzstein's invitation to Ragsdale to sing at a modern music concert assailed the barriers obstructing those performers. Blitzstein continued to knock down racial barriers. During World War II, he led a chorus of African American soldiers in several concerts in England.

Both the effects produced by the use of black and white singers and the general racial dynamics of the settings can be better understood by placing these works within the tradition of racial impersonation, which, after the decline of minstrelsy, was extended by the "coon song" and numerous genres and works incorporating blackface, including vaudeville and the film *The Jazz Singer*. The evocation of the "coon song" and the appropriation of jazz idioms directly tie Blitzstein's songs to that tradition. Besides such clear links, these works tap into the erotic currents of male homoerotic desire and miscegenation running through racial impersonation.[32]

Minstrelsy and its progeny were fueled in part by a white male fascination with black male sexuality. Although women appeared in racial masquerade, such entertainments were largely "an affair of male bodies," since many of the female roles were played by male transvestites.[33] Blackface concentrated on exhibiting the black male body, allowing white men not only to enjoy displays of sexual violence and potency but also to identify with the stereotyped sexual mastery of black men. The sanctity of white male sexuality, though, was never violated, because the staged presentation of black men was ultimately controlled by whites.

Similarly, Blitzstein's songs are "an affair of male bodies"—of Whitman's, the singer's, and his own. In this light, his appropriation of the "coon song," one of the few genres of racial masquerade dominated by female singers, is noteworthy, for Blitzstein completely erases the feminine presence in his works by using only male singers and setting highly male homoerotic texts. Moreover, the appearance of a black singer escalates the fascination with black male sexuality underscoring racial masquerade. It may further be suggested that the appropriation of black idioms allows Blitzstein the liberties that blackface entertainment affords—the liberty, in this instance, being the celebration of Whitman's homoeroticism. Yet these songs have an ironic relationship with racial impersonation. Whereas the latter uses erotic display to indulge in crude theatrical material designed to denigrate African Americans, Blitzstein's works draw on such display to vivify the homoerotic verse of a white cultural icon, a figure that would never be found on the minstrel stage.

The settings also respond to the lure of miscegenation raised by racial masquerade. Beyond its specific associations with heterosexual copulation, miscegenation can be viewed more broadly to encompass the mixture of white and black cultures. Yet even this general understanding has implications of sexual union. It is the threat of miscegenation, in both the sexual and cultural senses, that racial impersonation teasingly presents and attempts to quash, evoking physical union by bringing white and black bodies into close proximity. The anxiety over cultural mixture persisted, as the continual establishment of racial boundaries in blackface entertainment reveals.

During the 1920s, Blitzstein exploited the threat of miscegenation in several works, including the Whitman settings. He considered the proscriptions against miscegenation to be remnants of social and aesthetic traditions that needed to be swept away. The Metropolitan Opera production of Ernst Krenek's *Jonny spielt auf* provoked him for featuring "a black-face comedian, instead of a real negro, the dear trustees of the Met not being able to stand for a love scene between a black man and a white woman."[34] In the 1929 premiere of his chamber opera *Triple-Sec,* Blitzstein presented what the Met dared not.[35] Although race is not specified in the libretto by Ronald Jeans, Blitzstein cast the African American singer Albert Mahler in the lead role of Lord Silverside.[36] The climax of the light farce occurs when Silverside encounters both his wife, whom he has banished from his mansion, and his new fiancée, a confrontation that the opera leaves unresolved.

Although Blitzstein does not rely on blackface, his opera in many ways proves no more racially transgressive than the Met staging of *Jonny*. In its 1929 staging, *Triple-Sec* evinces strong connections to the tradition of racial masquerade. The casting of a black singer in the role of a foolish nobleman extends the mocking presentation of blacks in positions of white authority. Moreover, the licentiousness of the character reinforces the association between blacks and sexual uninhibitedness. The opera, however, goes a step beyond minstrelsy by presenting a black character married and engaged to white women, although these unions are depicted as nonsexual and comic. In his review of the opera, the critic H. T. Craven articulated the nonthreatening, farcical effects produced by this casting: "He [Lord Silverside] has a love scene, all in fun, mind you, with a white lassie. This is going the Metropolitan one better, since 'Jonny,' of *Spielt* fame, is, in the American production, only a Caucasian blacked up like a minstrel."[37]

In the "coon shout" settings, the threat of miscegenation proves more intimidating. Unlike *Triple-Sec,* in which that danger is comically contained on the stage, these songs venture into a troubling realm where black and white cultures merge, a space created by the convergence of Whitman, jazz, and the "coon song." Given the corporeal thematics in the selected Whitman texts and the physical associations of black idioms, this amalgamation of cultures takes on the guise of a union of white and black bodies, a perception heightened by the use of a black singer.

The threat of that union is partly countered by a white authoritative presence and gaze. In the Copland-Sessions performance, Blitzstein, appearing as accompanist, provided a declaration of such authority, visibly bolstering the "civilized" and "high art" terms used to define whiteness. The audience, on the other hand, exercised authority through its gaze, which largely reduced Ragsdale to an exotic object. Caught between the audience and the "controlling" composer, he was put on display to voice a sexual fantasy produced from the bond between a white composer and a white poet. In such a role and space, there was little or no room for resistance.

A performance with a white singer, like racial impersonation in general, is again an affair of white male bodies. Moreover, the locus of erotic desire shifts from the audience to the singer himself. Playing the part of a "coon shouter" and projecting jazz idioms, the white performer emulates the black body evoked by the musical appropriation. This transfer between performer and audience does not disconnect the erotic circuit between the two. On the contrary, the audience still erotically fixes on the individual, and the circuit connecting them in many ways has been charged, as concertgoers observe how one of their own has "transformed" himself into "a black male." Such a metamorphosis reveals how the drama of miscegenation is focused on the individual, within whom this racial alchemy occurs.

The tension between white and black bodies is only one of the corporeal factors in the "coon shout" settings. These songs also advance Whitman's efforts to manifest the body in his texts and to dispel negative corporeal attitudes. As Michael Moon describes it, Whitman not only offers readers a textual mold of his body but also heightens readers' awareness of their own bodies by implicating them in vivid corporeal depictions. This greater awareness, Whitman hoped, would encourage readers to question and ultimately to reject the prevailing notions of corporeality, which viewed the body, especially the nude body, as abject.[38]

In "As Adam Early in the Morning," Whitman distills his plea for acceptance of the body, namely his body, which he strips bare by means of a comparison to Adam.[39] Through a crescendo of imperatives, he implores readers to engage his naked body, first pleading with them to see him, then to hear and to walk toward him, and, finally, to touch him.

> *As Adam early in the morning,*
> *Walking forth from the bower refresh'd with sleep,*
> *Behold me where I pass, hear my voice, approach,*
> *Touch me, touch the palm of your hand to my body as I pass,*
> *Be not afraid of my body.*

Blitzstein incorporates this textual crescendo within a loose palindromic structure (ABCB'A') built around the impassioned plea to be touched (CD track 3). In the initial A section, he evokes the Edenic stroll by means of an ostinato in the accompaniment, which, as with the repeated bass figure in "As If a Phantom Caress'd Me," suggests the protagonist's tread. The prominence of the ostinato and its linkage with physicality are noteworthy, for, with the exception of a few stray measures, the accompaniment consists of a series of ostinatos. Building on the association with the body, these subsequent patterns enhance the pervasive corporeality of the text, not only suggesting the protagonist's continued walking but also his yearning for physical contact.

The new ostinatos of the B section launch the series of imperatives beginning with "behold." In addition to these short driving patterns, Blitzstein propels the textual crescendo with a musical one, moving from *mezzo forte* to *fortissimo*. The ostinatos and the increase in dynamics, in turn, fuel an explosive vocal glissando on the word "approach." Blitzstein may have intended that gesture to evoke the vociferous delivery of the "coon shouter," though if that is the case, he overshot the mark, for such an exaggerated, forceful gesture is rare, if not nonexistent, in that repertoire. His settings, however, clearly do not aim for a stylistic fidelity to that passé genre; rather, through such hyperbolic gestures, they exploit the racial and corporeal associations that it purportedly incorporates. In Blitzstein's songs, these associations "flesh out" the burgeoning corporeality of the text.

The glissando leads to both the culmination of the textual crescendo ("touch me") and the climactic central section of the setting, which is defined largely by extremes in range and dynamics. During the course of this brief passage, the voice attempts to isolate itself from the accompaniment, declaring significant phrases—"touch me" and "body"—in the terse silences of the ostinato. Resounding within those rests, these corporeal markers set the tone of the section, as the congruences between performance and textual physicality heard earlier multiply. The high vocal tessitura and the leaps of a major seventh expand on the physicality required and evoked by the glissando. The vocal strain produced by this passage for baritones like Ragsdale and Eddy captures the physical yearning expressed by Whitman. Moreover, the pianist's fleet left hand, vaulting more than three octaves, visibly displays "the palm of [the] hand" that Whitman desires to "touch [his] body." The entreaty "touch me" takes on a different corporeal significance given the use of a black singer, whose uttering of that plea directly articulates the desires for miscegenation underlying Blitzstein's settings.

The corporeal frenzy raised by Whitman's crescendo of imperatives is calmed by the return of the B material for the final injunction: "Be not afraid of my body." To emphasize that plea, the voice does not rely on such corporeal gestures as the glissando or a straining high tessitura; rather, it sustains pitches, a contrast to the rapid syllabic declamation of the C section. The reprise of the A section in the piano postlude brings further stillness, returning the listener to the Edenic scene before the crying of the impassioned physical call. Blitzstein similarly uses the piano postlude in "As If a Phantom

Caress'd Me" to bring listeners back to the original seashore scene. As in that earlier setting, the recapitulatory postlude has interpretative significance. In particular, it reinforces the palindromic structure of the song, a pattern at odds with Whitman's linear design. Rather than lopping off the superfluous or mismatched space created by this uniting of disparate shapes, Blitzstein's setting infuses it with meaning. The untexted rounded edge—the piano postlude—suggests cyclicity. Ending with the same suspended dissonant chord with which it begins, the song not only implies a repetition of the protagonist's plea but asserts that it needs to be restated. In other words, the possibility of endless repetition calls attention to the necessity of continually making that cry in the hope of eventually obliterating abject notions of physicality. Largely unheeded during Whitman's lifetime as well as in the late 1920s, that call is put in a symbolic perpetual repetition, awaiting the moment when the "touch" is finally made and the fears of the body overcome.

In "Ages and Ages," the desired touching hand belongs not to a distant body but to Whitman himself.

> *Ages and ages returning at intervals,*
> *Undestroy'd, wandering immortal,*
> *Lusty, phallic, with the potent original loins, perfectly sweet,*
> *I, chanter of Adamic songs,*
> *Through the new garden the West, the great cities calling,*
> *Deliriate, thus prelude what is generated, offering these, offering myself,*
> *Bathing myself, bathing my songs in Sex,*
> *Offspring of my loins.*

The autoerotic fantasy in the poem is stirred by such reflexive lines as "bathing myself, bathing my songs in Sex," a wash that induces the sexual "deliri[um]" enjoyed by the poet. This erotic self-gratification and seepage of sexual fluids suggest masturbation, a physical act, which falls within, rather than solely defines, the wide array of behaviors and acts that can be viewed as autoerotic. The connotation of masturbation, though, is significant, for it evokes an autoerotic behavior considered corrupt during and long after Whitman's lifetime. Viewed as sexual excess and as a danger to the reproductive heterosexual model, nineteenth-century anti-onanist literature terrorized young men and women with threats of physical and moral decay.[40]

Whitman and Blitzstein, on the other hand, embraced the perceived excessiveness of masturbation and its defiance of procreative heterosexuality, using masturbation, and autoeroticism in general, as a discursive means of approaching and exploring homoerotic desire, a linkage that ironically the antionanist tracts also saw and attempted to foreclose.[41] The autoerotic fantasy in "Ages and Ages" revolves around the male body, particularly the penis, which is described as "lusty" and "sweet" and depicted as the wellspring of the "bathing" sexual fluids. The male body also becomes a site of erotic flux. In the ecstasy of Whitman's autoerotic fantasies, bodies, body parts, objects, and actions often shift and merge.[42] Here, Whitman melds his "songs" and his body, the two being almost interchangeable: "offering these [his songs], offering myself, / Bathing myself, bathing my songs in Sex." He similarly conflates autoeroticism and procreation, at once gratifying himself and giving birth to his poems, the "offspring of [his] loins."

Blitzstein enhances Whitman's autoerotic frenzy through a heightened degree of racial appropriation and the formal design of his setting. "Ages and Ages" (CD track 4) incorporates jazz idioms, including blue-note inflections and syncopated rhythmic patterns. This appropriation supplements the "coon shout" vocality in vivifying the corporeality of the text. These borrowed racial elements cohere around a synecdochic figure, the stereotyped reduction of the black male body to the penis. "Lusty, phallic, with the potent original loins" bobs above a syncopated vocal melody, while a corporeal glissando like that in "As Adam" (an evocation of the "coon song" and African American vocal practices) rushes into the declaration of the final word "loins."

Blitzstein divides Whitman's text into two four-line units, contrasting them primarily by means of tempo. No thematic or dramatic break in the text, though, invites such partitioning. As in "As Adam," a disparate formal design is superimposed on the poem; unlike the earlier setting, however, this formal tension does not reorient Whitman's text but rather intensifies its erotic energies. In the first section, Blitzstein conveys the still timelessness conjured by Whitman in the opening lines with a slow tempo and static triadic harmonies. The atmosphere is one of quiescent sensuality in which slight breaths of jazz idioms stir the corporeal images in the text.

This tranquility gives way to the frenetic "deliri[um]" in the concluding section, a contrast that heightens the erotic fervor of the song. The arrival in "the West" and "the great cities" precipitates a change in the musical environment. Responding to the urban "call," Blitzstein sets loose a propulsive jazz idiom, featuring an offbeat stride pattern in the bass of the accompanimental ostinato. The texture of that ostinato and successive ones quickly thickens, a process culminating at the autoerotic line "Bathing myself, bathing my songs in Sex." Blitzstein also highlights this line by having the voice quickly repeat pitches, suggesting the obsessiveness and anxiety associated with the masturbator and the rapid, repetitive motions of the act.

The music after this orgasmic crescendo leads to an erotic rush or the "deliri[um]" described by Whitman. In the concluding measures, Blitzstein conveys the flux of autoerotic fantasy with a series of altered thematic reprises. Just as Whitman's body and "songs" merge in the text, musical sections shift, metamorphose, and amalgamate. After the "bathing in sex" statement, Blitzstein immediately returns to the stride ostinato, this time stated an octave higher and altered by a crescendo and an accelerando. This momentum leads directly to a surprising return of the opening static material, presented in its original slower tempo but now two octaves higher and played *fortissimo,* much like the "bathing in sex" ostinato. Having recast the opening material in the dynamics and range of that ostinato, Blitzstein follows it with an abrupt statement of the ostinato itself, thus fusing two previously unconnected sections. The ostinato returns in a new tempo vivo and in extreme registers. Unable to sustain such propulsion, it quickly wearies, ending in the convulsive hammering of four triads, which resemble the aftershocks of the song's orgasmic quake.

In contrast to the autoerotic "deliri[um]" of "Ages and Ages," "O Hymen! O Hymenee!" conveys an ambivalent mixture of psychic pain and pleasure arising from sexual contact with another body. That other body belongs to the Greek mythological character Hymen, a young man who is evoked by the eponymous cry quoted by Whitman, which was shouted during Greek wedding ceremonies.[43] Several myths, all focusing on the youth's beauty, explained how Hymen's name was incorporated into the marriage rite. So fair was Hymen that, in some stories, male deities, including Apollo, courted him.[44] In Whitman's text, though, this romance has gone painfully awry. The poem reverses the pedagogue/student, active/passive relationships in the Greek pedophilic contract, having Hymen "sting" the older man, who is reduced to a submissive position. The text builds its sadomasochistic fantasy around this pedophilic reversal, in which the older partner pleads, one frenzied question after another, to be "st[u]ng," and fixates on the rapturous death resulting from the fulfillment of that desire.

> *O Hymen! O hymenee! why do you tantalize me thus?*
> *O why sting me for a swift moment only?*
> *Why can you not continue? O why do you now cease?*
> *Is it because if you continued beyond the swift moment you would certainly*
> *    kill me?*

The protagonist's agitated pleading is at once a source of pleasure and the outgrowth of debilitating anxieties. This fluidity between pleasure and pain both fuels and sustains the sadomasochistic eroticism of the poem. The state of anxiety evoked in "O Hymen! O Hymenee!" corresponds to the paranoid positions that Moon finds in *Leaves of Grass.*[45] Drawing on Freud's studies of paranoia, Moon describes a state in which the subject experiences anxieties about being persecuted by figures to whom are ascribed inordinate powers and hostility. Overwhelmed by the weight of such fears, the subject disintegrates. In Whitman's poem, Hymen tortures the protagonist with his sexual teasing and is invested with the power to take the older man's life, which is the most sexually alluring of the youth's threats. No "I" surfaces in the poem; rather, the text presents a series of questions addressed to Hymen, which, with the exception of the final reflective one, convey no individual

agency or thought. The protagonist is reduced to the object of the boy's plea-
surable and painful "tantaliz[ing]," "sting[ing]," and "kill[ing]."

In evoking paranoia, Whitman ran the risk of reinforcing the cultural perception that "self-aware male homosexuality" is "by definition 'paranoid' homosexuality."[46] Freud tightened that linkage by viewing paranoia as primarily
a malady of homosexuals.[47] In Whitman's poetry, though, paranoia functions
not as a demented realm in which to sequester homosexual men but rather as
a privileged space, one opened up by the association of paranoia and homosexuality, where erotic bonds between men can be first rendered and then explored. Besides serving as a culturally sanctioned means of approaching
homosexuality, paranoia provides a forum in which to examine the cultural
attitudes toward erotic desires among men, particularly the prejudices that
place homosexual men in such agonized psychic positions.

By setting "O Hymen! O Hymenee!" (CD track 2), Blitzstein furthered
Whitman's exploration of paranoia; given the removal of the brief poem from
the dense network of paranoid texts in *Leaves of Grass,* however, the song
fails to register fully the expansive cultural critique made in Whitman's collective work. Nevertheless, the setting does succeed in heightening the psychic disintegration depicted in the poem. The listener is drawn into
Whitman's paranoid scene, impelled to identify with the protagonist and to
confront the prejudices crippling male-erotic bonds.

At the outset of the opening A section, Blitzstein captures Whitman's
frenzied shout in spasmodic phrases, vacillations in range, fluctuating meters,
and disruptive rests. The constricted phrases in the vocal part, consisting of
either single repeated pitches or alternations between two adjacent pitches,
suggest the protagonist's single-mindedness. The appropriation of African
American idioms now muted, the corporeality in "O Hymen! O Hymenee!"
does not emerge as vibrantly as in the other "coon shout" settings. This de-
emphasis of the body shifts the listener's attention from the corporeal to the
psychological.

The mention of the alluring sexual "sting[ing]" in the poem's second
question slightly calms the musical turbulence, as the protagonist recalls the
pleasure of that experience. In the less agitated B section, he pleads to par-
take again in that enigmatic act not with the short outbursts heard earlier but
with an extended legato line. This shift marks the first of several sudden
changes in vocal character, fluctuations that, as in "As If a Phantom Caress'd
Me," capture the protagonist's psychic instability. Although the vocal style
may have changed, the disjunct leaps and impetuous rush through ten chro-
matics in the voice part convey that the anxieties underlying the past parox-
ysms still linger. This winding vocal phrase is repeated throughout the B
section, suggesting a fixation on the desired "sting[ing]" with which that line
is linked.

Amid this obsessive echoing, the protagonist utters his next question:

"Why can you not continue?" His anxiety ramifies throughout the song and is conveyed by the tension between motion and pause. The first significant moment of such tension occurs immediately after the protagonist's third question, where the accompanimental statement of the B-section vocal phrase is suddenly stopped midway through by a measure of silence. Illustrating a failure to "continue," it suggests as well the protagonist's anxiety over his ability to "continue." With this sudden halting of motion, it becomes unclear whether or not the setting and the protagonist will resume.

A rocketing scalar run jolts the song back into motion, leading directly to a varied reprise of the A section. The reignited momentum of this section, though, is undermined by the textual question it advances: "O why do you now cease?" The anxieties over musical and psychic cessation again arise, and the setting responds, as it did to the previous question, with a disruption. The interpolation of a new formal section obstructs the song with a strange near silence.

The foundation of this C section is a bass chord that is to be played but not sounded: The keys are silently depressed, freeing the corresponding strings to resonate sympathetically with the voice. This silent-yet-sounding chord—itself a representation of the fluid oppositions in the setting, notably pleasure/pain—acts as a continuo accompaniment to a vocal recitative. Above the sustained chord, the voice asks the final question in a quick syllabic declamation, which suits the contemplativeness of that question, as opposed to the reactiveness of the previous ones. The new idiom also intensifies the vocal "schizophrenia" of the protagonist, revealing yet another side of his personality. In addition, the metric suspension of the passage heightens the disruption caused by the final interpolation and the related tension between motion and stasis.

Throughout the C section, the voice ascends tensely by half steps, interrupted only once by an anachronistic arpeggiated (and sounded) chord in the accompaniment. The semitonal grade steepens, capped by an augmented second that accentuates the concluding words "kill me." Raising the possibility of death, this question brings the anxiety over cessation to its highest pitch. The response to the question is startling. Answered characteristically by a disruption, the break in this case proves to be a resumption. The reprise of the A section, previously disrupted, now begins where it had left off. But the reprise falters. The next three measures present fragments of the A material, including the rhythmic outline of the first three measures and the three-note cell (E♭–E♮–A) that figures prominently in both the melodic and harmonic materials of the song.

This truncated, fragmentary reprise vividly illustrates the psychic decomposition brought about by the protagonist's paranoid response to Hymen. The rhythmic and melodic fragments can be seen as shards of the protagonist, who, during the course of the song, has irrevocably crumbled. The suggestion of death is reinforced by the last measure: a bar of silence, *Augenmusik* freighted with symbolic value.

Whose body collapses within that fatal silence? To this question and other possible ones regarding corporeal presence in Blitzstein's settings, this study has often evoked the unnamed "protagonist." Frequently that cloak of anonymity has dropped, and the revealed body has been identified as Whitman's, or Blitzstein's, or even some fusion of the two. The listener has now and then been placed in that fluctuating position. This last condition accords with Moon's description of how the attribution of "the body" constantly shifts between the poet and the reader in Whitman's verse.[48] A song setting, however, expands this interchange of identities: Now, "the body" might seem inhabited by Whitman, by Blitzstein, by the performers, or even by the listeners. Moreover, in the jazz-influenced works, a black body emerges, summoned to invigorate the celebration of the corporeal.

Such permutations, intrinsic to vocal settings, are especially suited to settings of Whitman's verse, which textualizes the body and dissolves the barriers between reader and poet. Blitzstein's works draw on this enhanced corporeality to amplify the erotic thematics and cultural critiques in the texts. In "Ages and Ages," the lines between poet and composer especially blur: With the exclamation "Bathing myself, bathing my songs in Sex," it becomes unclear whose sexual "songs" these are. "As If a Phantom Caress'd Me" produces a different effect, leading listeners to feel a haunting embrace and the anguish caused by social prejudices, and, most important, asking them whether or not they share that hatred. The performers' bodies add the most visible link to this corporeal chain. In "As Adam," for instance, the pianist materializes the desired hand that could satisfy the erotic yearnings being voiced.

Although that hand is not extended in the original Whitman poem, Blitzstein, through the act of setting "As Adam" and the other selected texts, offers his hand to the poet, fulfilling Whitman's desire to have his textualized body seen, felt, and heard. That metaphorical corporeal connection is a crucial part of Blitzstein's reclaiming of Whitman: Blitzstein, joining Alexander and Crane, liberates the poet from homophobic interpretations of his work and embraces him. Blitzstein also claims his own body, presenting it, like Whitman, in highly corporeal works. The songs similarly free his listeners from phobic views of sex and the corporeal. Blitzstein encourages them to experience a variety of sexual and physical sensations: an autoerotic rush, the magnetism of naked flesh, and the warmth of a lover's caress.

## Notes

An earlier version of this paper was presented at the Feminist Theory and Music II conference at the Eastman School of Music in June 1993. I would like to thank Philip

Brett, Matthew Head, Wayne Koestenbaum, and Greg Miller for their advice and encouragement.

1. Jeb Alexander, *Jeb and Dash: A Diary of Gay Life, 1918–1945,* ed. Ina Russell (Boston: Faber and Faber, 1994), p. 65.

2. A discussion of Blitzstein's activities during this formative period can be found in Eric Gordon, *Mark the Music: The Life and Work of Marc Blitzstein* (New York: St. Martin's, 1989), pp. 22–54. Gordon has produced a rare item in American music studies: A biography of a gay composer that deals openly and sensitively with the subject's sexuality. This article is indebted both to Gordon's candor and to his exhaustive research.

3. In 1928, Blitzstein began but never completed *A Word Out of Sea,* a cantata for women's voices and chamber orchestra based on texts by Whitman. This work was not available for study.

4. For discussions of the American response to Whitman's homosexuality, see Robert K. Martin, *The Homosexual Tradition in American Poetry* (Austin, Tx.: University of Texas Press, 1979), pp. 3–8; Thomas E. Yingling, *Hart Crane and the Homosexual Text: New Thresholds, New Anatomies* (Chicago: University of Chicago Press, 1990), pp. 7–13; and Byrne R. S. Fone, *Masculine Landscapes: Walt Whitman and the Homoerotic Text* (Carbondale, Ill.: Southern Illinois University Press, 1992), pp. 10–19.

5. Quoted in Fone, *Masculine Landscapes,* p. 12.

6. For an example of such a reading, see Martin, *The Homosexual Tradition,* p. 5.

7. Emory Holloway, "Walt Whitman's Love Affairs," *Dial* 69 (November 1920), 476–78.

8. The poem was often viewed as Whitman's remembrance of an affair with a woman of African American descent (an "octoroon") during his years in New Orleans.

9. Emory Holloway, *Whitman: An Interpretation in Narrative* (1926; rpt. New York: Biblo and Tannen, 1969), pp. 64–69.

10. Thomas Carl Whitmer, "Verse of Walt Whitman Holds Treasures for Composers," *Musical America* 34 (1921), 3.

11. This is especially the case with the corporeal poems "O Hymen! O Hymenee!" "As Adam," "I Am He," and "Ages and Ages," of which I have been unable to locate any earlier or contemporary settings. Frederick Delius, however, used lines from "As Adam" in his *Idyll* (1933). It also appears that Blitzstein was the first to set "After the Dazzle of Day," "What Weeping Face," and "Gods." For a discussion of settings of "As If a Phantom Caress'd Me," see n. 15 below. Compilations of Whitman settings can be found in Whitmer, "Verse of Walt Whitman," p. 4; Michael Hovland, *Musical Settings of American Poetry: A Bibliography* (Westport, Conn.: Greenwood Press, 1986), pp. 376–414; and the Clara Bella Landauer Collection in the Music Division of the New York Public Library.

12. For a study of the British reception of Whitman, see Eve Kosofsky Sedgwick, *Between Men: English Literature and Male Homosocial Desire* (New York: Co-

lumbia University Press, 1985), pp. 201–17; and Gregory Woods, " 'Still on My Lips':
Walt Whitman in Britain," in *The Continuing Presence of Walt Whitman,* ed. Robert K.
Martin (Iowa City: Iowa University Press, 1992), pp. 129–37.

13. For a discussion of Whitman's influence on Crane, see Martin, *The Homosexual Tradition,* pp. 136–63; and Yingling, *Hart Crane,* pp. 210–15.

14. Yingling, *Hart Crane,* p. 214.

15. The appeal of this text is obviously not limited to gay composers. In fact,
Carl Ruggles began but never completed a setting; see John Kirkpatrick, "The Evolution of Carl Ruggles," *Perspectives of New Music* 6 (1968), p. 153. Other composers
to set the text include Eugene Bonner (entitled "Phantoms") and Nicholas Douty (unpublished and unlocated). It is not clear whether or not either composer was homosexual.

16. This discussion of the closet and the discourse of "homosexuality" has been
significantly shaped by Eve Kosofsky
Sedgwick, *Epistemology of the Closet* (Berkeley and Los Angeles: University
California Press, 1990).

17. The brevity and light veiling of the quote accord not only with the text at
hand, alluding to the fading phantom, but also with Whitman's larger textual practice
of presenting established erotic discourses and symbols in unfamiliar—that is, homoerotic—environments.

18. On the "coon song," see Sam Dennison, *Scandalize My Name: Black Imagery in American Popular Music* (New York: Garland, 1982), pp. 354–424; and
James H. Dorman, "Shaping the Popular Image of Post-Reconstruction American
Blacks: The 'Coon Song' Phenomenon of the Gilded Age," *American Quarterly* 40
(1988), 450–71.

19. Quoted in Gordon, *Mark the Music,* p. 43. During the 1920s, Blitzstein
aimed to *epater les bourgeois* in other compositions. His *Percussion Music for the
Piano* features a passage in which the pianist shuts and opens the lid of the instrument
several times, marked *sempre forte* by Blitzstein. The shock intended by the casting of
an African American singer in his opera *Triple-Sec* is discussed in this chapter.

20. "Negro Choristers Singing for Copland," *World,* 30 December 1928, Metropolitan section, p. 9. Blitzstein's defense is also quoted in Gordon, *Mark the Music,*
p. 42.

21. Following Blitzstein's usage and that of white contemporary audiences in
general, "jazz" will be employed occasionally here as an ambiguous term encompassing a variety of African American repertories, including, as Blitzstein apparently does
in his defense, such white derivatives as the "coon song."

22. Blitzstein's "coon shout" settings are one example of the larger practice of
appropriating African American idioms during the early decades of the twentieth century. The racial dynamics shaping these works are not necessarily the same as those in
the borrowings of such contemporary composers as Copland, Gershwin, Ravel, and
Stravinsky. (On this topic, see Lawrence Kramer, "Powers of Blackness: Africanist
Discourse in Modern Concert Music," *Black Music Research Journal* 16 (1996),

53–70.) On the contrary, racial appropriation involves an intricate interplay of cultural, political, and sexual views, which, in each work, are arranged differently. By showing one possible arrangement, this study hopes to inspire similar analyses of borrowings by other composers.

23. For discussions of ambivalence in colonial discourse and racial representation, see Homi K. Bhabha, "The Other Question: The Stereotype and Colonial Discourse," *Screen* 24, no. 6 (1983), 18–36; Bhabha, "Of Mimicry and Man: The Ambivalence of Colonial Discourse," *October* 28 (Spring 1984), 125–33; Kobena Mercer, "Skin Head Sex Thing: Racial Difference and the Homoerotic Imaginary," in *How Do I Look? Queer Film and Video,* ed. Bad Object-Choices (Seattle: Bay Press, 1991), pp. 169–210.

24. Marion Bauer, "A Furious and Outraged Audience, a Debasing Program," *Musical Leader,* 3 January 1929, p. 8.

25. Olin Downes, "Young Composers Heard," *New York Times,* 31 December 1928, p. 8.

26. In this analysis of the racial transaction between Blitzstein and African American music, one crucial element has been omitted: Blitzstein's Jewishness. The incorporation of that element would lead this study far afield and steer it into the larger and potentially engulfing issue of appropriations of African American styles and stereotypes by early twentieth-century Jewish artists and performers, a diverse group including Blitzstein, Al Jolson, Aaron Copland, George Gershwin, and Sophie Tucker (a "coon shouter"). While complicating the white/black opposition used in this study, a discussion of such appropriation would ultimately uphold the use of that dualism. As Michael Rogin has described in his examination of blackface, Jewish artists participated in a variety of racial impersonation genres in order to polarize the racial spectrum into the white/black opposition. By mocking, exteriorizing, and distancing themselves from blackness, those artists achieved that polarization and settled onto the white side of the split, a move away from the extensive middle region in which dominant white racial attitudes placed them. It could be argued that Blitzstein's appropriation of both jazz and the "coon song" performs a similar function. On the other hand, the songs also could be viewed as outgrowths of the various political and social alliances that existed between blacks and Jews. See Rogin, "Blackface, White Noise: The Jewish Jazz Singer Finds His Voice," *Critical Inquiry* 18 (1992), 417–53; and idem, "Making America Home: Racial Masquerade and Ethnic Assimilation in the Transition to Talking Pictures," *Journal of American History* 79 (1992), 1050–77.

27. It appears that the Copland-Sessions concert was the last public performance of the four "coon shout" settings. During the 1950s, Blitzstein planned but did not succeed in recording the settings with the African American singer William Warfield. Gordon, *Mark the Music,* p. 412.

28. Gordon offers a sympathetic account of Blitzstein's motivations for marrying Goldbeck: "Marc's reasons for marrying were more complex. He entertained no illusions of changing his sexual preference; after five years of knowing Eva, he had no thought of suddenly being attracted to her. Marriage must simply have seemed the

next and only logical step, and it couldn't hurt him to be publicly perceived as heterosexual. As he had once expressed it to Jo [his sister], 'I go so far as to consider marriage for me as a possible social gesture.' The marriage did not alter the essence of the relationship. Rarely, but more likely never sexual with one another anymore, they simply found—Marc in Eva and Eva in Marc—the sharpest mind around with which to spar" (Gordon, *Mark the Music,* p. 83).

29. Quoted in Gordon, *Mark the Music,* p. 42.

30. Richard Dyer, "White," *Screen* 29 (1988), 44–64.

31. Gordon, *Mark the Music,* pp. 237–44.

32. This discussion of male homoeroticism and miscegenation in racial impersonation draws on Eric Lott, "Love and Theft: The Racial Unconscious of Blackface Minstrelsy," *Representations* 39 (1992), 23–50; and idem, *Love and Theft: Blackface Minstrelsy and the American Working Class* (Oxford: Oxford University Press, 1993).

33. Lott, "Love and Theft," p. 25. For a discussion of transvestism and blackface, see Marjorie Garber, *Vested Interests: Cross Dressing and Cultural Anxiety* (New York: Routledge, 1992), pp. 275–81.

34. Quoted in Gordon, *Mark the Music,* p. 41.

35. The work was published by Schotts Sohne under both the English title and the alternative German title *Die Sunde des Lord Silverside.*

36. As with the dual casting in the "coon shout" settings, Blitzstein featured a white singer in that role for a 1930 production. In order to show the effects of increased libation, the characters, during the course of the work, are played simultaneously by one or more singers, a multiplication process that culminates in the appearance of eight singers in the role of the maid. It is not clear if an African American performer doubled Albert Mahler in the role of Lord Silverside in the 1929 production.

37. Quoted in Gordon, *Mark the Music,* p. 45.

38. Michael Moon, *Disseminating Whitman: Revision and Corporeality in Leaves of Grass* (Cambridge, Mass.: Harvard University Press, 1991), pp. 69–74.

39. Blitzstein's setting of "I Am He" is in many ways similar to that of "As Adam." Given the close parallelism, only the latter work will be analyzed here. The texts of both songs concentrate on the desire for corporeal connection. Blitzstein sets "I Am He" in a ternary form and "As Adam" in a loose palindromic structure. In both formal patterns, the central section concentrates on an impassioned plea to touch another body. Moreover, each work has an extended piano postlude that draws on opening material. The two are also built on a series of ostinatos. Unlike "As Adam," "I Am He" borrows heavily from jazz idioms, a feature that it shares with "Ages and Ages." The use of jazz idioms, in addition to that of the "coon shout," is examined in the analysis of "Ages and Ages."

40. For a discussion of phobic attitudes toward masturbation, see Eve Kosofsky Sedgwick, "Jane Austen and the Masturbating Girl," *Critical Inquiry* 17 (1991), 818–37; Moon, *Disseminating Whitman,* 19–25; and Ed Cohen, *Talk on the Wilde Side: Toward a Genealogy of a Discourse on Male Sexualities* (New York, 1993), pp. 43–68.

41. On Whitman's relation to antionanist literature, see Moon, *Disseminating Whitman*, pp. 19–25. A discussion of the role of antionanist literature in the "construction of normative masculinity" can be found in Cohen, *Talk on the Wilde Side*, pp. 35–68.

42. M. Jimmie Killingsworth, *Whitman's Poetry of the Body: Sexuality, Politics, and the Text* (Chapel Hill: University of North Carolina Press, 1989), p. 38.

43. Consistent with Whitman's erotic obscurations, the poem is open to other interpretations than the homoerotic one explored here. Rather than summoning Hymen, the opening shout can be heard to evoke a married heterosexual couple; as the frantic questions in the poem reveal, however, that union is far from blissful. In her study of Whitman, Esther Shephard loosely supports a heterosexual reading, claiming that the poet took the opening line for his "intense little love lyric" from an "epithalamic song" in George Sand's *La Comtesse de Rudolstadt*, a work that Whitman owned. Shephard, though, is aware of the poet's "adhesiveness," a disturbing reality that impels her to invest in the universalist views of Whitman, calling him "the world's greatest lover, including and embracing all." Published eleven years after the composition of Blitzstein's setting, Shephard's study reveals once again the homophobic views that Blitzstein confronted. Shephard, *Walt Whitman's Pose* (New York: Harcourt, Brace, and Co., 1938), pp. 150, 179–80.

44. In his study of Greek homoeroticism, Symonds listed Hymen among a group of beautiful mythological youths. John Addington Symonds, *Male Love: A Problem in Greek Ethics and Other Writings* (1901; rpt. New York: Pagan, 1983), p. 10.

45. Moon, *Disseminating Whitman*, pp. 142–70.

46. Ibid., p. 157.

47. Sigmund Freud, "Psycho-analytic Notes on an Autobiographical Account of a Case of Paranoia (Dementia Paranoides)," in *The Standard Edition of the Complete Psychological Works of Sigmund Freud*, vol. 12, ed. and trans. James Strachey (London: Hogarth Press, 1958), pp. 3–82.

48. Moon, *Disseminating Whitman*, p. 71.

# CHAPTER 5

# A Visionary Backward Glance
## The Divided Experience in Paul Hindemith's
### *When Lilacs Last in the Dooryard Bloom'd:*
### *A Requiem "For Those We Love"*

*Philip Coleman-Hull*

After a 1960 performance at the Washington Cathedral of Paul Hindemith's choral composition *When Lilacs Last in the Dooryard Bloom'd: A Requiem "For Those We Love,"* popularly referred to as the "Lilacs" Requiem, critic Paul Hume responded: "I doubt if we shall ever mourn Abraham Lincoln's untimely death more eloquently than in the words of Walt Whitman set to the music of Paul Hindemith; it is a work of genius and the presence of the genius presiding over its performance brought us splendor and profound and moving glory."[1] The impression one receives from Hume's remark is that Hindemith's music simply operates as an aesthetic complement to the American poet's verse, not equally as a heartfelt response to Franklin D. Roosevelt's death and to the memory of the fallen soldiers of World War II. Because Hindemith was born in Germany, emigrated to the United States only in 1940, and eventually returned to his homeland as an expatriate after becoming a citizen in 1946, Hume's impression of the choral arrangement as an emotive halo or highlight might appear to have validity. Distanced from the historical context of 1946, the Requiem's date of composition, Hume communicates an ignorance of the music's personal and national significance through his reduction of it to a gloss, however splendid, on Whitman's patriotic reminiscence. But to give the composer his due, Hindemith's aesthetic achievement demonstrates not only artistry but also a complex of timely responses that begins within the private sphere of his personal emotions and his identity as an immigrant in America, and reverberates outward to voice the emotions of the larger public arena. Hindemith utilizes the voice of Whitman and expresses a nostalgia for the poet's worldview after the Civil War in order to reflect, if not discover a remedy for, the chaos and anomie that followed World War II.

The situation in which Hindemith found himself, first as a foreigner and then as a naturalized citizen, was not unlike that of the American public scrutinized by Alexis de Tocqueville in the early 1800s: "Picture yourself, my dear friend, if you can, a society which comprises all the nations of the world—English, French, German: people differing from one another in language, in beliefs, in opinions; in a word, a society possessing no roots, no memories, no prejudices, no routine, no common ideas, no national character."[2] The America that de Tocqueville describes is largely adrift and ambivalent toward traditions that could define it and its people. Donald Pease assesses this cultural milieu in his critical examination of the American Renaissance, *Visionary Compacts: American Renaissance Writings in Cultural Context,* in part to argue against the prevailing notion (forwarded by such critics as F. O. Mathiessen, Richard Chase, Richard Poirier, and John Carlos Rowe) that "inconsistencies in character, theme, and cultural action" embedded in nineteenth-century American literature arose from a Revolutionary mythos: a way of thinking that fostered methods of viewing the world and the nation in oppositional terms. The results of such thinking "produced citizens who believed in nothing but opposition—to family, environment, cultural antecedents, and even their former selves." But in the years preceding the Civil War, the threat of secession demanded a mythos—what Pease calls a visionary compact—that prompted "Americans to reflect upon cultural principles they could agree upon," rather than one that inspired separation, dissolution, and "negative freedom."[3] Pease, therefore, posits that writers during the American Renaissance, including Poe, Hawthorne, Whitman, Emerson, and Melville, turned to more positive examples of union in the national culture as a way of binding the nation together. Looking to the past, each of these authors attempted to tap into the collective memory of Americans, discovering those ideals that move the populace away from self-interest toward civic interest, and creating a new, valuable, and healing identity out of past compacts.

For Nathaniel Hawthorne, according to Pease, America was "a world without a past" in which "romance performed a necessary cultural task: it invested objects and persons with a cultural memory, without which persons in a culture . . . surge up before one another with all the durative qualities of ghosts." But Pease also makes clear the dichotomous nature of Hawthorne's writing. On the one hand, it is a public act to appeal to the masses for a "reactivation of a collective memory, enabling [Hawthorne] to remember the common purposes and motives from a shared past." On the other hand, it was mass action that precipitated Hawthorne's removal from his position in the Custom House, igniting his distrust in a populace who "believed in their passions much more than in democratic principles."[4] Hawthorne's own incompatibility with the present, his distrust of the masses, therefore compels him to explore a Puritan past, not a Revolutionary past, and to rediscover those elements vital to the nation's collective identity that have either been lost or submerged over time. So it is in Hawthorne's aversion to the public sphere of his own time that he explores the past in the private act of writing; yet that private act again turns outward, becoming a means of triggering in the public of his own time a remembrance of things past.

Walt Whitman's concept of the public and private spheres operates, according to Pease, on a completely contrary level. The renegade and egotistical poet's verse embodied the masses, spoke directly to them, encompassed them, and could not, indeed, have existed without them. His poetry feasted on and sang of the "body electric," America. And whereas Hawthorne delved into a Puritan past that, while noticeably American, still echoed its European roots, Pease observes that "in Whitman's preface, America is not opposed to Europe, but portrayed as the regenerative power enabling Europe to outgrow itself. . . . It existed in every European's aspirations for a better world. But once it fulfilled those aspirations, America enabled Europeans to separate the Americans in themselves from the Europeans in themselves."[5] So again in Whitman we find not the Revolutionary mythos that places Europe and America at odds with one another, but rather a natural progression allowing for freedom in the midst of separate national identities. Such a stance is echoed in Whitman's "Preface 1855—*Leaves of Grass,* First Edition" when he argues for a natural progression, not difference, between the past and the future: "Past and present and future are not disjoined but joined."[6] The past remains embraceable; but for Whitman the present and future contained their own triumph, as Floyd Stovall reiterates, in a "world led to democracy through the leadership of the United States, of liberty sweeping the world away from the past and into a glorious future, of singers that ignore the trailing glories of the feudal world for the triumphs of the new world of democracy."[7]

Pease's models of Hawthorne's discovery and recovery of the past and Whitman's visionary sense of the future aptly pertain to Hindemith and his composition of the "Lilacs" Requiem. As an immigrant in the United States, Paul Hindemith experienced American culture in terms potentially parallel to those that Alexis de Tocqueville witnessed and wrote about in the early 1800s. De Tocqueville recognized within the locus of the American experience a "palpable absence . . . of a usable past" coupled with a gravitation toward "private concerns and present circumstances" rather than the collective welfare of the community and of future generations.[8] As Kim Kowalke aptly points out in a recent study, the initial (unused) subtitle of Hindemith's composition, "An American Requiem," alluded not only to the Americanness of the work evident from Whitman, but also to the German-ness of the work in its structural, musical, and instrumental parallels to Brahms's *Ein deutsches Requiem,* completed in 1868:

> [One] might be tempted to (mis)interpret Hindemith's provocative subtitle
> as a signpost for an analogous attempt to define "American-ness" in music
> by alluding to a pivotal work defining musical "German-ness." . . . The im-

plicit double or triple entendre of "An American Requiem" thus seems to mirror the composer's ambivalence about his own national identity at this crucial point in his career. Whether Hindemith eventually realized that his music affirmed continuity with Germany's honorable past more than it expressed sympathy with the United States's present . . . he never again referred to the proposed subtitle "An American Requiem."[9]

Implicit in Kowalke's statement is the cultural and artistic fragmentation that followed in the wake of World War II, evoked predominantly by images of the holocaust and the A-bomb, and most immediately by the death of President Roosevelt and countless American (and European) soldiers. Equally notable, however, is the personal fragmentation or division that Hindemith feels between gratitude to his adopted country and identification with his homeland—a division that creates a need for him to reconcile public crisis with his own private, personal concerns. Thus, for a country in shock and still trying to find a way to mourn personal and national losses, Hindemith performs a dual task similar to what Pease describes Hawthorne and Whitman doing one hundred years earlier: He finds and taps into a usable past so that the collective needs of the people may be addressed. While the composer's status as an outsider jeopardized his ability to embrace fully a usable American past, he succeeded well enough in his immersion into American culture to create the "Lilacs" Requiem. On the one hand, Hindemith reaches back eighty years, like Hawthorne delving into his Puritan past, to tap into the voice of Whitman, expressive of another period of collective mourning barely dimmed in the public memory, as a way of both communicating the message of public grief in the war's aftermath and of finding an anchor for his own sense of belonging in America. On the other hand, he engages in the Whitmanian task of envisioning future healing for the masses in combination with personal healing and artistic integrity, a task accomplished in part through the adoption of Whitman's verse, but also through his understanding of modern musical culture and its infusion throughout the work.

### Hindemith's American Odyssey

Paul Hindemith's introduction to Whitman and thus to America did not begin with his emigration to the United States in 1940, or with his creation of the "Lilacs" Requiem six years later. While still in Germany, at the age of twenty-four, Hindemith composed but did not publish a song cycle entitled *Three Hymns by Walt Whitman,*[10] which marks the initiation of the artistic relationship between the American poet's verse and the German-born composer's musical art. Hindemith was not to invoke the talents of Whitman again until 1942, when he composed a solo song in English ("Sing on There in the Swamp") that would form the basis of the parallel movement in the "Lilacs" four years later. Nonetheless, according to Luther Noss, a close friend and critic, Hindemith's initial "chance discovery of these Walt Whitman poems sparked a keen and lasting interest in the work of the great poet. He immediately obtained a copy of *Leaves of Grass* and used it as a 'reader' for his studies in English he had now begun to undertake seriously."[11]

What *Leaves of Grass* offered Hindemith, besides a tutorial in the English language, was an opportunity to connect with American culture and to forge ties with a country as yet undiscovered. The poems of *Leaves of Grass* exposed Hindemith to the recurring tripartite themes of democracy, religion, and love that echo throughout the volume under the banner of freedom[12]— themes that became increasingly tantalizing as the composer suffered sustained attacks for "lacking proper respect for German traditions, associating and working with the Communist musicians and artists, writing simply for profit" and other supposed offenses under Adolph Hitler's burgeoning Nazi regime.[13] The strains of Whitman's "America" offered a stark contrast to the oppression Hindemith felt as an artist in Germany in the 1930s.

> *Centre of equal daughters, equal sons,*
> *All, all alike endear'd, grown, ungrown, young or old,*
> *Strong, ample, fair, enduring, capable, rich,*
> *Perennial with the Earth, with Freedom, Law and Love,*
> *A grand sane, towering, seated Mother,*
> *Chair'd in the adamant of Time.* (1–6)

On his arrival in Manhattan in 1937, the year of his first United States tour, Hindemith remarked in his journal:

> I went with Rudolph to see the most important work of man since the Temple of Karnak: New York at night from the top of the Empire State building. It is an incredible sight: the giant city and its harbors and bridges brilliantly illuminated with a million lights—tiny swarms of humanity in the streets surrounded by buildings that seem from this height to be moving—it is all unbelievably beautiful. The planet Venus stands alone and red in the east, almost a fixed part of the display of lights. At first it looks like the tower light of an even higher skyscraper, but then one realizes she goes her own way apart from the other lights and tells us more than the whole scene around her.
>
>    That people can accomplish all this for purely commercial purposes is shocking when you realize it was their religious faith that moved the Egyptians to their great achievements. Either God is trying to show today's heathen world what he has done or it is as worthless as it appears when you look at a tree or an animal. So many stones, such great hurry, so much noise—how great it is one can make music and thus possess a stronger counteragent against all the confusion of the old and new worlds than do the philosophers.[14]

This extended passage mirrors several of the themes evident in Whitman's poetry: religion, humanity, freedom, art, creation, universality. The final line even absorbs some the ideas on poetry and the poet found in his 1855 preface. Although Hindemith's phrase suggests the seclusion of the artist from the world's chaos, it appears to focus more intently on the need of the artist to rise above humanity and "indicate the path between reality and their souls," to act as "the equalizer of his age and land . . . suppl[ying] what wants supplying and check[ing] what wants checking."[15] Later journal entries and letters comment frequently on Hindemith's acceptance in the United States, his desire to move to America, and his pleasant surprise at the equal and familial treatment he receives during extended stays in the country, though he occasionally peppers his enthusiasm with less flattering references to America as the "land of limited impossibilities," a cryptic phrase, Noss admits, simultaneously suggesting Whitmanian vastness and a more modern disillusionment.[16]

### The Requiem: Genesis and Purpose

These early journal entries and Hindemith's early introduction to Whitman paved the way for a professional and personal attachment to America that solidified on his arrival in 1940. Letters to his wife Gertrude during his first few months in the United States indicate an initial phase of dissatisfaction with life in his new surroundings; at one point he confesses that "the last few days have really been wretched for me and I have concluded I could never feel at home here."[17] But Noss comments that such "pessimistic comments ceased abruptly after 12 March, when Hindemith's cycle of teaching and lecturing at Cornell, Wells, and Yale began," and six years later, when the Hindemiths were granted United States citizenship, they regarded it as "a distinction of which they were both proud and one they never relinquished." The manifestation of these feelings toward America can be felt in Hindemith's reasons for undertaking the composition of the "Lilacs" Requiem. Noss states that Franklin D. Roosevelt's death in April 1945 and the "terrible casualties suffered by both sides in World War II . . . deeply saddened" the composer. Rather than taking the means of expressing his emotions from the current cultural milieu, Hindemith summons memories and influences from the past through his most intimate and longest lasting connection with the country, Walt Whitman: "He . . . felt that [Whitman's] tribute to the memory of President Abraham Lincoln and the Civil War dead ["When Lilacs Last in the Dooryard Bloom'd"], with its eloquent plea for peace, brotherhood, and the reuniting of former enemies in a spirit of humanity and democracy, was an ideal text for the musical expression of his own reflections."[18]

Hindemith thus positions himself as Hawthorne had done almost a century earlier when he wrote *The Scarlet Letter,* tapping into the distant American past to resurrect icons and ideals in order to guide a misguided populace. But Hindemith's task does not immediately involve the task of reactivating a latent collective memory; rather its concern is discovering an adequate personal and artistic response to a sorrowful national event. Whereas Hawthorne escapes into the private sphere of writing out of an aversion toward his cultural present, Hindemith's retreat into the private arena of composition is initiated by a sincere desire to become a part of the national collective memory that he has so recently joined. Reaching back into the past and incorporating Whitman is only part of this process; making music—an exercise of Hindemith's personal talent—to complement Whitman's text and thereby join himself to the culture of America remains integral. The "Lilacs" Requiem, according to many critics, is Hindemith's most distinctly American work in form and structure, an orientation marked by the incorporation of "Taps" in an orchestral interlude. Many music critics agree that Hindemith succeeded in joining the past with the present to create a "profoundly moving work" that became "one of the finest compositions of its kind yet written in this country for use on occasions of national mourning or similar commemorations."[19] Hindemith shared such sentiments when he wrote, bitterly, years later: "Nobody ever bothered to call me an American musician, I always remained for them a foreigner, although I even wrote the piece that in due time . . . may well become one of the few musical treasures of the nation."[20]

In this letter (its wounded vanity aside), Hindemith bridges the gap between the privatized emotive act of composition and the presentation and subsequent reception of the work in public. And the piece, from its inception, possessed an inevitable public life, for like the author Hawthorne who marketed his art, Hindemith devoted himself to making a living producing music. Indeed, the "Lilacs" Requiem was perhaps more, or at least equally, a product of public culture than of Hindemith's intellectual and artistic vision. Although the piece found inspiration in Hindemith's feelings, its genesis was a commission from Robert Shaw, director of the Collegiate Chorale, in December 1945. Writing the oratorio took about four months, from 17 January to 20 April 1946, and the piece premiered at the New York City Center on 14 May of that same year.[21] About two weeks later, on 2 June, the "Lilacs" Requiem saw more national recognition when broadcast over the airwaves in a performance with the CBS Symphony.[22] As Hawthorne had shifted from the private act of writing and rediscovering his past to exposing his finds to the public, Hindemith transports his work from the stasis of a musical score to the influential stage of public presentation. His own emotional expression, realized by rummaging through both personal and collective pasts, emerges; whether it accomplishes the composer's intended mission of promoting "peace, heralding the reconciliation of enemies and the awakening of a new spirit of brotherly love" is, of course, moot.[23] The *New York Times* music critic Howard Taubman, however, commented in a review that "since this music was written only last winter, one feels that the composer was thinking of another fallen war leader of our country, just as Whitman was writing of Lincoln."[24] Apparent in Taubman's response, and demonstrated by the omission of Franklin Roosevelt's name, is the collective memory of the American people for the recently dead president and the power of Hindemith's music, set to Whitman's lyrics, to resurrect and communicate their shared sentiments of grief and remembrance.

Though Hindemith shares Hawthorne's desire to retrieve and valorize historical events and icons, the composer's sights are set on the future as well. In this respect, Hindemith mimics Whitman's fascination with and devotion to succeeding generations of Americans. Whereas Hawthorne involved himself in a process of reflecting back into the past, Whitman posited a philosophy, engendered throughout his poetry and prose, of regeneration. Pease says, "America does not 'reflect' previous forms. Everything in America subsists within two simultaneous contexts: Everything is itself and is on the way to becoming all. In apprehending this world, individuals—or at least those in Whitman's poetry—do not reflect upon things but project them into what they can be, thereby extending what we more usually call memory, or the work of reflection, into the future."[25] This philosophical position is put forward repeatedly in the 1855 preface, and its artistic application can readily be seen midway through "When Lilacs Last in the Dooryard Bloom'd." The poet has already engaged in the act of remembering Lincoln's death, the procession with the coffin, and the multitude of other war dead. Now his attention turns toward the ever-growing West, the "far-spreading prairies cover'd with grass and corn" (92), and the gray-brown bird announcing as well as symbolizing that extension into the future:

> Sing from the swamps, the recesses, pour your chant from the bushes,
> Limitless out of the dusk, out of the cedars and pines. . . .
> Yet each to keep and all, retrievements out of the night,
> The song, the wondrous chant of the gray-brown bird,
> And the tallying chant, the echo arous'd in my soul,
> With the lustrous and drooping star with the countenance full of woe,
> With the holders holding my hand nearing the call of the bird,
> Comrades mine and I in the midst, and their memory ever to keep, for the
>      dead I loved so well,
> For the sweetest, wisest soul of all my days and lands—and this for his dear
>      sake. (100–01, 198–204)

In his own writing on music, Hindemith demonstrates a distinct affinity with Whitmanian beliefs in the purposes and power of art, whether of poetry or music. He incorporates such promise for the future into the oratorio simply by his adaptation of the Whitman lyric, suggesting an allegiance to the poetry's underlying philosophical tenets. In *A Composer's World: Horizons and*

*Limitations,* Hindemith explores the multifaceted world of the musician: the composing process, attention to instruments, the reality of music as business as well as art, the emotions of the listener and the author, the performers of the piece, and so forth. A chapter entitled "Perceiving Music Emotionally" discusses in depth the complex relationship between the feelings of the composer, the performer(s), and the listeners and further gives an indication of Hindemith's own motives for writing the "Lilacs" Requiem. According to Hindemith, it is a common perception that music allows the mutual feelings of the composer and audience to be expressed. But in composing a piece, the artist "himself is not only reproducing the feelings of other individuals, but is actually having these same feelings, being obsessed by them whenever he thinks he needs them. . . . He believes that he feels what he believes the listener feels . . . and consequently he does not express his own feelings in his music."[26] Musical compositions, in other words, arise in part from the consciousness of the artist, but invariably arise also from the feelings of the dominant culture as they are reflected back onto the composer. Music is not insulated from culture, but rather has a symbiotic relationship with it. Ultimately, musical attempts at expressing "true" feelings, either of the composer or the larger culture, never materialize, for the composer's feelings are modified by those of the general public, and those in turn by the composer's.

What Hindemith perceives music to accomplish is not the evocation of real feelings, for "[r]eal feelings need a certain interval of time to develop," but instead reactions that "may change as fast as the musical phrases do" and are "images, memories of feelings." In fact, the meaning we gain from music depends on the supply of memories that music restores in our collective and individual minds. And woven into this process of restoring memories is the composer's own attention to those "creative geniuses of the past who in our imagination are the dearest examples of a most gracious human mind," together with a realization that a "composer's horizon cannot be far-reaching enough."[27] Thus the patterns of Whitman's deference to the past, combined with an unyielding hope in a limitless future, reemerge in Hindemith's own thoughts. Not surprising, then, is Hindemith's admission that the Requiem not only expresses his own feelings, but also emanates outward as "an ode to peace, heralding the reconciliation of enemies and the awakening of a new spirit of brotherly love."[28] Certainly, as the Taubman review indicates, Hindemith succeeded, if only for a moment, in bridging the gap between the private sphere of his personal feelings and the public sphere of restoring the collective memories of the American people.

## The Musical Context

Musically, the oratorio functions on yet another level in the public sphere: that of the current movements governing contemporary musical composition.

Two days prior to the "Lilacs" Requiem premiere, Olin Downes, in the *New York Times,* wrote a column entitled "American Music Survey: A Study of Conditions in This Field Is Made by Dr. Hugo Leichtentritt," in which he highlights the latest trends in the American (classical) music scene. According to Leichtentritt's theory, the first wave of Americanism hit in the 1920s with Charles Ives and Carl Ruggles. Composers Aaron Copland, Roy Harris, Walter Piston, and Virgil Thompson, all schooled in Paris, went a step further in the 1930s by trying to reconcile their learned modernist approach with desires to inject an American flair. By the 1940s, an established milieu existed in which "American composers are more than ever before becoming conscious of the fact that the richest source of inspiration is in their homeland."[29] Not a native American, Hindemith nevertheless composed the "Lilacs" Requiem within this cultural climate.

As a native of Germany, Hindemith grew up under the influences of the European Romantic tradition and wrote works evolving out of that tradition. Yet in response to an admonition that he return to Germany from America in order to compose a more "German" work, Hindemith replied: "The Rhine is not any more important than the Mississippi, Connecticut Valley, or the Gobi Desert—it depends on what you know, not where you are." His own knowledge of Germany and German tradition served him well throughout his career. But the "Lilacs" Requiem differs markedly from the other works in his canon as "a distinctly 'American' work in its concept and construction,"[30] his "only profoundly American work."[31] What constitutes it as an American piece is not so much Hindemith's utilization of characteristically American modes of expression, such as are found in Dvořák's *New World Symphony* or various works by Aaron Copland, nor even his choice to set Whitman. Rather, the Requiem achieves this national character through an "uncharacteristically tight motivic-thematic integration" between Hindemith's "generative method" of composition and the "consistent mood and recurrent imagery of Whitman's text."[32] As Robert Shaw, the director and commissioner of the piece, stated, "Tonalities and rhythmic and melodic motives have insistent and conscious significance. The smaller sections of the work have their own logic and construction, and there is a grand and unifying architecture throughout."[33] Music and poetry, then, intertwine in a reciprocal relationship, so that the "Americanness" of Whitman's poetry infuses Hindemith's musical response, and the music, in turn, illuminates Whitman's text.

### The Requiem: A Reading

Taking Shaw's comments into account, the listener-reader of the Hindemith and Whitman texts may begin, indeed, to appreciate the logic, construction, and architecture of Hindemith's piece by focusing on associative tonalities and text-soloist-chorus interrelations. Kim Kowalke remarks that Whitman's poem "is one of the most musical of poems, as the very act of singing structures the text from within. Three leitmotivic images of loss, mourning, and death—the fallen western star, the sprigs of lilac, and the singing of the hermit thrush—recur and transform (in what some critics have called 'sonata fashion') before coalescing in 'death's outlet song' in the swamp."[34] Divided into eleven distinct solo or choral pieces, the "Lilacs" Requiem uses Whitman's "When Lilacs Last in the Dooryard Bloom'd" in its entirety. And, as if following Whitman's example, it is from within—in arioso no. 5, "Sing on, there in the swamp"—that Hindemith structures his composition. Interweaving text, song, and music to emphasize themes and concerns both universal and personal, public and private, he crafts a requiem that, from the inside out, at times deftly mirrors Whitman's own literary purposes, while at other times it takes compositional liberties (especially with the chorus) in order to forward Hindemith's own vision as he gradually builds toward an interpretation more communal than the one implied by the solitary narrator in Whitman's verse.

Significantly, Whitman's strophe 9 (Hindemith's arioso no. 5) figures as a structural center for both the poem and the oratorio, forming the pivot-point in an emotional exploration of death. Gay Wilson Allen refers to this section in the poem as the moment where the "*tension* which Whitman had actually experienced begins to control the form of the poem, giving it a dramatic structure."[35] In the opening lines of the strophe, Whitman anticipates the reassuring hymn of the thrush, a carol that views death as natural, "lovely," and "soothing" (135). Yet these reassurances are undercut by the recurrence of the evening star, a symbol of grief and tragedy opposing the hopefulness of the bird:

> *Sing on there in the swamp,*
> *O singer bashful and tender, I hear your notes, I hear your call,*
> *I hear, come presently, I understand you,*
> *But a moment I linger, for the lustrous star has detain'd me,*
> *The star my departing comrade holds and detains me.* (66–70)

Symbols coalesce, and one senses both movement toward reconciliation (the bird) and suspension or atrophy in grief (the star).

Arioso no. 5, "Sing on, there in the swamp," is similarly the defining point of the "Lilacs" Requiem. Hindemith uses this central strophe, and not the opening arioso or prelude, as the place where all the major musical motives and tonal centers for the entire Requiem may be found. From a literary perspective, this is an appropriate starting point for analysis, for we find the narrator at a juncture between mourning "The star my departing comrade" (70) and anticipating the song of the gray-brown bird, the "singer bashful and tender" (67). Similarly, Hindemith bifurcates the strophe musically, using a mirrored, accented melodic pattern mimicking birdlike sounds with flute,

bassoon, and piccolo—one set of notes rising as the other falls—to emphasize both difference and continuity in the verse. The irregular rhythms of this
pattern contrast with the dirgelike sound of the pulsing strings. These musical
contrasts correspond to the contrasting poetic themes as they occur in Whitman's lyric. The soloist, singing in A minor, begins, "Sing on, there in the
swamp! / O singer bashful and tender" (66–67; mm. 1–4). The wind instruments help to sustain a sense of fluidity and movement throughout the mezzo-
soprano solo, in spite of their often unsettling nature; meanwhile the tonal
center continually ascends through m. 8, beginning with A, with the dirge
supporting these upward shifts as the whole vocal and musical ensemble
works to communicate the difference in subject. Also in the opening measures, Hindemith incorporates a falling minor third, "an ancient musical em-
blem for a bird call," thus mimicking the thrush.[36] Movement—both forward
in expectation of the death carol and backward in reflection on the past—
punctuates Whitman's verse and surfaces in Hindemith's use of instrumentation. He couples the musical sounds of the thrush in the flute, bassoon, and
piccolo with the words suggestive of hope and anticipation: "I hear your
notes, I hear your call, / I hear, I come presently, I understand you" (67–68;
mm. 5–8). Conversely, as the other woodwinds die out, an English horn
emerges to accompany the more mournful and reflective refrain, "But a moment I linger, for the lustrous star has detained me" (69; mm. 9–11). Hindemith finishes his brief arioso by conjoining these disparate images,
returning to the trills of the flute and piccolo as the English horn trails off and
the soloist completes her line, "The star my departing comrade holds and de-
tains me" (70; mm. 11–16). A signal rather than a climactic piece, this central
solo thus replicates musically the tension and continuity exhibited in Whitman's text, recalling what came before and anticipating what will follow.

    Arioso no. 5 provides the principal tonalities for the rest of the Requiem,
which are based on the relationship between C# minor (equated with images
of death) and A minor (equated with the thrush).[37] Structurally, the changes in
tonal center correspond with the changes Whitman institutes throughout the
poem as he moves between the human narrator's voice and the bird's carol.
Numbers 1–3, 8, and 11 (corresponding with strophes 1–7, 13, and 16 of
Whitman's text) utilize a principal tonality based on C# minor, and all contain
stanzas in which Whitman focuses on death, grieving, and war. As Allen
states in *The Solitary Singer,* the three basic symbols permeating the poem—
lilacs, the western star, and spring—present themselves in the opening stanza,
where the occasion of mourning is also introduced. The melancholy C#-minor
scale that begins Hindemith's work similarly initiates memories of grief and
mourning. Compounding the tonal quality is Hindemith's use of chromaticism and slow tempos throughout the first three pieces, emphasizing somber-
ness through the repetition of dirgelike music. Rarely does Hindemith break
from the ultralinear sequence of notes, except when referring to lilacs, spring,

or the star; uncharacteristic intervals such as full octaves, fifths, and fourths highlight these as important thematic images.

Even when Whitman introduces the thrush, a harbinger of hope, in the fourth strophe, Hindemith (in arioso no. 2, "In the Swamp") refuses to deviate from the solemnity presented in the baritone arioso and chorus. While suggesting movement beyond the interiority of personal human grief, Whitman's solitary thrush still imitates the mourning and parallels the seclusion of the narrator: "Solitary the thrush, / The hermit withdrawn to himself" (20–21). And here the thrush motive, the falling minor thirds to be heard in no. 5, surfaces proleptically. Whereas Hindemith will center no. 5 in A, he casts no. 2 in C♯ minor, in keeping with the theme of death evidenced in the strophe: "Song of the bleeding throat, / Death's outlet song of life (for well dear brother I know, / If thou wast not granted to sing thou would'st surely die)" (23–25; mm. 15–20). In mixing the melancholy tonality and the lilting thrush motive, Hindemith subtly begins the blending of images and emotions that becomes more evident as text and music progress.

Further blending occurs with the mixture of voices in no. 3, the march, when the chorus returns to sing Whitman's strophes 5 and 6, strophes telling of the "Coffin that passes through lanes and streets" (33; mm. 57–59). To "the rhythms of the syllables, and the very syntax" of the lyrics that "give the reader the sensation of traveling,"[38] all of which it replicates, the march adds drum taps, giving a patriotic and nationalistic flavor to the piece. The music emphasizes Whitman's shift from the voice and thoughts of the individual toward the collective voice and thoughts of the nation. Such collectivity is brief, however, and the final measures of the march return to the solo baritone voice: "Here, coffin that slowly passes, / I give you my sprig of lilac. / . . . All over bouquets of roses, / O death, I cover you over with roses and early lilies" (44–45, 49–50; mm. 118–22, 138–48). On the one hand, this return to the individual suggests an inability to grieve publicly, the narrator's hesitation to join in community, a retreat inward after tentative steps outward. On the other hand, and more positively, both Hindemith and Whitman envision the broader dimensions of grief, beyond the individual and toward the universal. Restoration of the individual humanizes the universal and recognizes that both tribute and homage to the dead and their outcome in a reconciliation with death are ultimately personal acts, performed in the public arena.

Conversely, in nos. 4–7 and 9 (Whitman's strophes 8–11 and the thrush's song in 14), the tonal centers derive from A minor, and it is here that incidents involving the bird arise. Whereas nos. 1–3 allow Hindemith to complement musically the textual references to death and mourning, nos. 4–7 evidence the possibilities of hope and restoration hinted at in the aforementioned baritone solo. As mentioned earlier, these sections lead to the dramatic crossroads of the poem, the moment (in arioso no. 5, Whitman's section 9) where the narrator is caught between the tragedy and joyfulness of death. And it is during this

transition that we find the narrator alone again, walking "in silence the transparent shadowy night" (57), wondering "how shall I warble myself for the
dead one there I loved?" (71), and asking "what shall I hang on the chamber
walls?", wanting to make some kind of contribution (78). Still to come in the
final strophe, resulting from the thrush's solitary song, is the speaker's assurance that "it is not the dead who suffer but the living. Death is the end of suffering."[39] For now Whitman isolates his narrator.

While Whitman's text clearly warrants the interpretation of a speaker
dangling in limbo, Hindemith interprets the lyric from this moment onward
as a gradual crescendo toward greater unity, community, and hope for the future. The baritone solo with chorus (no. 4), highlights the soloist, adding the
chorus sparingly for the repetition of key phrases:

B: As my soul, in its trouble, dissatisfied, sank,
C:                                    . . . sank,
B: as where, you, sad orb,
C:          . . . sad orb,
B: Concluded
C: Concluded,
B: dropt in the night, and was gone
C:                    . . . was gone. (Hindemith, "Lilacs" Requiem, mm. 81–98)

Awakening slowly, the chorus stresses endings and images of sadness, center-
ing on and sharing in the narrator's emotional nadir. It then rests during the
central arioso no. 5, gaining more intensity in the course of the sixth song,
based on Whitman's strophes 10 and 11. Here the baritone, a lone figure,
searches for appropriate responses to the president's death: "And how shall I
deck my song for the large sweet soul that has gone?" (72; mm. 7–13). Rather
than imply answers coming from within, Hindemith invokes the community
of singers at the end of no. 6 and the beginning of no. 7, sections that resound
with lines telling the speaker to decorate the walls of the tomb with pictures
of the land and the people around him:

*With floods of the yellow gold of the gorgeous, indolent, sinking sun,*
*burning, expanding the air,*
*With the fresh sweet herbage underfoot, and the pale green leaves of the*
*trees prolific.* (83–84; no. 6, mm. 81–87, no. 7, mm. 1–7)

The emotional climax for the chorus occurs in the seventh song, a fugue,
the contrapuntal texture of which becomes an image of hard-won community.
Hindemith generates power and a grand sensation of movement and expansion through the repetition of key phrases and the continuous layering of
voices, adding to the feeling of westward movement and the joining together
of diverse peoples:

S:                              O —
A: Lo! body and soul! this land! My own Manhattan, with
T:           O    — hi — o's,        O —
B: [tacit]

S: hi — o's      shores,              and flashing Mis-
A: spires, and the sparkling and hurrying tides; O —
T: hi — — — o's                    shores, O —
B: [tacit]

S: souri, And ever the far-spreading prairies, and
A: hi — o's shores, Ohio's shores And ever-
T: hio's shores, Ohio's shores,              O —
B: [tacit]

S: ever the far-spreading prairies cover'd with grass and corn.
A: spreading prairies cov — er'd with grass and corn. Ohio's
T: — hio's shores, and flashing Missouri, And ever the far-spreading prairies
        and ever the far-spreading prairies . . .
B:                                  And ever . . . .
    (Hindemith, "Lilacs" Requiem, mm. 48–57)

When the chorus enters, the multiplicity of voices signals a gradual shift in perspective from the introspection of the narrator, resonating outward, toward the national community, embracing the land and the people.

The culmination of this choral extravaganza comes during the brown bird's carol (no. 9), assumed in Whitman's text to be a solitary voice, but interpreted by Hindemith as the multiple and mellifluous cries of the people. The choral arrangement announces a unity and collectivity that does not arrive lyrically for Whitman or Hindemith until the fifteenth strophe and tenth arioso, respectively. The many-voiced carol is indicative of Hindemith's conviction that only choral singing "is able to touch the collective feelings of large groups of people."[40] Thus we find Hindemith promoting through his music the sensation not only of moving beyond the introspection of the narrator and the solitude of the bird, but also of recognizing and anticipating Whitman's public voice. The popular response in the choral sections absorbs the solitary figures, making them part of a collective identity that discovers a response in rejoicing at death.

In no. 10, the baritone solo and chorus "To the tally of my soul," a tonal crisis arises as if in response to the death carol of the bird. This song is unique in that it lacks a tonal center. Eventually it segues into F♯ as the narrator remarks on the thrush and finally settles into the key of B♭. Unlike the other songs that employ this melancholy tone, "To the tally of my soul" completes its refrain not with the lonely, searching voice of the bird or the narrator, but rather with the determined, hopeful, collective voices of the chorus. Echoes of death and suffering, though never canceled, nevertheless find a reconciliation in the collective memory of the people. The no. 10 solo and chorus stands as a transitional piece that, through chromaticism and unsettling key changes, brings the listener uneasily full circle to the poem's final stanza. And it is in the final stanza of the no. 11 "Finale," after eighty-two measures of baritone solo, that Hindemith unites all the voices—narrator, bird, and chorus—for the first time. With the chorus singing "Lilac and star and bird twined with the chant of my soul, / There in the fragrant pines and the cedars dusk and dim" (205–06; mm. 84–111), the baritone and mezzo-soprano complement their phrase with the opening line, "When lilacs last in the dooryard bloom'd," signaling Hindemith's perception of the ultimate interconnectedness of the poem. Likewise, concluding on this phrase emphasizes the duality of the public and private spheres, the Whitman-Hawthorne difference, as "last" implies not only a reflection on memories of the past, but also finality, completion, resolution, and the need to embrace the future.

**Aftermath**

Close scrutiny of the "Lilacs" Requiem thus reveals both nuances between the text and the music and places where Hindemith clearly uses poetic license in interpreting the text. There is more to this piece than its overall architecture as a series of contrasting and congruent tonalities. Hindemith painstakingly committed himself to producing art in accord with Whitman's ideas. Perhaps his composition did not—how could it?—serve as an impetus for universal peace; but Hindemith appears to have achieved his goal of transferring private reflections into public sentiment. The "Lilacs" Requiem succeeds as a "plea for peace, brotherhood, and the reuniting of former enemies" not because it materially accomplishes those tasks, but because it resolves toward a sense of community rather than retreats back into the composer's private world. To recall a critical accolade cited earlier, the piece has become "one of the finest compositions of its kind yet written in this country for use on occasions of national mourning or similar commemorations."[41] At best, the "Lilacs" Requiem sustains itself by seeking to inspire collective mourning and, subsequently, healing.

Ironically, Hindemith eventually experienced estrangement from the United States, becoming an expatriate from 1953–58. Recall his complaint of 1956: "I was fourteen years in America and did my best to collaborate in the development of American music. . . . Nobody ever bothered to call me an American musician, I always remained for them a foreigner, although I even wrote the piece that in due time . . . may well become one of the few musical treasures of the nation."[42] What cannot be ignored, and what Hindemith clearly asserts, is that the "Lilacs" Requiem, while a private emotional response, operates equally on a public level. The work graduates from the interiority of the narrator and the thrush and rises to the level of universality through the blending of choral and individual voices. The expectations for recognition as an "American" composer that Hindemith rather unrealistically hangs on this piece betoken his desire for both a public persona and an initiation into collective American memory. He not only wishes to join Americans in discovering and sharing their collective, usable past and present, but also desires induction into the continuum that encompasses the likes of Whitman and Hawthorne by creating an artwork that becomes part of the collective memory of future generations. Whitman's poetry initially acts as a means through which Hindemith, in spite of his German heritage, connects with the American culture; "When Lilacs Last in the Dooryard Bloom'd" serves as an impetus, model, and tool for shaping his music and gaining the basis for creating an American artwork. But whereas the "Lilacs" Requiem finds acceptance by a part of the musical public, it is this same work, lauding peace and kinship, that contributes to Hindemith's general souring toward the American public—something partially though never fully healed. Hindemith may celebrate with America over its collective past, but complete acceptance in envisioning the future seems reserved for those born in the boroughs of New York, not the industrial town of Hanau, Germany.

## Notes

1. Luther Noss, *Paul Hindemith in the United States* (Chicago: University of Illinois Press, 1989), p. 188.

2. Letter from de Tocqueville to Count Chabrol; quoted in Donald E. Pease, *Visionary Compacts: American Renaissance Writings in Cultural Context* (Madison: University of Wisconsin Press, 1987), p. 163.

3. Ibid., pp. ix, x.

4. Ibid., pp. 81, 50, 108.

5. Ibid., p. 124.

6. Walt Whitman, "Preface 1855—*Leaves of Grass*, First Edition," in *Leaves of Grass*, ed. Sculley Bradley and Harold W. Blodgett (New York: W. W. Norton, 1973), p. 718.

7. Floyd Stovall, introduction, in *Walt Whitman: Representative Selections, with Introduction, Bibliography, and Notes*, by Walt Whitman, ed. Floyd Stovall (New York: American Book Co., 1939), p. xxix.

8. Pease, *Visionary Compacts*, p. 81.

9. Kim Kowalke, "For Those We Love: Hindemith, Whitman, and 'An American Requiem'," *Journal of the American Musicological Society* 50 (1997), 143.

10. Includes the pieces *Der ich in Zwischenraumen an Aeonen, Schlagt! Schlagt! Trommeln!* (Beat! Beat! Drums!), and *O, nun heb du an* (Now Lift You Close).

11. Noss, *Paul Hindemith*, p. 199.

12. See Floyd Stovall's introduction for a discussion of these themes in Whitman's poetry; also see *Starting From Paumanok,* esp. lines 129–47.

13. Noss, *Paul Hindemith,* p. 10.

14. Journal entry, 6 April 1937; quoted by Noss in *Paul Hindemith,* p. 19.

15. Whitman, "Preface 1855—*Leaves of Grass,*" pp. 716, 714.

16. Letter from Hindemith to Willy Strecker, 21 February 1938; quoted by Noss in *Paul Hindemith,* p. 32.

17. Letter 3 March 1940; quoted by Noss in *Paul Hindemith,* p. 81.

18. Noss, *Paul Hindemith,* pp. 81, 158, 124.

19. Ibid, p. 124.

20. Letter from Hindemith to Oscar Cox, 14 December 1956; quoted by Geoffrey Skelton in *Paul Hindemith: The Man Behind the Music, A Biography* (London: Victor Gollancz, 1975), p. 278.

21. Noss, *Paul Hindemith,* p. 124.

22. Robert Shaw, "Aims of Choral Singing: Director of Collegiate Group Discusses Paul Hindemith's New Work," in *New York Times,* 5 May 1946, sec. 2, p. 5x.

23. Skelton, *Hindemith: The Man Behind the Music,* p. 219.

24. Howard Taubman, "Work By Hindemith In World Premiere," *New York Times,* 15 May 1946, p. 51, sec. A.

25. Pease, *Visionary Compacts,* p. 129.

26. Paul Hindemith, *A Composer's World: Horizons and Limitations* (Garden City, N.Y.: Anchor Books, 1961), p. 43.

27. Ibid., pp. 45, 52, 53.

28. Skelton, *Hindemith: The Man Behind the Music,* p. 220.

29. Olin Downes, "American Music Survey: A Study of Conditions in This Field Is Made by Dr. Hugo Leichtentritt," in *New York Times,* 12 May 1946, sec. 2, p. 5x.

30. Letter from Hindemith to Wally Strecker, 20 January 1947; quoted by Noss in *Paul Hindemith,* pp. 123, 124.

31. Skelton, *Hindemith: The Man Behind the Music,* p. 216.

32. Ibid., p. 233.

33. Shaw, "Aims of Choral Singing," p. 5x.

34. Kowalke, "For Those We Love," p. 141.

35. Gay Wilson Allen, *The Solitary Singer: A Critical Biography of Walt Whitman* (New York: New York University Press, 1967), p. 356.

36. David Neumeyer, *The Music of Paul Hindemith* (New Haven: Yale University Press, 1986), p. 216.

37. As shown by Neumeyer in his analysis of Hindemith's Requiem, the arioso no. 5 begins in A and ends on C♯, the two tonalities on which the entire piece is based. "On the largest structural level, the arioso [no. 5] supplies the principal tonalities for the Requiem, though the relation of A and C♯ is reversed" (p. 218):

Arioso Nos.: 1 2 3 4 5 6 7 8 9 10 11
Keys: C♯——— A——— A–E C F ?–F♯–B♭
C♯

The "?" designates a moment of uncertain tonality, and thus a moment of unrest and unresolved conflict within the piece.

38. Allen, *The Solitary Singer,* p. 356.

39. Richard P. Adams, "'Lilacs' As Pastoral Elegy," in *Critics on Whitman: Readings in Literary Criticism,* ed. Richard H. Rupp (Coral Gables, Fl.: University of Miami Press, 1972), p. 76.

40. Hindemith, *A Composer's World,* p. 200.

41. Noss, *Paul Hindemith,* p. 124.

42. Letter from Hindemith to Oscar Cox, 14 December 1956; quoted in Skelton, *Hindemith: The Man Behind the Music,* p. 278.

# CHAPTER 6

# "I'm an American!"
## Whitman, Weill, and Cultural Identity

*Kim H. Kowalke*

I

*Revolt! and the downfall of tyrants!*
*The battle rages with many a loud alarm, and frequent*
  *advance and retreat,*
*The infidel triumphs—or supposes he triumphs,*
*. . . . . . . . . . . . . . . . . . . . . . . . . . . . . . . . . . .*
*The named and unnamed heroes pass to other spheres,*
*The great speakers and writers are exiled.*
                    —Whitman, "To a Foil'd European Revolutionaire"

On 27 August 1937, after months of planning and preliminary paperwork, Kurt Weill and his wife Lotte Lenya reentered the United States from Toronto, Canada, each on a newly granted immigrant's visa. Since their arrival in New York in September 1935, a temporary visitor's visa (with several extensions) had sufficed, as they waited for the oft-postponed production of *The Eternal Road* to open. But now, as conditions in Europe deteriorated and family members pressured Weill for help emigrating to the United States, Weill and Lenya decided to stay. Reentry would be the first mandatory step toward American citizenship.[1] Weill allowed the lease on his apartment outside Paris to lapse and asked Madeleine Milhaud to arrange for his belongings to be shipped to the Weills' new duplex apartment on East 62nd Street. By year's end, Weill and Lenya had filed their "first papers" for citizenship.[2] In a detailed résumé of his activities during the previous two years, Weill explained his decision to Universal Edition, his former publisher in Vienna:

> I have become fully acclimated here in America and feel very much at home. Here on Broadway last season I had two extraordinary personal successes that firmly established my name with the public and the press. The

first was *Johnny Johnson,* a musical comedy that I wrote last summer with the well-known American author Paul Green. It was a sensational success, won the drama prize for 1937 and was named third among the ten best plays of the year. The second was *The Eternal Road,* the Reinhardt pageant, which, despite the fantastic reception by the press, did not have the desired financial success, but was definitely a personal success for me. A few weeks after *The Eternal Road* premiere I went to Hollywood and wrote music for a film [*The River Is Blue*] that will be filmed next fall. Then I began work on a film with Fritz Lang, for which I have already finished some of the music [*You and Me*]. At the moment I am working here in New York on a play with the Spewacks, who are among the best known Broadway authors and in the fall I have to return to Hollywood in order to complete the Fritz Lang film. As you know, it is very difficult here, especially for someone who speaks his own musical language, but the situation in the theater is still better and healthier than anywhere else, and I believe I can get to the point here where I can continue what I began in Europe.[3]

Weill does not mention that he and Green were currently at work on another project, *The Common Glory,* a large-scale musicodramatic portrayal of the beginnings of the American Constitution, intended for the Federal Theatre Project but never finished.[4] Prior to his trip to Toronto, Weill had visited Green in Chapel Hill to collaborate on an outline of the play. On 19 August, he wrote to Green, "You remember what I said in Chapel Hill, that I have the feeling that most people who ever came to this country came for the same reasons which brought me here: fleeing from the hate, the oppression, the restlessness and troubles of the Old World to find freedom and happiness in a New World." Weill suggested that a recent speech by Franklin Delano Roosevelt offered a "complete ideological outline of the play," which he now envisioned in three parts, concluding with "the world-events of the nineteenth and twentieth centuries which all bring new people to the shores of this country. . . . And that should go right up to Hitler and Mussolini."[5]

On Weill's return from Canada the following week, Green presented him with a commemorative gift, the Universal Library edition of *Leaves of Grass.* Green inscribed it, "For Kurt Weill, May his trouble increase on account of me being so troubled! Hail Columbia! P.G. 8/31/37."[6] This was certainly not Weill's introduction to Whitman. Celebrations of the Weimar Republic's birth had coincided with those for the centenary of Whitman's in 1919. Hans Reisiger's new German translation of *Leaves of Grass,* as well as dozens of critical essays reinterpreting Whitman as an archetypal utopian socialist, reenergized the long-standing "Whitmann-Tradition" in Germany. The Spartacists even transformed "To a Foil'd European Revolutionaire" (1856) into a tribute to the fallen Karl Liebknecht. Weill was nowhere near so ardent an admirer of Whitman as were Franz Werfel and Paul Hindemith. Still, in November 1926, in his capacity as Berlin correspondent for the German radio journal *Der deutsche Rundfunk,* he warmly previewed an upcoming broadcast reading of Whitman's poetry by the actress Gertrud Eysoldt: "Walt Whitman was the first truly original poetic talent to grow out of American soil. He was the first who discovered poetic material in the tempo of public life as well as in the landscapes of the New World. . . . Because he openly expresses things normally kept secret, he is openly chastised."[7]

## II

> Long, too long, O Land,
> Traveling roads all even and peaceful, you learn'd from joys and prosperity
> only;
> But now, ah now, to learn from crises of anguish—advancing, grappling
> with direst fate, and recoiling not;
> And now to conceive and show to the world what your children en-masse
> really are.
>
> —Whitman, "Long, Too Long, America"

On 27 August 1943, exactly six years after Weill had reentered the United States on an immigrant visa, he was awarded U.S. citizenship. Long before his translation was legally formalized, however, Weill had claimed "I'm an American!" on a radio series with that title sponsored by the United States Department of Justice. As the announcer explained (over "hurrahs and cheering of crowd") when script no. 43 was broadcast on the NBC Blue Network on 9 March 1941, "we have invited a number of distinguished naturalized citizens to talk about the American citizenship which they have recently acquired. . . . Today's guest of *I'm an American!* is the well known German-born composer, Mr. Kurt Weill, whose most recent work, the music for *Lady in the Dark,* is now delighting Broadway. Mr. Weill will tell our interviewer, Mr. William Marshall, Assistant District Director of the Immigration and Naturalization Service of New York, what his American citizenship means to him."[8] At no point in the program did anyone hint that Weill was not yet actually a citizen—and would not even be eligible for citizenship for another two and one-half years. Instead, Weill claimed he "never felt as much at home in my native land as I have from the first moment in the United States. . . . Those who come here seeking the freedom, justice, opportunity and human dignity they miss in their own countries are already Americans before they come."[9]

So visible had been his many patriotic activities subsequent to the abandoned *Common Glory* project that even the Justice Department and Immigration Service were willing to overlook the technicality of the actual oath. With the exception of *Lady in the Dark,* virtually every project begun after Weill's initial application for citizenship in 1937 had focused on an American theme, or, after Britain and France declared war on Germany in September 1939, had been intended to rally the nation against his former homeland: "Davy Crockett" (unfinished, play with music by H. R. Hays, 1938), *Knickerbocker Holiday* (musical play by Maxwell Anderson after Washington Irving, 1938), *Railroads on Parade* (pageant by Edward Hungerford for the 1939 World's Fair), "Ulysses Africanus" (unfinished musical by Anderson after a novel by Harry Stillwell Edwards, 1939), *The Ballad of Magna Carta* (radio cantata, text by Anderson, 1940), *Fun to be Free* (pageant by Ben Hecht and Charles MacArthur for "Fight for Freedom," 1941), *Your Navy* (radio program with Anderson, 1942), *We Will Never Die* (pageant by Ben Hecht, "Dedicated to the Two Million Jewish Dead of Europe," 1943). Weill also contributed directly to the war effort, composing for films, broadcasts, and recordings made by the Office of War Information and the War Department. He served as a Civil Defense plane-spotter in Rockland County, New York and as production chairman of the "Lunchtime Follies," which presented shows intended to boost morale and productivity in military-related industries. He even registered for the draft, allowing him to conclude the broadcast interview: "I know for myself that I would be ready to fight if ever this American freedom would be threatened. And since I have never felt this way before in my life, I think I may have the right to say, 'I'm an American.' "[10]

Because Weill's comments in the script of *I'm an American!* so closely match his private expressions of affirmation and assimilation, and are so specific in their references to his own work, it's clear that he was no ventriloquist's dummy on this occasion. In June 1940, for example, he had written to Thomas Mann's daughter, Erika, proposing an organization to mobilize and coordinate the efforts of émigré artists in America: "What can we do to prove to our American friends that we are loyal citizens of this country? My idea is to form immediately an organization called something like 'Alliance of Loyal-Alien Americans' with the purpose of convincing the authorities and the public in this country that we are strongly anti-Nazi, that they can count on us in every effort to save American democracy and that they can consider us in every way as faithful American citizens."[11] The following year he proposed to the shortwave division of CBS, "What I would like to do is to mobilize all this talent for a cultural attack on the German people. We would write radio plays, pamphlets, songs."[12]

Midway through the *I'm an American!* program, in reply to the question "Do you think that America's spiritual defenses can be strengthened by music?," Weill declared:

> When I first studied American music, I was astonished at the richness and
> beauty of the American folksongs, and when I learned to know the national
> songs in this country, I found that they express much more the soul of the

people than in those European countries where they change their national anthems every time they get a new ruler. To me the "Battle Hymn of the Republic" is the most exciting, stirring hymn I've ever known, and "The Star-Spangled Banner" is a dignified, proud melody. The music as well as the words are far superior to those martial hymns of hate that are coming out of Europe lately. Any new national song written in the same spirit and with the same dignity would be an enormous contribution to the welfare of the country because it seems to me when people sing a song together they are sharing a common emotion and songs that express devotion to our great ideals of liberty and justice would certainly help to unite Americans of all races and occupations in a strong determination to defend these ideals.

Weill concluded with almost Whitmanesque images and diction: "Music could help to give the word 'liberty' once more the solemn, passionate meaning it had when Sam Adams wrote it in his letters of correspondence to the humble, hardworking, simple blacksmiths and farmers and fishermen in New England who talked of the rights of men and human dignity by candlelight and campfire, in taverns and town meetings."[13]


## III

> *How you sprang! how you threw off the costumes of peace with indifferent*
> *   hand,*
> *How your soft opera-music changed, and the drum and fife were heard in*
> *   their stead,*
> *How you led to the war, (that shall serve for our prelude, songs of soldiers,)*
> *How Manhattan drum-taps led.*
> *   —Whitman, "First, O Songs, for a Prelude"*

"I've written some orchester [*sic*] music but I threw it away," Weill confided to Ira Gershwin shortly after *Lady in the Dark* had opened. "It seems so silly just to write music in a time like this."[14] But he also told Gershwin that he was thinking of composing "a book of songs (not popular songs but 'Lieder') for concert singers."[15] There is no further mention of the project, but shortly after the bombing of Pearl Harbor in December 1941, Weill turned to the edition of *Leaves of Grass* that Paul Green had given him in 1937. Preserved in that volume are two three-by-five-inch sheets torn from a note pad, on which Weill jotted down the titles (or abbreviations thereof) for ten poems: on the first, "To a Foil'd European Revolutionare," "Beat! Beat! Drums!," "Drum-Taps (3)," "O Captain! My Captain!," "O Star of France!"; on the second, "France: The 18th Year of These States," "Europe: The 72d and 73d Years of These States," "Drum-Taps: First, O Songs, for a Prelude," "Rise, O Days, from Your Fathomless Deeps," "Long, Too Long, America."[16]

On Christmas Day, 1941, Weill presented playwright Maxwell Anderson and his wife, Mab, with the holograph score of "O Captain! My Captain!" A month later, on 28 January, he reported to Lenya (who was on tour in Anderson's *Candle in the Wind* with Helen Hayes) that he was going "to the watch tower with Max" and that "I'm finishing another Whitman song (Dirge for Two Veterans), which I think will be the best, and I started working on the MacLeish song."[17] The following week Weill wrote to his parents: "Everybody tries to help the enormous war effort in his own way. Among other things, I've written some songs to poems by Walt Whitman, the great American poet."[18] On the same day he reported to Lenya: "The three Whitman songs will be printed and I'll try to get Paul Robson [*sic*] to sing them first."[19] When Weill visited Lenya in Detroit in March, he performed "O Captain! My Captain!," "Beat! Beat! Drums!," and "Dirge for Two Veterans" for her and Hayes. Lenya reported that "[Helen] loved the songs (so did I—I think they are the best songs you have ever written. They are the most effortless, at least that's how they sound, songs you ever wrote). I'll sing 'My Captain' all day, the other ones are too difficult to remember after one hearing."[20]

In fact, Hayes was so impressed that she immediately asked Weill to compose underscoring for patriotic recitations she was going to record for RCA Victor as a benefit for the American Theatre Wing War Service. On only a few days' notice, Weill arranged three musical icons ("America," and, no surprise, "The Star-Spangled Banner" and "Battle Hymn of the Republic"), as well as his own "Beat! Beat! Drums!," as "spoken songs." He then supervised Hayes's recording with the Victor Concert Orchestra in Chicago on 30–31 March; the four "spoken songs" were released in May as a two-record set entitled "Mine Eyes Have Seen the Glory: Four Patriotic Recitations."[21] In a lengthy commentary on his settings (most of which never appeared in the liner notes), Weill singled out his setting of "Beat! Beat! Drums!" as the perfect example of the "spoken song": "I was inspired for this composition by the extraordinary timeliness of Whitman's poem, which is a passionate 'call to arms' to everybody in the nation."[22]

Indeed, as the nation mobilized for war in the months after the attack on Pearl Harbor, Whitman moved up to the front lines. New editions of *Leaves of Grass* flooded the market, and biographies of the poet competed for readers under such overtly nationalistic titles as *Walt Whitman: Poet of Democracy*.[23] Weill's music publisher, Chappell and Company, lost no time in issuing, at the price of one dollar, "Three Walt Whitman Songs" for medium voice and piano, leading off with Whitman's most anthologized poem at the time, "O Captain! My Captain!" and concluding with the "Dirge for Two Veterans." *Musical America* reviewed the set favorably:

> These are elaborate settings perhaps rather less distinguished melodically,
> in at least two instances, than in the vividly moodful background created by

the accompaniments. The dramatic essence of each poem, however, is keenly sensed in every case and effectively projected, with a climax reached in the "Dirge for Two Veterans," in which a poignancy of musical utterance is achieved which parallels that of the texts. The three are large-scale musical delineations of the poems, and they provide rewarding material of potent appeal for the singer with a dramatic voice and a dramatic temperament.[24]

That's what Lenya had in mind after she had heard Helen Hayes's spoken version of "Beat! Beat! Drums!" She exclaimed in her newly acquired English, "It just lifts you right out of your sit." But she also tried to reassure Weill that RCA Victor surely "will do it over again with [Lawrence] Tibbett or [John Charles] Thomas," both of whom were leading baritones at the Metropolitan Opera.[25] In May Weill informed Ira Gershwin that indeed "the Whitman songs will be recorded by John Charles Thomas."[26] It's likely that Weill's masterful but hastily copied orchestrations for the three songs were intended for this recording, which then apparently never occurred (or was never released).[27] In fact, there is no record of any public performance during the composer's lifetime.

The volume of Whitman went back on Weill's shelf until 1947. His postwar rereading of Whitman was again occasioned by personal experience, as he wrote the Andersons on returning from his first and only visit to Europe: "Coming home to this country had some of the same emotion as arriving here 12 years ago. . . . Strangely enough, wherever I found decency and humanity in the world, it reminded me of America. . . . I'll write a few more Whitman songs (which will be recorded) and a symphonic suite from *Street Scene*."[28] All of the poems annotated in this pass through *Leaves of Grass* stemmed from the Civil War collection *Drum-Taps* and depicted the tragedy or dehumanization of the individual soldier: "By the Bivouac's Fitful Flame," "In Midnight Sleep" ["Old War-Dreams"], and "Come Up from the Fields, Father." Although by mid-July Weill told Anderson that he had completed "some more Whitman songs" and mentioned the upcoming recording, only "Come Up from the Fields, Father" has survived.[29]

The four Whitman songs were then recorded by tenor William Horne and Adam Garner for Concert Hall Records with Weill's participation, including not only upward transpositions of "O Captain! My Captain!" (minor third) and "Dirge for Two Veterans" (semitone) but also a new sequence—a crucial reordering that converts the group into a genuine "dramatic" cycle (see Figure 1). Horne's annotated "blue print" of Weill's holograph of "Come Up from the Fields, Father" contains, in addition to the expected markings of a singer learning a new song, a crucial change that also is evinced on the recording. At the climax of the mother's reading from the letter, the agitated accompaniment stops dead in its tracks on the downbeat, as if paralyzed by the preceding status report of her son's condition: "At present low." Once the following phrase, "but will soon be—" is heard without accompaniment over collective halted breathing, then completed as the accompaniment resumes to contradict its last word, "better," Weill's original idea simply sounds wrong (see Figure 2).[30] But because "Come Up from the Fields, Father" remained unpublished until 1984 (and Horne's copy unknown until 1994), this crucial revision is not reflected in any recordings or published scores.[31]

Weill's plan to make a symphonic suite from his opera *Street Scene* would seem unrelated to the Whitman project. But when the opera opened on

**Figure 1.** Kurt Weill accompanying tenor William Horne in Weill's *Whitman Songs*. Photo courtesy of Weill-Lenya Research Center, New York. Reprinted by permission of the Kurt Weill Foundation for Music.

Broadway on 9 January 1947, the inside front and back covers of the souvenir program book featured photographs of lilac sprigs illustrating two stanzas of "When Lilacs Last in the Dooryard Bloom'd," Whitman's famous elegy in memory of Abraham Lincoln, which is recited, but only in small part, by Sam at the climax of Act I in both the 1929 play by Elmer Rice and the opera.[32] In describing *Street Scene* as his "most experimental" play, a "patterned mo-

**Figure 2.** Kurt Weill, "Come Up from the Fields, Father," © 1994 European American Music Corp. All rights reserved. A page from William Horne's "blue print" of Weill's holographic score. Photo courtesy Weill-Lenya Research Center, New York. Reprinted by permission of the Kurt Weill Foundation for Music.

saic" that depended on "concealed architectonics," Rice characterized its constructive technique in Whitmanesque terms as "symphonic," "the statement, restatement and development of themes."[33] Although Rice insisted that he himself adapt the play as a libretto, he agreed to bring in a lyricist, someone, Weill said, who could "lift the everyday language of the people into simple, unsophisticated poetry."

That they offered the task to the African-American poet Langston Hughes, who had no previous experience writing song lyrics, has been portrayed as a bold choice: two "outsiders" of German-Jewish descent commission a representative of the quintessential American "Other" to give voice to the play's underlying Whitmanesque vision of the urban American melting pot. Langston Hughes may have been a Broadway novice, but he was widely recognized as the foremost Whitman disciple of his generation. Hughes claimed that at a crucial point in his life he had thrown away every book he owned except *Leaves of Grass.* He celebrated its centenary by writing "Old Walt" and concluded his first poetry collection, *The Weary Blues,* with an epilogue: "I, too, sing America. / I am the darker brother. / They send me to eat in the kitchen. / When company comes."[34] During the two years he worked on *Street Scene,* Hughes edited and introduced two collections of Whitman's poetry and proposed (unsuccessfully) to Doubleday a third Whitman anthology on Negro and Indian themes entitled "Walt Whitman's Darker Brothers."[35]

Whitman had helped to shape all three collaborators' impressions of the American scene, and by the time the opera opened a web of Whitmanesque imagery linked dialogue, lyrics, and music, stretching from the black janitor's opening urban blues, "I Got a Marble and a Star," to the final strains of Act II, where Rose consoles Sam with "Don't forget the lilac bush bright in the morning air," an impassioned reminiscence of the utopian pastoral Whitman duet from Act I. In its eclectic attempt to embrace "a great variety of music, just as the streets of New York themselves embrace the music of many lands and many people," *Street Scene* aspired to be Weill's "Whitman opera."[36]

**IV**

> *With music strong I come, with my cornets and my drums,*
> *I play not marches for accepted victors only, I play great marches for*
> *    conquer'd and slain persons.*
>
> —Whitman, "Song of Myself" (sec. 18)

If the *Walt Whitman Songs* do indeed represent the realization of Weill's plan to "compose a book of songs (not popular songs but 'Lieder') for concert singers," they beg a number of questions concerning genre, audience, and performance practice. As both "Lieder" and "songs" (but not "popular songs"), these settings reflect Weill's own dilemma, resituating himself in

America as a Jewish, German-born, classically trained composer for the musical theater, during and immediately following a world war incited by his fatherland. Like virtually every one of his works for the stage, the *Whitman Songs* are hybrids, negotiating the notoriously ill-defined boundaries between "serious" and "popular," "high" and "low," "cultivated" and "vernacular," "European" and "American," "autonomous" and "occasional." Not "rousing" enough to be patriotic anthems, not "folklike" enough to be baubles of Americana, and not "arty" enough to stand next to sets of Schumann and Brahms, they have recently generated more controversy than performances (with either piano or orchestral accompaniment). Though indeed requiring "concert singers," they still seem ill-at-ease on the recital or symphonic platform, too aware of their "melting pot" origins, too self-conscious of their "otherness."[37] Echoing the jaunty clichéd rhythmic patterns of "How Can You Tell an American?" in *Knickerbocker Holiday* as audibly as the constructive ostinatos of Hugo Wolf's setting of "Alles endet, was entstehet" in *Drei Gedichte von Michelangelo,* the *Whitman Songs* challenge performer, audience, and critic with their range and admixture of idioms, tone, harmonic vocabulary, and intertextuality.

The three songs in the initial collection ("O Captain!," "Beat! Beat! Drums!," and "Dirge for Two Veterans," in that order) share common imagery and idioms, each invoking musical instruments in tandem with a march trope of some kind. In the orchestrated poetry selected by Weill, drums and bugles, which burst like a ruthless force into church, school, and home for a quick-march off to war in "Beat! Beat! Drums!," also accompany a sad procession toward the double grave in "Dirge for Two Veterans." What Weill's mentor Ferruccio Busoni had described as its "fanatical tone" permeates "Beat! Beat! Drums!" Whitman's narrator demands that nothing, no individual's protest or entreaty, be allowed to interfere with the mass summons to war. Whitman had written the poem in 1861 shortly after the Battle of Bull Run, when he was as caught up in the patriotic fervor of mobilization as the narrator seems to be; the antepenultimate line of the poem's first published version was "Recruit! Recruit!"[38] The imagery is almost entirely aural, as the "terrible" drums are exhorted through incessantly repeated phrases and obsessive iambic-anapestic meter to beat, burst, rumble, rattle, whir, pound, and thump quicker, wilder, heavier, climaxing in a crescendo that leaves the reader breathless. The poem's critical subtext, warning of war's barbaric threat to individual autonomy, is simply overwhelmed, and few composers who have set the text have been able to take issue with the narrator. This, and the poem's own intrinsic music, surely accounts for some of the striking similarities of Weill's setting to those of Ralph Vaughan Williams (1936), Howard Hanson (1930), and especially Paul Hindemith (1919)—none of which would have been familiar to him in 1942.

Weill initially seems to have deflected the threat that this "reveille" poem poses to the maternal values of family and civilization (subsequently embodied in "Come Up from the Fields, Father") into his setting of its "wound-dresser" counterpart, the "Dirge for Two Veterans." By placing the "Dirge" last in both orderings of his songs, Weill rounds off their overall progression with a transformation of the opening musical images. In the first ordering, the bells and bugle trills of "O Captain! My Captain!" herald the arrival of the ship of state safely in port, but its captain, "fallen cold and dead" on the deck, does not hear their exultant tones. Before the third stanza of the poem can begin, what Whitman might call a "strong dead-march" ("Dirge," 24) has stolen, unwelcome, into the drumlike figuration of the bass line of the song, vividly documenting Weill's erstwhile claim that "every text I've set looks entirely different after it's been swept through my music."[39]

"Come Up from the Fields, Father" precedes the "Dirge" in the second ordering, which also differs from the first by beginning with "Beat! Beat! Drums!" "Come Up" is the only setting that parades no diegetic music or musical instruments. Rather than marching, its breathless characters race headlong to hear the dreaded news that will prompt the "Dirge" that must inevitably follow on it—a necessity that Weill built into the inconclusive cadence of the song. As the narrator arrives on the expected tonic in D minor, the accompaniment arpeggiates a C-major triad; the final sonority, a five-note, fifth-generated chord (C–G–D–A–E), is virtually a signature harmony in many of Weill's works from 1920–27. By reversing the original order of "O Captain! My Captain!" and "Beat! Beat! Drums!" and by inserting "Come Up from the Fields, Father" into third position as the point of highest tension and climax in the set as a whole, Weill, like so many *Liederkreis* composers before him, converted a group of disparate poems into a dramatic narrative.[40] A fanatical call to battle in "Beat! Beat! Drums!" precipitates the individual tragedies of two veterans, the father-captain and soldier-son, whose deaths are announced in the two middle songs and who are mourned simultaneously in the "Dirge for Two Veterans." With such an implicit plot, Weill's *Whitman Songs* owe as much to the tradition of American theater song as to that of the German *Lied*.

Whitman's poetry challenged the formal expectations and structural paradigms of both those traditions and thus inspired solutions more imaginative than had been required of Weill when working within either of them. The three seven-line stanzas of "Beat! Beat! Drums!," each of which begins with the refrain, "Beat! beat! drums!—Blow! bugles! blow!," appear to be more regular than they really are. As the decibel level escalates from the final line of each stanza to the next ("fierce and shrill" to "quicker and wilder" to "terrible and loud"), any routine expectations for syllable count, meter, or mode of discourse are frustrated. Although they may appear to be strophic, the poems cannot be set strophically. Weill's ingenious formal response wraps a double-refrain envelope (for lines 1 and 7) around the irregular free verse of lines 2–6 in each stanza. He then uses these markers expressively and dynamically: the opening refrain of each respective stanza (*mf, f p, f*) is intensified in each case by the closing refrain ( *f >, ff pesante, f* ), Weill then repeats an expanded opening refrain ("Beat! beat! drums! Beat! beat! drums! Blow! bugles! blow!") as a climactic coda, *fortissimo* and "wildly." The bugle calls that responded to the imperatives at the end of the first stanza grow ever more invasive, unable to wait for the singer to finish at the end of the second stanza, then competing with him for priority in the opening refrain of the third.

"O Captain! My Captain!" became Whitman's most popular poem during his lifetime, much to his chagrin. It was also one of his most "regular": three eight-line stanzas, each subdivided four plus four, and ending with the refrain "Fallen cold and dead." In early editions of *Sequel to Drum-Taps*, certain lines were grouped and progressively indented so as to outline on the page the shape of a ship. Perhaps this intentional "naiveté," evinced also in clichéd rhymes and metaphors, prompted Weill to respond with a setting that wears its show-business costume uneasily. The result is an unstable hybrid indeed. Weill treats the first two stanzas strophically, but with varied accompaniment; he mirrors the change in mode of address in the third stanza by composing entirely new music for the first half and then reverting to strophic material for the final four lines, modified to accommodate the irregularities of "Exult, O shores, and ring, O bells!" The result is, of course, an expanded bar form (A A B, where the B section incorporates some of A at its close). The song's Germanic roots are emphasized also by Weill's coloration of its F-major tonality with the flatted submediant (D♭), a commonplace in nineteenth-century German practice (see, for example, the ubiquitous D♭ in the first movement of Brahms's Symphony No. 3 in F). Weill introduces D♭ on the second beat of the introduction, and it then generates the motive, F–E♭–D♭–C, that permeates the song and recurs prominently in the vocal line at the beginning of the second half of each strophe.

Schubert and Brahms are standing in the wings, readily apparent, and this makes Weill's compositional choices for the first strophe all the more puzzling. Although the generic piano accompaniment might have been lifted from a hundred different Broadway "charm songs" or ballads of the day, I suspect that it had a particular association for the composer. It appears, rhythm-for-rhythm and nearly note-for-note, in the bridge section of "Johnny's Song" at the end of *Johnny Johnson,* where Paul Green's banal lyric (for the Gump-like title character) reads, "And we'll never lose our faith and hope and trust for all mankind. We'll work and strive while we're alive that better way to find." (That Weill's melody for Whitman's "our fearful trip is done" is nearly identical to that for Green's "As up and down I wander" only reinforces the intertextual connection.) But the strategy doesn't succeed. The topic is too profound for so casual a presentation; in that sense, the setting is apt for the poem but not the subject.

In a 1948 letter defending *Down in the Valley* against its "corniness," Weill quotes his mentor Ferruccio Busoni: "The fear of triviality is the greatest handicap for the modern artist." Weill also asserts that "form" is at once "the personal expression of a composer" and "the most important element of dramatic music."[41] The textual design and rhetoric of "Come Up from the Fields, Father" presented Weill with formidable compositional problems. In the Universal Library edition of *Leaves of Grass,* the poem appears in five irregular sections, ranging in length from two to eleven lines and, in several cases, further subdivided into smaller groupings.[42] Weill treats the poem as a tragic scene from a verse drama, more a libretto than a *Ballade,* though he was certainly not unaware of its obvious resonances with *Erlkönig.* As was so often the case in his settings of Brecht in the context of musicodramatic pieces, Weill wielded his scalpel and excised the entire fourth section of Whitman's poem, which focused on the "single figure" of the grieving mother. Reassigning its affective task to the music, Weill was able to juxtapose the climactic line from the letter "but will soon be better" with the omniscient narrator's report, "Alas, poor boy, he will never be better . . . he is dead already." Once one has heard Weill's version, it is hard to imagine a musical setting that could preserve the fourth section, so riveting and escalating is the dramatic tension from the opening of the letter until the *pianissimo* reverberation, "The only son is dead." Schubert's and Loewe's analogous responses to Goethe's "Das Kind war tot" hover phantomlike in the pauses within Weill's vocal line.

At several other points in his setting, Weill ignores or subverts Whitman's formal divisions. The omnipresent triplet figuration of the opening $\frac{4}{4}$ Agitato breaks off at the end of Whitman's first section, but resumes only with the second line of the third section; Weill has, in effect, detached the first line, "Down in the fields all prospers well," and joined it to its pastoral predecessors in section 2 (*Meno mosso, subito p* $\frac{3}{4}$—$\frac{9}{8}$). No section is allowed to close; all are open-ended. There are no unelided internal cadences in the song; in fact, triads are only slightly less rare than the tonic chord. Weill does not try to characterize each of the leading players in the drama, just as Whitman does not always make clear who is actually speaking. (The narrator sometimes appropriates the distraught voice of the farmer's daughter, but at other times offers the dispassionate reportage of an observer.) Instead Weill underscores changes of scene and developments of plot. As the narrator urges the mother to "open the envelope quickly," intertextual references to Schubert's *Erlkönig* and *Street Scene* intertwine. The mother reads the broken sentences in a dazed monotone while the accompaniment admits its own horror in incessantly reiterated augmented triads, punctuated first by a tritone motive and then by frenzied chromatic cells. Reminiscence of the $\frac{9}{8}$ pastoral music of section 2 returns, now *Molto meno mosso,* as the narrator tells us, calmly, what we already fear to be the case. The mother's subsequent "midnight waking, weeping, and longing" recall with increasing urgency the triplet figuration that had accompanied the letter. This final section gradually thickens in texture, gaining weight, speed, and dynamics until the narrator can no longer control his emotions. On the heels of a climactic allargando, he bursts forth with quasi-Puccinian passion. With a rare espressivo marking, Weill gives the singer explicit permission to identify with the mother as she yearns "to be with her dear dead son." A masterful musicodramatic conception, this scena would not have been out of place in *Street Scene.*

Weill also omits a stanza (number seven) of Whitman's "Dirge for Two Veterans," thereby allowing the final line of the sixth quatrain, "And the strong dead-march enwraps me," to segue (with a monumental crescendo to *fortissimo*) into "O strong dead-march you please me!" By linking the sixth and eighth stanzas into a single musical unit, the climax of both song and cycle, Weill brings into close proximity four recurrent images within the "Dirge": the moon, bugles, drums, and the dead-march. "What I have I also give you" summons the work's highest note for the singer and loudest dynamic for the piano (or orchestra). The final stanza of text is reserved for the completion of the rondo structure of the "Dirge"; it also does double duty as an epitomizing coda for the set as a whole:

> *The moon gives you light,*
> *And the bugles and the drums give you music;*
> *And my heart, O my soldiers, my veterans,*
> *My heart gives you love.* (33–36)

In one of the most exquisite passages in his *œuvre,* Weill marks the vocal part *dolce,* the piano *dolcissimo.* In the ethereal orchestral version, harp and woodwinds seem almost capable of miraculously refracting moonbeams, and in such a setting Weill's and Whitman's hushed voices seem to merge with the singer's. The bright lights of Broadway are far removed. Nonetheless, the "Dirge" does manage to bring Old and New World topics and techniques together one last time. In the fifth stanza, standing at the center of the song, the dynamic level shifts suddenly from *forte* to *pianissimo.* In this quietude, as "the son is brought with the father," the piano sounds "Taps," the Civil War melody first used by the Army of the Potomac in 1862, but fourscore years later again echoing graveside around the world. The material is indeed pointedly American, but its treatment is serenely Mahlerian. In yet another sense, a son has been brought with the father.

**V**

> *Through me many long dumb voices,*
> *Voices of the interminable generations of prisoners and slaves,*
> *Voices of prostitutes and of deformed persons,*

> *Voices of the diseas'd and despairing, and of thieves and dwarfs,*
> *Voices of cycles of preparation and accretion,*
> *And of the threads that connect the stars—and of wombs, and of the father-*
> *  stuff,*
> *And of the rights of them the others are down upon.*
>
> —Whitman, "Song of Myself" (sec. 24)

"I feel completely like an American and no longer look back," Weill said in an interview published in New York's German-language newspaper *Aufbau*—at precisely the time he was writing the *Whitman Songs*. "For me, America is the continuation of Europe, and I am happy that it is my country."[43] Few exiled German intellectuals shared Weill's opinion. Many dismissed so radical an assimilation and redefinition of cultural identity as self-deception, a "sell-out," a prime example of "Schnellamerikaner." For Adorno, perhaps the most extreme of Weill's critics, "the profile of this composer, who died in America, can hardly be encompassed by the concept of a composer at all."[44] Harold Clurman phrased it in less Eurocentric but equally uncomprehending terms; for him, Weill is a musical Gulliver, "characteristically twentieth century" in his adaptability: "He could write music in any country so that it would seem as if he were a native. If he had landed among the Hottentots, he would have become the outstanding Hottentot composer of the Hottentot theater. Weill was all theater and all 'mask.' "[45] In such an interpretation, Weill's vociferously American identity is not real, but rather yet another masterful impersonation—a new act, one good enough to be taken "on the road" again if it were to become necessary.

Weill would have disagreed vehemently. In fact, he had already done so, obliquely and unwittingly, in an interview in the *New Yorker* in 1944: "If I were removed to a place like off the earth, I would never be homesick for Berlin or Dessau or Lüdenscheid, I would be homesick for the drugstore in New City."[46] At a time when European civilization seemed on the brink of extinction, the drugstore in the hamlet near Weill's house in Rockland County must have epitomized the Whitmanesque democratic visions and values he so admired. Such a drugstore was no mere pharmacy, but a microscopic melting pot, a classless gathering place for rich and poor alike; a veritable cornucopia of the basic necessities of life, yet offering few of its luxuries—except for the "queen of the drugstore," ice cream, the virtues of which Weill and Langston Hughes extolled at length in the "Ice Cream Sextet" in *Street Scene*. Nowhere within the private or public documentation that Weill left behind at the time of his untimely death in 1950 is there a scrap of paper or shred of other evidence that Weill's American identity had been "scripted" as a mask for suppressed convictions or genuine self. If his American identity was only a role, Weill played it so convincingly that it became his only reality. If it was self-deception, it was total.

There had been talk of the American Weill not being the "real" Weill since his success with *Lady in the Dark.* So it was not surprising that Boris Goldovsky touched on this topic during an "Opera News on the Air" intermission interview in 1949. After discussing with Weill "what makes Puccini Puccini," Goldovsky inquired, "Tell me, Mr. Weill, as a composer yourself, are you conscious of [what] brings forth the most characteristic in you; what brings out the Weill in Weill, so to say?" Weill replied with a spontaneity uncharacteristic of this scripted genre: "Well, I'm not conscious of it when I actually write music, but looking back on many of my compositions, I find that I seem to have a very strong reaction in the awareness of the suffering of underprivileged people; of the oppressed, the persecuted."[47] Commenting in particular on *Lost in the Stars* but reflecting (just three months before his death) on what would turn out to be his entire *œuvre,* Weill identified his artistic response to human suffering as the underlying constant bridging his Old and New World careers.

"Good songs are but the dreams, the hopes, and the inner cries deep in the souls of all peoples of the world," Langston Hughes wrote in an essay about "My Collaborator, Kurt Weill." He suggested that Weill's activity in the popular arena spiraled not downward toward the "commercial," but outward toward the "universal": "He had something to say and he said it in the simplest and most direct terms, in the surface language of each country in which he lived, but also in the universal language of that world beyond worlds in which all human souls are related. . . . That is why Germany can claim Kurt Weill as German, France as French, American as American, and I as a Negro."[48] In these terms, Hughes might have been describing Whitman, in whom Weill found so kindred a sensibility. Fifty years after his death, most people tend to think of Weill as a "Brecht-composer." He would surely have preferred to be remembered as a "Whitman-composer."

> *Come, said the Muse,*
> *Sing me a song no poet yet has chanted,*
> *Sing me the Universal.*
>
> —Walt Whitman, "Song of the Universal"

## Notes

1. On 31 May 1937, Weill wrote to his brother Hans in Mannheim, Germany: "I'm going to take care of my immigration affairs as soon as I get back to New York. This is one of the reasons why I would want to get back as soon as possible (not to mention the fact that I like New York much better than Los Angeles). I'll let you know as soon as it's been taken care of. . . . According to today's papers, things in Europe are looking grim again, but I hope that it will not lead to a catastrophe." And on 24 July: "We're still waiting for a certain paper, so that we can take care of all our affairs,

but I'm hoping that we'll get it soon, so that we can go to Canada possibly already
next week. With this, one more major difficulty would also be taken care of as far as
you're concerned. How do things stand with you now? Have you already made some
decisions and have you also made arrangements, which could secure you a temporary
existence?" On 4 September Weill reported on their reentry: "We came back from our
trip to Canada this week. Everything went very smoothly, and we finished all our business there within two days. I'm so glad we have finally done it. Meanwhile, I've talked
to several people in connection with the plan you talked about in your last letter, and
I'm glad to tell you that it will be possible to get the money, which is necessary for
your immigration, for a few weeks and hold it in a special bank account for you. Of
course, I have to take responsibility for paying it back immediately after your arrival
here" (Hans and Rita Weill Collection, Weill-Lenya Research Center, series 45). All
correspondence and documents in the Weill-Lenya Research Center are quoted by
permission of the Kurt Weill Foundation for Music. Unless otherwise noted, translations from the German are my own.

2. In a letter of 14 November 1937 to his brother Hans, Weill wrote: "This
week we're getting our own first citizenship papers. It will probably take one week
until I have all the documents together and then I'll send them off immediately."

3. Letter from Weill to Alfred Kalmus, director and owner of Universal Edition in Vienna, 29 July 1937 (photocopy in Weill-Lenya Research Center, series 41).
Although for a few weeks in January 1937 Weill did have two productions running
simultaneously on Broadway, he exaggerated the success of the Group Theatre's production of *Johnny Johnson,* which lasted only sixty-eight performances. *The Eternal
Road* opened on 7 January 1937; drama critic Brooks Atkinson wrote: "Let it be said
at once that the ten postponements are understood and forgiven. Out of the heroic
stories of old Jewish history Max Reinhardt and his many assistants have evoked a
glorious pageant of great power and beauty." It closed in May, after 153 performances.

4. A decade later Green eventually finished his own outdoor historical pageant
with the same title; it premiered in Williamsburg, Virginia.

5. Letter from Weill to Green, 19 August 1937; Paul Green Papers, University
of North Carolina Library, Chapel Hill. In a postscript Weill informed Green that "We
are leaving on Saturday. You will hear from us from Canada."

6. The volume was among those the present author found in Brook House,
New City, New York, after Lenya's death in 1981. It is now housed in the Weill-Lenya
Research Center. "Hail Columbia" is a march said to have been composed in honor of
George Washington. According to the *International Cyclopedia of Music and Musicians,* the composer was either Johannes Roth or a Professor Phylo, both of Philadelphia. Its words were written in 1798 by Joseph Hopkinson: "Hail, Columbia! happy
land! / Hail, ye heroes! heaven-born band! / Who fought and bled in Freedom's cause, /
And when the storm of war was gone, / Enjoyed the peace your valor won. / Let inde-
pendence be our boast, / Ever mindful what it cost; / Ever grateful for the prize, / Let
its altar reach the skies!" In light of the occasion for the gift, however, Green's "Hail

Columbia" might also refer, improbably and ironically, to the Alma Mater of Columbia University, "Stand Columbia!," a tune composed in 1797 by Joseph Haydn. The Weimar Republic adopted the same melody as the German national anthem in 1922 under the title "Deutschland, Deutschland über alles." It was retained as the anthem of Nazi Germany. "Stand Columbia!" contains the verses, "Many a grateful generation / Hail thee as we hail thee now!"

7. Kurt Weill, "Berliner Rundfunkprogramme: Kritik der Woche—Vom kommenden Dingen," *Der deutsche Rundfunk,* 14 November 1926, p. 3253.

8. *I'm an American!,* script no. 43. National Broadcasting Company. WKZ—New York City, Sunday, 9 March 1941, 12:15 to 12:30 p.m. EST, Blue Network (typescript, with annotations, as well as a recording of the actual broadcast, in the Weill-Lenya Research Center, p. 1).

9. *I'm an American!,* script no. 43, pp. 2–3.

10. In a letter to Lenya of 15 February 1942, Weill reported that he had completed two songs ("Schickelgruber" and "The Song of the Free") and was hard at work on *Your Navy.* "This war is very serious. Yesterday I registered for the draft" (*Speak Low (When You Speak Love): The Letters of Kurt Weill and Lotte Lenya,* ed. and trans. Lys Symonette and Kim H. Kowalke [Berkeley and Los Angeles: University of California Press, 1996], letter no. 237, p. 296).

11. Letter from Weill to Erika Mann, 17 June 1940 (Weill/Lenya Archive, Yale University Music Library; series IV.A., box 47, folder 11). Weill wrote similar letters to Bruno Frank and others. On 6 June, Weill wrote to his friend Frank Cahill in London: "This is just a reminder that we are thinking of you a lot during these dark days. I wanted to write to you for a long time, but things were moving in such a breathtaking tempo that it seemed silly to write letters, and even now there is so little to say for an onlooker, except that we are with you, that your fears are our fears and your hopes our hopes, and that we all have an enormous admiration for what you are doing over there and that we all know that you are fighting the last battle for civilization. This sounds like big words, but you know it is the simple truth" (photocopy in the Weill-Lenya Research Center, series 40).

12. Letter from Weill to Robert Sherwood, 12 December 1941 (Weill-Lenya Archive, Yale Music Library, series IV.A., box 47, folder 17).

13. *I'm an American!,* script no. 43, pp. 5–6.

14. Letter from Weill to Ira Gershwin, 28 May 1941.

15. Letter from Weill to Ira Gershwin, 20 February 1941; photocopy in Weill-Lenya Research Center, series 40; original in the Library of Congress, Music Division.

16. I discovered these lists while packing Weill's library in 1982; the sheets had lain between the same pages for so long that they had imprinted a three-by-five discoloration on each pair of pages.

17. Letter no. 221 from Weill to Lenya, 28 January 1942, *Speak Low,* p. 281. The "MacLeish song" was "The Song of the Free," with text by Archibald MacLeish (1892–1982), then Librarian of Congress. Whitmanesque in its tone and imagery,

though amateurish all the same, "The Song of the Free" enjoyed widespread performances denied to Weill's settings of Whitman during his lifetime.

18. Weill to Albert and Emma Weill, 5 February 1942; Weill-Lenya Research Center, series 45.

19. Letter from Weill to Lenya, 5 February 1942. On 11 June 1942, Weill wrote to Mrs. Robeson: "I have tried many times, through Mr. Rockmore, to get hold of Paul because I wanted to show him those three Walt Whitman songs and also the 'Song of the Free' which I wrote with Archibald MacLeish, but he never seemed to have time for me and I am afraid he is not interested. The songs are printed now and will be sent out by the publisher. I will send him copies" (carbon copy in Weill-Lenya Research Center, series 40).

20. Letter from Lenya to Weill, 6 March 1942. On 12 March 1942, Brecht sent Weill a copy of a new poem "Und was bekam des Soldatenweib." Weill thanked Brecht for the "marvelous song" and said that he would set it and offer it to the War Department for broadcasting behind enemy lines. It makes an interesting "control" for comparison with the *Whitman Songs* dating from the same period.

21. Weill wrote: "When Helen Hayes asked me to write the music for her recordings of national songs, I decided to use the form of the 'spoken song.' I took the words of 'The Star-Spangled Banner,' 'America,' and the 'Battle Hymn of the Republic' as if they were fresh material, and set them to music, emphasizing the meaning of the words and their emotions. For instance, in 'The Star-Spangled Banner' I based my musical setting on the dramatic situation that gave birth to the poem: a man looking out into the dim light of the early dawn and discovering that 'our flag was still there.' Of course, I used as much as possible of the original tunes of the songs, but I had to make them a part of my own form which had to be different from the original songs because the reading of a poem does not allow any holds, any 'long notes' or pauses. So I discovered, for instance, that a natural, simple reading of the words of 'The Star-Spangled Banner' called for a $\frac{4}{4}$ rhythm instead of the $\frac{3}{4}$ rhythm of the song, and I had to change the rhythm of the original tune accordingly" ("Notes about the musical settings for Helen Hayes' recordings," unpublished typescript; Weill/Lenya Archive, Yale Music Library, series VIII, box 68, folder 11).

22. Weill reported to Lenya on Archibald MacLeish's reaction to both "The Song of the Free" and the "Four Patriotic Recitations": "My visit in Washington was extremely successful. When I had played the song MacLeish sprang up and said: That's what we've been waiting for all the time. He was in ecstasy, and so was his wife. He is going to do everything to get a big start for the song, probably he will write himself one of the 'This Is War' programs around the song. I also played the Helen Hayes records. He thought they are absolutely unique, and they should be spread all over the country, in schools, factories, and private homes. . . . About the music he said it was miraculous what I had done. Well, all this is very important and very promising. He is Roosevelt's closest friend, and a wonderful man." "The Song of the Free" was included in a revue that opened at the Roxy Theater in New York on 4 June 1942, and Weill reported that "Our song is a very big success at the Roxy. I went to see it yester-

day and I must say it has a very stirring effect on the audience, although the singer is far from first-rate and the production is typical Roxy." In the same letter of 9 June, Weill wrote: "The publisher tells me that the first reaction from singers and conductors is quite favorable. But we have to overcome a certain resistance to patriotic songs on the part of radio sponsors and the recording firms." But on 14 June 1942, when twenty-six nations signed the charter of the United Nations, the song was declared "The United Nations Anthem," and the holograph score inscribed to Gertrude Lawrence "as a token of my undying affection" carries that annotation. Walter Mehring translated the text into German, and in this version it was featured on the first broadcast of the radio series, "We Fight Back," the German-American Loyalty Hour, 27 September 1942.

23. See my "For Those We Love: Hindemith, Whitman, and 'An American Requiem'," *Journal of the American Musicological Society* 50 (1997), 133–74.

24. "Three Poems by Whitman Are Set by Kurt Weill," *Musical America,* 10 February 1943, p. 207. The precise date of publication is unknown; the publication was registered for copyright on 7 August 1942. In June 1942 Weill sent Paul Robeson a copy of the printed score, inscribed "For Paul Robeson, with all good wishes, Kurt Weill" (Weill-Lenya Research Center, series 13, folder 42).

25. Letter from Lenya to Weill, 3 April 1942 (*Speak Low,* letter no. 257, p. 316).

26. Letter from Weill to Ira Gershwin, 2 May 1942; photocopy in Weill-Lenya Research Center, series 40.

27. Maurice Abravanel conducted the first known performance of the orchestrated version of the songs with the Utah Symphony and baritone Arthur Kent, in a concert on 19 March 1955, in celebration of the 300th anniversary of Jewish settlement in the United States. Weill completed only the first seven pages of the full score of the "Dirge for Two Veterans"; the final eleven pages of the manuscript are in the hands of his assistant Irving Schlein.

28. Letter from Weill to Max and Mab Anderson, 22 June 1947 (photocopy in Weill-Lenya Research Center, series 40).

29. In a letter to Anderson of 10 July 1947, Weill reported: "I have written some more Whitman songs lately. They will be recorded by Concert Hall Records. Now I am working on the symphonic suite from *Street Scene.* I have turned down three shows in the last two weeks" (photocopy in Weill-Lenya Research Center) "Come Up from the Fields, Father" had immediately followed "Beat! Beat! Drums!" as its antidote in the first edition of Whitman's *Drum-Taps,* but in Weill's volume the poems are widely separated.

30. William Horne's annotated score is held by the library of the Jerusalem Rubin Academy of Music and Dance; the Weill-Lenya Research Center holds a photocopy.

31. The song seems to have been unperformed until 1956, when Carlos Surinach orchestrated it, utilizing the same instrumentation as the first three songs. My newly ordered and annotated reprint of *Four Walt Whitman Songs* for voice and piano, EA 584, was published by European American Music Corp. in 1996. The orchestral version is available only on rental.

32. Curiously, in King Vidor's famous film version of 1931, with music by Alfred Newman, the poem is replaced with something far less "elevated" and "pastoral."

33. Elmer Rice, *Minority Report: An Autobiography* (New York: Simon and Schuster, 1963), p. 237.

34. George B. Hutchinson, "Langston Hughes and the 'Other' Whitman," in *The Continuing Presence of Walt Whitman,* ed. Robert K. Martin (Iowa City: University of Iowa Press, 1992), p. 22.

35. The two collections were published by Young World Books and International Publishers. Both Doubleday and Oxford University Press rejected the anthology of African-American poetry. Arnold Rampersad, *The Life of Langston Hughes,* vol. 2, 1941–67 (New York: Oxford University Press, 1988), pp. 109*ff.*

36. Kurt Weill, "Score for a Play," *New York Times,* 5 January 1947. For a detailed discussion of Weill's treatment of the "Lilacs" fragment in *Street Scene,* see my "Kurt Weill, Modernism, and Popular Culture: *Oeffentlichkeit als Stil,*" *Modernism/Modernity* 2 (1995), 27–69.

37. Even among Weill scholars the *Whitman Songs* prompt dissent. David Drew, mistaken in his assertion that these were intended as propaganda songs for the *Fight for Freedom* organization, asserts that Weill's settings "are clearly not intended as 'art songs' in the European sense" (*Kurt Weill: A Handbook* [Berkeley and Los Angeles: University of California Press, 1987], p. 321). On the other hand, Jürgen Thym suggests that they "are not what in German would be called 'songs' but what in English would be called 'Lieder'" ("The Enigma of Kurt Weill's Whitman Songs," in *A Stranger Here Myself: Kurt Weill Studien,* ed. Kim H. Kowalke and Horst Edler [Hildesheim: Georg Olms, 1993], p. 291). For yet a third opinion, see Werner Grünzweig, "Propaganda der Trauer: Kurt Weills Whitman-Songs," in *A Stranger Here Myself,* pp. 297–313.

38. The poem was first published in the *Boston Daily Evening Transcript* on 24 September 1961. This version is reprinted in William White, "Beat! Beat! Drums!: The First Version," *Walt Whitman Review* 21 (1975), 43–44.

39. Undated letter (May 1933) from Weill to Erika Neher; Weill-Lenya Research Center, series 30.

40. Although Weill frequently used tonality as an associative or symbolic device and usually grounded cyclic structures in their opening key, here there is no evidence of such intent. Weill sanctioned transposition of two of the songs for Horne and reordered the published settings for the recording. The new ordering, however, does make connections between adjacent songs seem stronger than they were intended to be; for example, at the end of "Beat! Beat! Drums!," the conflict between the bass line D and the A-minor tonality remains unresolved, but is immediately mediated by the first note, F, of "O Captain! My Captain!," which, in turn, concludes with an unambiguous F-major chord at the midpoint of the set that acts as pivot to the D-minor tonality of "Come Up from the Fields, Father." And finally, the double dirge is mirrored by what Robert Bailey calls a "double-tonality," in this case, G major and E minor; the composite four-note "double-tonic complex" is articulated at major struc-

tural downbeats and is the concluding sonority. This, too, remained a constant component of Weill's vocabulary throughout his career.

41. Letter from Weill to "Mr. Sablosky," 24 July 1948. Copy of draft in Weill/Lenya Archive, Yale University Music Library, series IV.A., box 47, folder 14.

42. The first section comprises only two lines; the second begins with "Lo, 'tis autumn" and encompasses eight lines (subdivided 6 + 2); the eleven-line third stanza opens with "Down in the fields all prospers well" and subdivides 3 + 2 + 6, with the final phrases, broken sentences that the mother reads from the letter, printed in italics; the fourth, beginning with "Ah, now, the single figure to me," includes seven lines (4 + 3); the nine-line fifth section, commencing with "Alas, poor boy, he will never be better," is presented as a single unit.

43. A. H., "Gespräch mit Kurt Weill," *Aufbau,* 16 January 1942. The words "my country" were printed in English; the remainder is my translation.

44. Theodor W. Adorno, "Kurt Weill," *Frankfurter Rundschau,* 15 April 1950. For a résumé of responses to Weill in America by his fellow émigrés, see my "Formerly German: Kurt Weill in America," in *A Stranger Here Myself: Kurt Weill Studien,* pp. 35–57; and "Kurt Weill, Modernism, and Popular Culture," pp. 27–34.

45. Harold Clurman, *All People Are Famous* (New York: Harcourt Brace Jovanovich, 1974), pp. 128–29.

46. "Pensacola Wham," *New Yorker,* 10 June 1944, p. 16.

47. Tape recording of the intermission feature for a Texaco broadcast of the Metropolitan Opera's production of *Manon Lescaut,* 10 December 1949 (Weill-Lenya Research Center, series 114/24; a transcription is filed in series 31, box 3).

48. Langston Hughes, "My Collaborator: Kurt Weill," typescript dated 10/27/55 and annotated "For Germany" (James Weldon Johnson Collection, Beinecke Library, Yale University: MSS Hughes, folder 729). It was translated and published in German in the program book for European premiere of *Street Scene* in Düsseldorf. There it stood next to Adorno's retrospective essay about Weill, "Nach einem Vierteljahrhundert," a refunctioning of his obituary of Weill in which he dismissed the musical as "merchandised nuisance."

CHAPTER 7

# Three American Requiems
Contemplating "When Lilacs Last in the
Dooryard Bloom'd"

*Kathy Rugoff*

In 1981 the 100th anniversary of Whitman's completion of what would be the
definitive edition of the *Leaves of Grass,* poetry and essays by eighty writers
addressing his work appeared in the collection *Walt Whitman: The Measure
of His Song.* Writers with varying perspectives on poetics including Theodore
Roethke, Derek Walcott, Diane Wakowski, Langston Hughes, Robert Bly,
and June Jordan contributed.[1] In addition, Whitman's poetry had a considerable role in the course of American, British, and European musical composition; it has been set to music more than the work of any other American poet,
prompting over one thousand compositions. In 1997, over a century after the
poet's death, baritone Thomas Hampson and pianist Craig Rutenberg released the compact disc *To the Soul* with settings of Whitman's poetry by
composers such as Charles Ives, Ralph Vaughan Williams, Ned Rorem, and
Paul Hindemith.[2]

What is it about Whitman's work that elicits so great a response among
so many composers and writers, many of whom are major voices in the world
of twentieth-century arts? While numerous contemporary literary critics are
preoccupied with issues related to modernism and postmodernism, Whitman's spectral presence has relatively little to do with this critical perspective. Instead, it reveals something about twentieth-century American and
European culture that harks back to a nineteenth-century concept of the artist for which Whitman, then as now, was a prominent spokesman. This self-
concept is associated with the desire for political, social, and sexual freedom
among many late nineteenth-century poets, painters, and musicians.

## Whitman and Music

Both Whitman's poetry and his prose regularly suggest that the construct
of music was central to his view of himself as an artist, to his perspective on

poetics, and to his perception of the world. Many twentieth-century poets and composers have responded to this and shared some of his cultural assumptions about the artist. Whitman's attention to sound in poetry in alliteration, assonance, and parallelism, together with repeated allusions to the music in nature, has drawn the attention of a wide variety of composers. Finally, for practical reasons, Whitman's poetry lends itself to music. His predilection for the long end-stopped line, unlike regular accentual-syllabic verse or free verse with enjambment, has musical parallels. Compositions in Western music are often characterized by the limitation of a regular pulse dictating a measure conjoined with the freedom of different phrase rhythms from measure to measure. Whitman's flexible, varied, but end-stopped line is similarly paradoxical.

The poet's statements about music show that it had important social, political, and spiritual associations for him. In his 1845 essay "Art-Singing and Heart-Singing," he praised and advocated a "heart-singing" consisting of "simple music sung by family trios and quartettes."[3] In this essay and elsewhere, Whitman celebrated popular music and exhorted Americans to pursue a national idiom; he maintained that "the subtlest spirit of a nation is expressed through its music—and the music acts reciprocally upon the nation's very soul."[4]

But Whitman also was drawn to European opera. He heard the soprano Marietta Alboni perform in the 1850s, and years later he said, "I wonder if the lady will ever know that her singing, her method, gave the foundation, the start, thirty years ago, to all my poetic literary effort since."[5] In "Out of the Cradle Endlessly Rocking" (1881, original 1859), Whitman reveals the song of the bird to be at the heart of his self-concept as a poet; his awareness of the unity of life and death is associated with the song of the bird mourning the loss of his mate, which mingles with the implicit music of the ocean waves in the image of "an old crone rocking the cradle." The nexus of life, death, music, and maternity runs like a Leitmotiv throughout Whitman's work.[6]

These themes, along with the song of the bird, are also key elements in "When Lilacs Last in the Dooryard Bloom'd," the elegy Whitman wrote for Abraham Lincoln and the soldiers who died in the Civil War, first published in *Sequel to Drum-Taps* in 1865 and appearing later, with some revision, in *Leaves of Grass*.[7] The 206-line poem, in strophes of varying length, has a broad scope and incorporates a strongly characterized speaker, a complex narrative action, and an array of highly lyrical images. The speaker expresses his sorrow over the death of "him I love" and reveals his growing consciousness of his own sense of the meaning of death and the consolation he paradoxically finds in death itself. The narrative action depicts the journey of Lincoln's coffin without mentioning the president by name and portrays visions of "the slain soldiers of war" without mentioning either the Civil War or its causes. The identifications are assumed to be superfluous, even tactless; no American could fail to understand what war was meant. Finally, in the "carol of the bird," the speaker recounts the song in which death is invoked, personified, and celebrated. The treatment of death abandons the world of human affairs; the bird invokes death as a tranquilizing power: "Approach strong deliveress" (147), "Come lovely and soothing death, / Undulate round the world, serenely arriving . . ." (135–36). By employing the persona of a bird, Whitman intimates that his response to death is not tempered by reason and the language of logic, but by another way of perceiving the world. The recurrent images of nature—of the lilacs, the star, and the bird—and their variation throughout the elegy reveal the poet's mindfulness of the objects of the world and their play on his senses and emotions.

The repetition and variation of these images have received a great deal of critical attention. Robert Faner (1951), Robert Carlile (1971), Justin Kaplan (1980), and Manuel Villar Raso (1994), following Whitman's friend John Burroughs (1866), have pointed out that "When Lilacs Last in the Dooryard Bloom'd" is structurally analogous to music, with passages comparable to arias and oratorio numbers. Calvin Brown initiated the series of twentieth-century comparisons between "When Lilacs Last in the Dooryard Bloom'd" and music in 1948 in his book *Music and Literature: A Comparison of the Arts,* devoting a chapter to the poem. He considers at length "the three principal symbols of lilac, star, and bird." According to Brown, the poem is not "written with any specific musical analogy . . . but nevertheless conforming to certain general structural principles which are more musical than literary."[8] Faner and Raso associate the treatment of poetic motives with specific musical structures. Faner claims that "When Lilacs Last in the Dooryard Bloom'd" parallels sonata form, with an exposition, development, and recapitulation.[9] Raso points out that the poem is simultaneously an elegy, "a work on the theme of the poetic process," and "a musical piece." Like Faner, he maintains that the poem appears "to follow the principle of the sonata form."[10] These observations, however, are rendered somewhat tenuous by the critics' use of metaphors to describe the figurative language of Whitman's poem. A more significant sign of the phenomenological kinship between Whitman's poetry and music is the sheer number of settings of his work.

Literary critics discussing "When Lilacs Last in the Dooryard Bloom'd" in relation to music tend to stress the repetition and variation of images. Musicologists, who address the poem via a particular musical setting, point out further connections established by the composition's melodies, harmonies, and rhythms. They also may observe that parts of the text are highlighted and allied by consistencies in instrumentation, and textual passages are connected each time they are sung by the same voice or voices. Thus, the reading of the literary text by musicologists is informed by images and phrases stressed by a composer. Musical settings are, on one level, a reader's response to a poem and afford the attentive listener not only the pleasure of the musical text but also an interpretation of the written text. The interpretation lingers long after the musical performance is over.

It is important to keep in mind that musical color, texture, and rhythm concretely affect a listener's emotions. The settings of Whitman's "When Lilacs Last in the Dooryard Bloom'd" by George Crumb (b. West Virginia 1929), Roger Sessions (b. New York 1896, d. 1985), and Paul Hindemith (b. 1895 Hanau near Frankfurt, Germany, d. 1963) reveal that the poem's appeal to these composers was not only intellectual but also, more important, emotional. As Wallace Stevens succinctly put it in "Peter Quince at the Clavier," "Music is feeling, then, not sound."[11] The importance of feeling is intimated by Whitman himself in "Out of the Cradle Endlessly Rocking" and in "When Lilacs Last in the Dooryard Bloom'd": in both, the purely emotive song of the bird, which the poet "translates," has a major role. The three settings of "When Lilacs Last in the Dooryard Bloom'd" emphasize this aspect of the text, so that the notion of language as sound and feeling as opposed to language as semantics and intellect comes to the fore.

The compositions embody three distinct approaches to setting a text. They illustrate each composer's unique style of attentiveness to Whitman's words; they represent three different interpretations of the poem; and, to use Ned Rorem's Quaker phrase about his own vocal music, they reflect the varying ways in which Whitman's work "spoke to the condition" of each composer.[12] Whitman's perspective on social, political, and spiritual matters as well as his consciousness of himself as a poet deeply engaged Crumb, Sessions, and Hindemith as they contemplated "When Lilacs Last in the Dooryard Bloom'd."

Each composer enters into his own dialogue with the poem. Considering different settings of the same passages helps illuminate variations in individual response and musical strategy. But even the titles are clues. Crumb makes no reference to the text in his title, *Apparition, Elegiac Songs and Vocalises for Soprano and Amplified Piano.*[13] He takes great liberties with the text, setting only a small portion of it in a work that lasts about twenty minutes. In contrast, both Sessions and Hindemith wrote a large-scale work for vocal soloists, chorus, and orchestra and set almost every word of Whitman's long poem. Sessions's work is simply called *When Lilacs Last in the Dooryard Bloom'd* and subtitled "Cantata for Soprano, Contralto, Baritone, Mixed Chorus and Orchestra."[14] Its sections are identified only by their tempos. Hindemith leans more toward the invocation of specific musical conventions; he uses Whitman's title and adds to it, *A Requiem "For Those We Love."*[15] Identification as a Requiem places the piece in the context of a long musical tradition. In the same vein, Hindemith identifies the piece's sections as instances of conventional musical subgenres such as prelude and march.

## George Crumb: Overtures and Echoes

Crumb's *Apparition* (CD tracks 9–17) is the most recent setting. Because it has received the least critical attention, the most space will be devoted to it here. Composed in 1979, it was premiered early in 1981 by Jan DeGaetani and Gilbert Kalish; DeGaetani had asked Crumb to write a piece for her.[16] Previously many of the texts he had set were from the highly imagistic, dreamlike poetry of Federico García Lorca, one of the many artists murdered in fascist Spain. Crumb, who is drawn to both American and world music, gravitates toward poetry that contemplates the marriage of life and death and their cosmic significance.

*Apparition,* through its unusual musical textures and rhythms, stresses Whitman's archetypal imagery. The piano is amplified, enhancing the duration of its overtones. In various passages the pianist strums specified strings, thereby creating a dronelike effect; this is stressed by the composer's instructions in the score that the piano is to be "welling, pulsing; like a sound of nature." In the first and last parts of the piece, the soprano is accompanied by glissandos on the piano, but, as Crumb writes, "these sections are *not* [vocally] synchronized with the piano."[17] Such a holistic approach renders musical time more cosmic than linear. In addition, by including various lengthy rests, Crumb liberates the piece from any rigid sense of meter. Another strategy is that in a few places the time signature changes from measure to measure, thus creating a large metric sequence and liberating rhythm from obedience to measurement; in addition, Crumb abandons linearity by starting and ending the piece with roughly the same textual and musical passage. Once again, time is more cosmic than linear. Some of the individual sections are also cyclical, such as the third one, "Dark mother, always gliding near with soft feet," which begins and ends on practically the same phrase both from the poem and in the music. Finally, similarities in rhythm, melody, and tone color echo from section to section; notable here are the occurrence of quadruplet figures and the same tone clusters. And although it may be either sustained or highly percussive, a massive tone cluster with the same ground note constitutes the beginning of three sections.

In *Apparition,* Crumb sets only twenty lines of the poem, namely parts of five strophes, with major changes in sequence. In addition, he alters the order of lines and repeats selected phrases. Although he is literally the least faithful to the text of the three composers under scrutiny, his setting is ironically the most faithful in two important respects: first, to Whitman's sonoric strategy in the extensive use of repetition in rhyme, half rhyme, parallelism, and motivic imagery; and second, to the poet's approach to the theme of death.

*Apparition* consists of six sections setting verse by Whitman and three in which the vocalist articulates sounds and syllables evocative of birds and other sounds in nature. The imitative passages are entirely free of words;

Crumb identifies them as vocalises. In the passages that do set Whitman's words, Crumb also includes pure syllabic sounds imitating the sound of the poem's bird. He thus takes text painting to its logical extreme and indeed selects most of the text he sets from the song of the bird.

Section 1 is based on the sixth strophe of the bird's death carol:

> *The night in silence under many a star,*
> *The ocean shore and the husky whispering wave whose voice I know,*
> *And the soul turning to thee O vast and well-veil'd death,*
> *And the body gratefully nestling close to thee.* (155–58)[18]

This is followed by "Vocalise 1: Sounds of a Summer Evening." Section 2 sets lines one and three of the first strophe of the poem, "When lilacs last in the dooryard bloom'd," and "I mourn'd, and yet shall mourn with ever returning spring" (1 and 3). Section 3 is based on the third strophe of the bird's song:

> *Dark mother always gliding near with soft feet,*
> *Have none chanted for thee a chant of fullest welcome?*
> *Then I chant it for thee, I glorify thee above all,*
> *I bring thee a song that when thou must indeed come, come unfalteringly.*
>    (143–46)

This is followed by "Vocalise 2: Invocation to the Dark Angel." Section 4 is a setting of the fourth strophe of the song of the bird:

> *Approach strong deliveress,*
> *When it is so, when thou hast taken them I joyously sing the dead,*
> *Lost in the loving floating ocean of thee,*
> *Laved in the flood of thy bliss O death.* (147–50)

The final vocalise, "3: Death Carol ('Song of the Nightbird')" follows. Section 5 is based on the first strophe of the bird's song:

> *Come lovely and soothing death,*
> *Undulate round the world, serenely*
>    *arriving, arriving,*
> *In the day, in the night, to all, to each,*
> *Sooner or later delicate death.* (135–38)

*Apparition* concludes cyclically with a near repetition of the first part.

*Apparition* is transparent and atmospheric as it contemplates death through the repetition and elaboration of musical figures. Joan Heller, a soprano who has often performed the piece, is struck by the ethereal atmosphere of a live performance and by its dramatic effect on audiences that become practically spellbound as they listen.[19] Crumb's compositional strategy parallels Whitman's in "When Lilacs Last in the Dooryard Bloom'd," a poem in which the speaker himself is almost mesmerized by his rhythmically recurrent consciousness of objects in the natural world, and particularly of the chant of a bird. The repetition and elaboration of the image-motives of the lilacs, star, and bird are emphasized on an aural level through the poem's alliteration, rhyme, half-rhyme, and repetition of words and phrases. In effect, the poet incorporates sound and semantic cells on both the micro and macro levels.

This strategy also is at the heart of Crumb's *Apparition*. Each section of the piece is composed of discrete rhythmic, melodic, and harmonic cells that are elaborated on in various ways. In addition, various rhythmic, melodic, and harmonic figures appear in more than one section; most obvious is the close repetition of the first section to constitute the last. Kristina F. Szutor, in a discussion of the "principal motives" of the piece, suggests that Crumb's own description of his "mosaic technique" very much applies to the composition of *Apparition*. "Basically," says Crumb, "this method of construction consists of the elaboration and expansion of minute pitch and rhythmic elements. From these I tend to build larger shapes as opposed to beginning with and working with larger units."[20]

In the first section, with the soprano singing over a piano glissando, musical phrases correspond to lines of poetry. Crumb elaborates on the initial melodic phrase for each line by repeating Whitman's initial phrase; this is accompanied by a musical phrase variation. All the musical phrases consist merely of two or three tones. At the end of each line are groups of melismas on the vowel sound "ah." This is anticipated by a similar, shorter embellishment that separates the repetition of the first phrase from the rest of the line.

Septuplets predominate in both the voice and piano lines of the first vocalise, "Sounds of a Summer Evening"; the voice here intones pure syllables, including "Tikiuwi," "a" and "u—u," for the last of which Crumb calls for a "turtle-dove effect" while "executing a delicate Monteverdi trill."[21] (Also known as a *trillo caprino*—goat's trill—this is a vocal ornament in which a single note is sustained in staccato fashion as it accelerates, slows, and resolves.) These sounds also resonate in the two other vocalises. In "Vocalise 3: Death Carol," a Monteverdi trill is called for and an "a" sound initiates the section. This vowel is the voice's only sound in "Vocalise 2: Invocation to the Dark Angel." The vowel prefigures and stresses the opening of the fourth section, "Approach strong Deliveress," which begins with "Ap-proach."

Like the first section, the third, "Dark mother" includes many three-tone melodic sequences. These occur both in the piano part and in the vocal line. The phrase "Dark mother" occurs only once in Whitman's text, but Crumb repeats it three times at the beginning of the section and four times subsequently, two paired. The combination of the repetition of Whitman's image and melodic similarity among the three-tone figures puts great emphasis on the words, transforming Whitman's strophe into a meditation on the image;

the semantics of the strophe serve to do something similar as the speaker first describes the mother, then addresses her. In effect, Whitman and Crumb follow different strategies to a similar end. The composer also tone-paints considerably in this section; for "gliding" he uses a series of slurred eighth notes, and for "with soft feet" he uses quarter and half-note triplets and writes "whisper (sustain!)" in the score.[22]

The fourth section, "Approach strong deliveress," like "Dark mother," incorporates three-note figures. Again, although the phrase is only found once in Whitman's strophe, Crumb includes it five times and ends the section with it. His tempo marking for "Dark mother," section 3, is "Adagio molto [♩ = 40]; hushed, reverential"; the section is marked *ppp* in many places. Section 4, "Approach strong deliveress!" is, on the other hand, marked "Alla marcia [♪ = 170]; with great energy, implacable," and ends *ffff*.[23] Running sixteenth-note triplets predominating in the piano part lend the section a sense of inexorable movement as opposed to the previous section in which whole and half notes predominate in the piano. By setting Whitman's portrayals of death as dark mother and deliveress in pointed musical contrast, Crumb emphasizes the transcendental notion of death as both an ending and a beginning—as a ruler and a liberator.

Section 5, "Come lovely and soothing death," harks back tonally and rhythmically to previous sections and incorporates several strongly pronounced contrasting figures that give it a considerable dramatic range in a mere five minutes. Figures built of semitones, whole tones, minor thirds, fifths, and parallel rising and descending fourths comprise the gestural variety, and these figures, linked to Whitman's words, thereby also constitute, to borrow Pound's phrase, "the intellectual and emotional vortex" of the section. "Come lovely and soothing" is set as a series of identical two-note phrases in descending sixteenth notes spanning a whole tone. "Death" is set to a pair of eighth notes, also descending a whole tone, followed by an identical setting for the syllable "mm." The invocation crystallizes into the utterance of both the key word "death" and its inarticulate counterpart. Soon after, these words and musical figures are repeated up a half tone. For "Undulate," Crumb once again text-paints by incorporating thirty-second notes, again using two pitches, here semitones. This is followed by the phoneme "mm," also enunciated on the same two pitches. "Round the world" and "mm" are then set with the same melodic and rhythmic figure taken down a minor third. Crumb places the same musical emphasis on the pure sound, "mm," as he does on the words, echoing the nonverbal dimension of Whitman's insight into death, just as he does in the three nonverbal vocalises.

"Serenely arriving, arriving" is set to three parallel three-tone figures involving a seventh and a minor third. The second "arriving" is accompanied by a D♭-major chord in the bass in stark contrast to the angular three-note figures and preceding alternating semitones. As a contrast to these passages, Crumb gives the piano a series of descending and ascending parallel perfect fourths marked "delicatiss.," thus once more intimating the dual nature of death.

Another contrast in this section occurs in the timbre of the piano. The section opens with a pedal-sustained cluster, with the instruction "strike strings gently with palms."[24] This ghostly atmospheric sound is followed by a knock on the soundboard. The piano plays *fff* in places, and in other places *ppppp*, as in the series of fourths. The section ends with the contrast of the percussive sound of piano beams struck followed by the ethereal sounds of the strings struck. This atmosphere is maintained in the penultimate soprano passage, a descending glissando to the words "Come lovely and soothing," which Crumb directs to be indistinct in pitch. Just as the composer breaks down the distinction between words and pure sound through the syllables of the bird elsewhere in the piece and the "mm" figures in this movement, he also breaks down the boundaries of pitch through this series of slurred indistinct tones. Section 5 concludes with "death" and "mm" on the same whole-tone descent in eighth notes.

Without a break there follows the glissando over the piano strings by which, as noted earlier, the last section suggests the return of the first. Crumb thereby intimates the cyclical nature of death and his own oceanic consciousness of it. To convey this holistic perspective requires a musical language that resists tonal linearity, closure, and chronological resolution. The dronelike effect of the piano and the timbre of the voice and repeated tonal figures give the music the required non-Western quality. The use of relatively small note clusters in extensive elaboration and ornamentation is reminiscent of Far Eastern and Middle Eastern music; here it sounds vatic.

Just as Crumb's description of his compositional technique, quoted above, is borne out by this piece, so, too, are his more general accounts of his musical predilections and aesthetic perspectives. Many of his perceptions are consistent with Whitman's. He points out that he is engaged by the idea of reintroducing "the ancient idea of music being a reflection of nature." He continues: "Although technical discussions are interesting to composers, I suspect the truly magical and spiritual powers of music arise from deeper levels of our psyche." Crumb also relates music to culture and observes that "today there are more people who see culture evolving spirally rather than linearly. Within the concentric circles of the spiral, the points of contrast and the points of departure in music can be more readily found."[25] The notion of concentric circles overlaps Crumb's technique of evolving cell clusters, and this perspective is reflected in his notation. For example, sections of the score of his composition *Makrokosmos I* are fashioned as spirals, and the staffs of *Apparition* form large arcs (see Examples 1 and 2).

Like Whitman, Crumb is very much aware of the connection between the mind and the body and does not underplay the significance of the body. He maintains that music relates to "our central nervous system," and that it is rhythm, "of all the most basic elements of music," that "most directly affects our central nervous system."[26] Oliver Messiaen is mentioned among several composers whose rhythmic approach Crumb admires; Messiaen, he notes, was much inspired by Hindu music. Crumb's predilection for Eastern music and philosophy has parallels in Whitman.

Although there is some controversy because of contradictory statements made by the poet about his familiarity with "ancient Hindu poems," Gay Wilson Allen points out that "many critical readers of the *Leaves,* from Thoreau to Malcolm Cowley . . . have thought of parallels in Indian literature." In his foreword to V. K. Chari's book, *Whitman in the Light of Vedantic Mysticism,* Allen agrees with this assessment and claims the following:

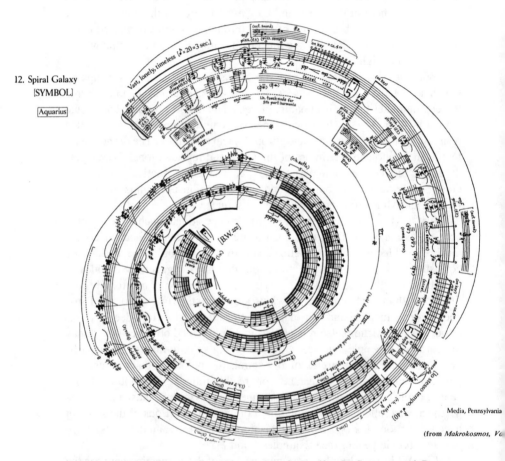

**Example 1.** *Makrokosmos,* from *George Crumb: Profile of a Composer,* ed. Don Gillespie, p. 48. Copyright 1974; reproduced by special permission of C. F. Peters Corporation.

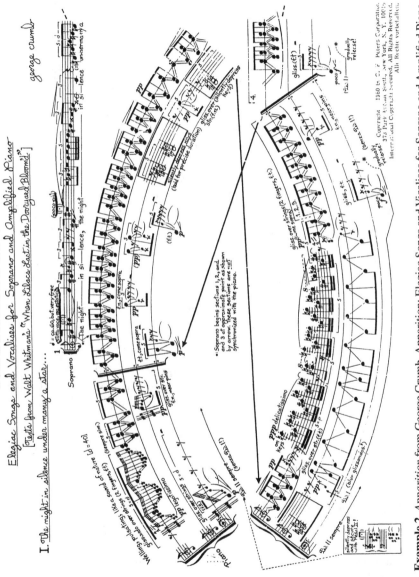

**Example 2.** *Apparition* from George Crumb, Apparition: Elegiac Songs and Vicalises for Soprano and Amplified Piano, p. 1. Copyright 1974; reproduced by special permission of C. F. Peters Corporation.

> The question of Whitman's reading of the "Hindu poems" still remains
> unanswered, but it is not really important whether he read them or not;
> whether he absorbed the ideas or attitudes directly, or indirectly, at second
> or third hand, through American, British, and German Transcendentalism;
> or—most directly of all—through his own psychology, which enabled him
> to intuit some of the oldest spiritual truths in human experience.

Chari himself goes on to suggest that Whitman's poetry, "under the influence
of Neo-Platonic and Hindu ideas, conceived a mystical doctrine of intuition
or unitary vision that is genuinely 'transcendental' in that it is above the dualisms inherent in rational thinking."[27] A similar perspective on dualism
emerges in an interview with Edward Strickland in which Crumb says that he
views the world "as immensely beautiful and immensely tragic at the same
time." Crumb indicates an interest in Eastern religion and in the use of the
drone in Eastern music. He maintains that there is a significant tie between
music and religion. In response to a question on whether or not he is a theist,
Crumb replies that he is, but "divorced from any particular creed." He continues that "there's some spiritual energy that's burning all over the world
that takes different forms. I can see it in music. I can say music is equally
religion."[28]

*Apparition* is an intensely intimate piece of chamber music in which the
composer reveals his consciousness of death in musical terms. Whitman,
through the personification of the bird and the sonoric quality of his verse,
also intimates that music is connected to his consciousness of death. Although Crumb, unlike Sessions and Hindemith, does not name Whitman's
elegy in his title, the title is still very much in keeping with it. "Apparition"
not only suggests death as something strange or ghostly but also refers to
the nature of consciousness in relationship to all that appears. Thus Crumb
seems to focus on the phenomenological dimension of death. Sessions and
Hindemith, on the other hand, who are in another respect truer to Whitman's
text in that they set practically every word of it, seem to respond to Whitman
more historically, focusing on his response to the deaths of Lincoln and of
countless young men.

### Roger Sessions: Past and Present

Sessions's work premiered in 1971. In 1964 he was commissioned to write a
choral/orchestral piece to commemorate the founding of the University of
California at Berkeley. He dedicated it "To the memory of Martin Luther
King Jr. and to Robert F. Kennedy," who were assassinated while he was
working on the piece, but he had thought of setting "When Lilacs Last in the
Dooryard Bloom'd" fifty years earlier.

The forty-five-minute composition is divided into three movements of unequal length. The third movement, the longest, includes the two voices in Whitman's poem, that of the speaker or poet and that of the bird. Whitman's persona, introducing the bird's death carol, says:

> *And the charm of the carol rapt me,*
> *As I held as if by their hands my comrades in the night,*
> *And the voice of my spirit tallied*
> > *the song of the bird.* (132–34)

The lines are sung by the baritone. The bird then says, in the poet's low-pitched slow vowels:

> *Come lovely and soothing death,*
> *Undulate round the world, serenely*
> > *arriving, arriving,*
> *In the day, in the night, to all, to each,*
> *Sooner or later delicate death.* (135–38)

Sessions emphasizes this passage in several ways. First of all it is sung by a contralto, who has sung very few lines up to this point. Her solo, which includes the seven strophes of the bird, is framed by the baritone solo and a tonally related soprano solo. Passages of the contralto solo are marked by large intervallic leaps to low pitches, making these passages very soft. Sessions's setting of "serenely arriving" pointedly contains such large intervals. For the phrase "O vast and well-veil'd Death," the contralto leaps a twelfth from E♭ above middle C to A♮ below. As Andrea Olmstead observes, this is followed by the lowest pitch in the solo, G♭ below middle C.[29] This climatically sets the word "thee" in the line "And the body gratefully nestling close to thee." The voice "nestles" within its own depths. Harold Powers maintains that "Sessions has obviously designed 'Come, lovely and soothing Death' as the crucial point of the cantata."[30]

Sessions addresses this passage and the entire Whitman text minutely in his technique of linking measure to measure. First, in regard to rhythm, one-syllable nouns and verbs are generally given longer note values than the endings or prefixes of words. Second, virtually every comma in Whitman is treated as a rest. Third, each subsection of Sessions's piece is full of time signature changes at a rate of practically one per measure so as to conform to the poem's rhythms. In other ways as well, Sessions echoes the Whitman text in fine detail. For example, textual references to the bird are often accompanied by flute, whereas references to the lilacs are signaled by oboe and English horn. In melodic progressions, there is a great deal of tone painting: for example, the word "rising" is expressed in rising pitches. Whitman's reference to "tolling bells" is realized by the percussion section of the orchestra. In addition, as Andrew Porter's analysis of Sessions's twelve-tone technique reveals, the inversions and retrogrades of the row are carefully related to the text.[31]

Sessions also attends to the words in his directions to the performers that the vocal music should be interpreted "in terms of the unforced inflections of the English language" and "freely in terms of natural English diction, respecting the subtleties of rhythm and stress which are inherent in the words themselves."[32] Finally, some of the passages for chorus have little contrapuntal echoing or division; they articulate textual passages in large, univocal, note-by-note units, so that the chorus sounds like a large crowd, the speaking voice of a nation. Sessions even employs this technique where the poet uses the first person pronoun, as in a passage following the bird's carol.

Both Whitman and Sessions address the social and political ramifications of Lincoln's death within the context of American democracy. This dimension of the poem is particularly important to the composer because it had two sad parallels during the time he was working on the piece, the aforementioned murders of Martin Luther King and Robert Kennedy. Sessions mentioned that Kennedy's "funeral train was passing through while I was writing the second part, and I was affected by it."[33] The health of a democracy for both its populace and its leaders was an ongoing concern to Sessions, who had lived in Italy and Germany before World War II. He had responded to the death of Franklin D. Roosevelt in the Adagio of his Second Symphony and to the assassination of John F. Kennedy in his Third Piano Sonata. Clearly, the composer admired American leaders who represented social and political liberalism.

For Sessions, as for Whitman, the arts are innately allied to democracy. This conviction emerges in Sessions's 1933 essay "Music and Nationalism," which supported conductor Wilhelm Furtwängler's protest against Joseph Goebbels's banning of Jewish musicians from German orchestras. Sessions claimed that the Nazis' propaganda and their interference in the enterprise of art were anathema. He argued that art "must be conscious of its responsibilities, competent, close to the people, and combative in spirit . . . [and] it must be rooted in the soil, and in the deepest human impulses that spring from man's contact with the soil and with other human beings."[34]

## Paul Hindemith: Memories of War

Hindemith shared Sessions's belief in democracy and its connection to the arts, and he had firsthand experience with a government's dictating what would and would not be performed. His work was banned in Nazi Germany, but in 1934 Furtwängler nonetheless conducted *Mathis der Maler* and published a strong defense of Hindemith. Shortly thereafter, the conductor was relieved of his duties and Goebbels launched a verbal attack against the composer at a rally. A few years later, Hindemith emigrated to Switzerland (he would eventually return) and then to the United States, where he became a citizen. In 1946 he composed *When Lilacs Last in the Dooryard Bloom'd: A*

*Requiem "For Those We Love"* in response to a commission from the choral director Robert Shaw to write a choral/orchestral work. Hindemith viewed it as an elegy for both Roosevelt and for those who had died in World War II. Like Whitman, he mourned the deaths of both a great leader and of legions of fighting men. At the same time, however, the poem resonated on another level for Hindemith; he had been drawn to Whitman's work decades earlier, as evidenced by his settings of Whitman in Three Hymns, op. 14 (1919), and by several other pieces, including two songs based on "Sing on, there in the swamp!" from "Where Lilacs Last in the Dooryard Bloom'd."

Hindemith's Requiem is not quite as sensitive to the natural inflections of the words as Sessions's, partly because English was his second language, but also because he took other liberties with the text. As Andrew Porter incisively maintains, Hindemith's "grave, impressive, dignified, formal piece" reflects "the subordination of the words to his musical designs."[35]

Whitman's poem is cast into four movements during the hour-long Requiem. Like Sessions, Hindemith maintains the structural integrity of the seven strophes that are uttered in the voice of the bird; they appear in the third movement in a subsection entitled "Death Carol." Unlike Sessions, Hindemith does not use a soloist but sets the carol for a large four-voice chorus. The passage is introduced by an F and C in the strings, an open fifth with a tonal focus on F, the tonal center. This passage and others in the "Death Carol" assume religious overtones by evoking organum, the texture employing primarily open fourths and fifths that is typical of much early church music. In addition, as Klaus George Roy notes, Hindemith employs another convention from earlier music, the passacaglia, a seventeenth-century form built on a figured-bass progression. A large portion of the carol is built on such a progression in the lower strings and brass; thus the choral parts are driven by this musical gesture rather than by the syllabic stress of the words in the text. Finally, quite in contrast to some of Sessions's homophonic choral passages, Hindemith's chorus is often polyphonic, with both musical and verbal phrases repeated and imitated from part to part. The musical texture thus overbears Whitman's text.

But the composer is still mindful of the organization of the poem in both the breadth of his musical design and his treatment of the motives of the lilacs, star, and bird. The piece begins with a long C♯ pedal in the timpani, low strings, brass, and winds, and C♯ (minor) is the tonal basis for the Requiem. As Roy points out, the initial theme is related to tonalities developed in later movements.[36] Like Sessions, Hindemith also employs motivic tone painting with, for example, flute passages accompanying Whitman's mention of the bird and a bugle playing offstage when a bugle is mentioned in the poem.

Whitman's poem clearly spoke to what Rorem terms "the condition" of these composers. Their actions and opinions show that both Hindemith and Sessions shared Whitman's enthusiasm for democracy. As already intimated,

Sessions wrote several essays in the 1930s and 1940s criticizing Fascism and celebrating the integrity of art that the Nazis banned. Furthermore, in his essay "Art, Freedom, and the Individual" (1957), a depiction of the artist's role in society that would not be at all alien to Whitman in its paradoxical combination of fierce individualism and social solidarity, Sessions maintains that the artist has "obligations to society," and that these are fulfilled by meeting the responsibility "to seek and to follow his own vision . . . and to follow it with no deviation, whatever the demand." Whitman's and Sessions's perspectives on the source of music are also synchronous. Like Whitman, Sessions claims in "The Composer and His Message" (1939) that music "reproduces for us the most intimate essence, the tempo and the energy, of our spiritual being."[37]

Hindemith was directly confronted by the tyranny of a Nazi Germany hostile to his music, his philosophy of music, and the musicians with whom he worked. Shortly after emigrating, he wrote a large-scale piece dedicated to Roosevelt, the American president who was instrumental in liberating Europe from the grip of Nazism, its horrific daily murder of thousands, and its monstrous assault on art and artists.

But perhaps it is Crumb and Whitman who have the closest kinship. Suzanne Mac Lean is insightful in her observation that "a transcendental view of the world pervades Crumb's music" and is right to emphasize the composer's claim, "I feel intuitively that music must have been the primeval cell from which language, science, and religion originated."[38] Thus, the twentieth-century composer expresses, both in discussions of his music, and more importantly, in the music itself, an aesthetic that is firmly rooted in the tradition of nineteenth-century American Transcendentalism.

Finally, the music of the three composers studied here suggests not only the perspectives they share with Whitman but also their profound respect for him. Their scores reveal that they read Whitman's "Lilacs" with great care and entered into a genuine dialogue with the nineteenth-century innovator through their own innovative settings of his words.

## Notes

1. *Walt Whitman: The Measure of His Song,* ed. Jim Perlman, Ed Folsom, and Dan Campion (Minneapolis: Holy Cow Press, 1981).

2. *To the Soul: Thomas Hampson Sings the Poetry of Walt Whitman,* Thomas Hampson, baritone and Craig Rutenberg, piano, EMI Classics compact disc 724355502827.

3. Justin Kaplan, *Walt Whitman, A Life* (New York: Simon, 1980), p. 175.

4. Walt Whitman, Brooklyn *Daily Eagle,* 8 September 1847, in Walt Whitman, *The Gathering of the Forces,* ed. Cleveland Rodgers and John Black, 2 vols. (New

York: G. P. Putnam's Sons, 1920), II, 345. Quoted in Robert D. Faner, *Walt Whitman and Opera* (Carbondale: Southern Illinois University Press, 1951), p. 39.

5. Kaplan, *Walt Whitman, A Life,* p. 178.

6. On this nexus, with specific reference to Alboni, see Lawrence Kramer, *After the Lovedeath: Sexual Violence and the Making of Culture* (Berkeley and Los Angeles: University of California Press, 1997), pp. 58–59.

7. The original fourteenth, fifteenth, and sixteenth strophes were combined into the fourteenth strophe; the original seventeenth and eighteenth strophes were combined into the fifteenth strophe; and the original nineteenth, twentieth, and twenty-first strophes were combined and shortened, comprising the sixteenth and final strophe of the 1881 version. Sessions and Hindemith used the 1865 version; both cut some passages. See Walt Whitman, *Drum Taps (1865) and Sequel to Drum Taps 1865–1866,* a facs. reproduction, ed. and intro. F. DeWolfe Miller (Gainesville: Scholars' Facsimiles and Reprints, 1969). In the discussion below, strophe and line numbers refer to the 1881 version; quotations from "When Lilacs Last in the Dooryard Bloom'd" are from Walt Whitman, *Leaves of Grass and Selected Prose,* ed. and intro. John A. Kouwenhoven (New York: Modern Library, 1950), pp. 259–66.

8. Calvin Brown, *Music and Literature: A Comparison of the Arts* (Athens: University of Georgia Press, 1948), pp. 185, 193.

9. Faner, *Walt Whitman and Opera,* pp. 154–58.

10. Manuel Villa Raso, "Musical Structures of Whitman's Poems," in *Utopia in the Present Tense: Walt Whitman and the Language of the New World,* ed. Marina Camboni (Rome: Editrice Il Calmano, 1994), pp. 196–97.

11. Wallace Stevens, *The Collected Poems of Wallace Stevens* (New York: Vintage, 1982), p. 90.

12. Ned Rorem, "Words Without Song," in *The Artistic Legacy of Walt Whitman: A Tribute to Gay Wilson Allen,* ed. Edward Haviland Miller (New York: New York University Press, 1970), p. 18.

13. References and discussion are based on George Crumb, *Apparition: Elegiac Songs and Vocalises for Soprano and Amplified Piano* (New York: Peters, 1980).

14. References and discussion are based on Roger Sessions, *When Lilacs Last in the Dooryard Bloom'd: Cantata for Soprano, Contralto, Baritone, Mixed Chorus and Orchestra,* vocal score arranged by the composer (Bryn Mawr: Merion Music, 1974).

15. References and discussion are based on Paul Hindemith, *When Lilacs Last in the Door-yard Bloom'd: A Requiem "For Those We Love,"* mezzo-soprano and baritone soli, chorus, and orchestra, piano score (London: Schott, 1974).

16. See *George Crumb: Songs, Drones and Refrains of Death, Apparition, A Little Suite for Christmas, A.D. 1979: Apparition,* Jan DeGaetani, mezzo-soprano and Gilbert Kalish, amplified piano, Bridge Records compact disk 9028.

17. Crumb, *Apparition,* p. 1.

18. In Crumb's score "nestling" is written as "nesting."

19. Personal interview with Joan Heller, soprano, Wilmington, N.C., 7 January 1998.

20. Kristina F. Szutor, *Musical Coherence and Poetic Meaning in George Crumb's* Apparition (D.M.A. diss., University of British Columbia, 1994), p. 14. Crumb's passage is also quoted in Robert V. Shuffett, *The Music, 1971–1975, of George Crumb: A Style Analysis* (D.M.A. diss., Peabody Institute, 1979), p. 499.

21. Crumb, *Apparition,* p. 3.

22. Ibid., p. 5.

23. Ibid., pp. 5, 7.

24. Ibid., p. 11.

25. George Crumb, "Music: Does It Have a Future?" in *George Crumb: Profile of a Composer,* ed. Don Gillespie, intro. Gilbert Chase (New York: Peters, 1986), pp. 19, 16.

26. Crumb, "Music: Does It Have a Future?" p. 18.

27. V. K. Chari, *Whitman in the Light of Vedantic Mysticism,* intro. Gay Wilson Allen (Lincoln: University of Nebraska Press, 1964), pp. vii, viii, 20.

28. Edward Strickland, *American Composers: Dialogues on Contemporary Music* (Bloomington, 1991), pp. 172–73, 168.

29. Andrea Olmstead, *Roger Sessions and His Music* (Ann Arbor: UMI Research, 1985), p. 160.

30. Howard S. Powers, "Current Chronicle," *Musical Quarterly* 58 (1972), 304.

31. Andrew Porter, "Musical Events: An American Requiem," *New Yorker,* 16 May 1977, pp. 134–35.

32. Sessions, *When Lilacs Last in the Dooryard Bloom'd,* p. iii.

33. Andrea Olmstead, *Conversations with Roger Sessions* (Boston: Northeastern University Press, 1987), p. 110.

34. Roger Sessions, *Roger Sessions on Music: Collected Essays,* ed. Edward T. Cone (Princeton: Princeton University Press, 1979), pp. 274–75.

35. Andrew Porter, "Sessions's Passionate and Profound Lilacs," *High Fidelity Magazine,* February 1978, p. 70, and idem, "Musical Events: An American Requiem," p. 139.

36. Klaus George Roy, "When Lilacs Last in the Dooryard Bloom'd, a Requiem for 'Those We Love'," *Cleveland Orchestra Program Notes,* 21 February 1963, pp. 583–84.

37. Sessions, *Roger Sessions on Music: Collected Essays,* pp. 118, 19. Also quoted in Tracy Pinchman, "Sessions's Vocal Music," *Kent Quarterly* 2 (1986), 18.

38. Crumb quoted in Suzanne Mac Lean, "George Crumb, American Composer and Visionary," in *George Crumb: Profile of a Composer,* p. 20. Originally in Oliver Daniel, "George Crumb," *Brochure of Broadcast Music,* 1975.

CHAPTER 8

# Like Falling Leaves
## The Erotics of Mourning in
## Four *Drum-Taps* Settings

*Lawrence Kramer*

Walt Whitman regarded *Drum-Taps* (1865), his cycle of Civil War poems, as the fulcrum of his life's work, even declaring it superior to the first three editions of *Leaves of Grass* (1855, 1856, and 1860). "Although I had made a start before," he wrote, "[it was] only from the occurrence of the Secession War, and what it show'd me as by flashes of lightning, with the emotional depths it sounded and arous'd . . . [that] the final reasons-for-being of an autochthonic and passionate song definitely came forth."[1] The book was successful with mainstream nineteenth-century reviewers as *Leaves of Grass* had not been, but twentieth-century literary critics, intent on celebrating what the nineteenth-century mainstream had deplored and deploring what it had celebrated, proved relatively indifferent. The cornerstones of the twentieth-century Whitman canon would be "Song of Myself," "Out of the Cradle Endlessly Rocking," and "When Lilacs Last in the Dooryard Bloom'd," the latter more often regarded as heir to a line of English elegies including Milton's "Lycidas" and Shelley's "Adonais" than as a text of the American Civil War. In the last years of the century, the "Calamus" poems also came to the fore because of their open homoeroticism—a topic pertinent to *Drum-Taps* as well—but this welcome development was shaded by a certain irony, since the kind of homoeroticism celebrated in these poems was to a large extent a part, though a forgotten part, of the nineteenth-century mainstream.[2]

Whitman's musical reception followed a different course. The poet's primary musical persona has not been the inspired roughneck who gallivants through "Song of Myself" with a "barbaric yawp" but the modernist mystic who chants credos of oceanic union with the nation and the cosmos in the postbellum editions of *Leaves of Grass*. This version of Whitman rationalizes and renders programmatic his raw pleasure in human diversity, in material and bodily existence, and in all the minute particulars of American experience—a pleasure rampant in the first three editions of the book but already subject to a certain discipline by the second. Whitman himself was well aware of the temporizing process, which he would ground in the revelation about his own purposes granted him by his war experience. The successive editions of *Leaves of Grass* (which include *Drum-Taps* after 1867) do not so much renege on the intuitions of the first one as buffer it, enveloping it in tissues of explanation, sublimation, and ideology. The resulting image of Whitman as sage, the substance of what David Reynolds calls the Whitman Myth, is the one inherited by most twentieth-century composers, who, in contrast to the literary critics of the age, sought more to perpetuate the myth than to circumvent it.[3]

This is the image promulgated in the century's first decade by Ralph Vaughan Williams's settings for voices and orchestra, the grave "Toward the Unknown Region" (1907) and the grandiose "A Sea Symphony" (1910). In its climactic passages, the symphony's finale explicitly gives Whitman's primary image of modern spiritual and material adventure, his dialogue with his own soul, a traditional mythographic form. Impassioned dialogues for solo baritone and soprano realize the trope of hierogamy, the mystic, divine, or cosmic marriage, in terms reminiscent of the duets in some of Bach's cantatas between Jesus and the soul. Frederick Delius's slightly earlier "Sea Drift" (1903), though drawing its text from "Out of the Cradle," realizes the same large prophetic stance in more sensuous, more frankly eroticized terms. The Whitman of these works is something like the formative spirit of the new century, paradoxically both forward-looking and steeped in archaic images of the soul's journey; as the London *Times* reviewer put it after the premiere of "A Sea Symphony," in language sounding oddly like D. H. Lawrence: "In both [poet and composer] there is the distaste for the old-fashioned forms, both are striving for the newer poetic life."[4] The same persona in its wartime guise, chastened but undaunted, is still discernible in Paul Hindemith's midcentury setting of the "Lilacs" Requiem (1946), as it is, to a lesser degree, in the ritualistic gravity that threads the poem itself.

The persona of *Drum-Taps,* a lover of union, a seeker of reconciliation, a mourner over a fragmented community symbolized traumatically by the fragmented bodies of its young men, has figured importantly in this tradition almost from its inception. Yet here, too, a certain irony shades the historical development. The majority of *Drum-Taps* settings have been expressions of antiwar sentiment; *Drum-Taps* itself is nothing of the sort. As John Adams observes in reference to his setting of a long excerpt from "The Wound-Dresser," Whitman's war poetry is

> remarkably honest in that it expresses not just the horror and degradation of war but also the thrill of battle and the almost manic exhilaration of one caught up in a righteous cause. Whitman hated war—this war of all wars—

but he was no pacifist. Like his idol, Lincoln, he never ceased to believe in the Union's cause and the dreadful necessity of victory.[5]

Yet there is more at stake even than this. For Whitman, the fratricidal character of the Civil War demanded a special, personal, intimate reckoning with its dead. As his poems delineate them, these war dead belong to a sacrificial process that is, paradoxically, both a bringer of absolute loss and yet regenerative. To borrow a suggestive turn of phrase from Robert Pogue Harrison, the force of regeneration gives the absoluteness of the loss its absolution:

> *Over the carnage rose prophetic a voice,*
> *Be not dishearten'd, affection shall solve the problems of freedom yet,*
> *Those who love each other shall become invincible,*
> *They shall yet make Columbia victorious. . . .*
>
> *One from Massachusetts shall be a Missourian's comrade,*
> *From Maine and from hot Carolina, and another an Oregonese, shall be*
> *    friends triune,*
> *More precious to each other than all the riches of the earth.*
> ("Over the Carnage," 1–4, 9–11)[6]

Grief for the fraternal dead becomes the medium of possibility for a renewal of fraternal love.

For the leading composers drawn to Whitman's Civil War writings, however, among them Vaughan Williams, Ned Rorem, and Adams, whose settings (together with one of my own) form the focal points of this essay, no absolution is possible. The mourner of the dead can do no more than bear them witness in the hope that such deaths as theirs may not be repeated in the future. This act of witness, however, depends on an intimacy between the living and the dead or dying that is, indeed, projected in Whitman's poems, derived in part from a culture of such intimacy endemic to the Civil War and in part from Whitman's own gift—plain enough in the lines just quoted from "Over the Carnage"—for intense, homoerotically inflected compassion. Whitman and the modernist composers who set him simply draw different conclusions from the premise of this intimacy. But even in Whitman the moment of intimacy tends toward a self-sufficiency in which the question of being "for" or "against" the war, any war, temporarily makes no sense. Although the moment of loving fraternal care does not "transcend" the carnage of war—what could?—it briefly transforms the space around the body for which the battle is over, the body wounded or dead, into a kind of transient haven.

In "Vigil Strange I Kept on the Field One Night," a soldier returns to the spot on the battlefield where his comrade has fallen. He sits by the body all night long, gazing intently at the dead man's face: "long, long I gazed, / Then

on the earth partially reclining sat by your side leaning my chin in my hands, /
Passing sweet hours, immortal and mystic hours with you dearest comrade"
(11–13). The survivor's love literally takes the form of witnessing, of testify-
ing by his vigil that his comrade has been; this alone makes it possible to bury
the dead, which the survivor does at dawn. The act of witness is (fictitiously)
repeated by the poem, which also is a form of testimony; and this, too, is in a
sense necessary, because it allows the strange pleasure, the "sweetness," of
the "mystic hours" to find intelligible form in the chanting rhythms of the
verse, through which the poem becomes a kind of secular liturgy for the vigil.
So powerful is the bond thus expressed that it easily encompasses strangers,
even enemies. The survivor and fallen soldier in "Strange Vigil" are father
and son, at least figuratively. In "The Wound-Dresser," based on Whitman's
experience as a nurse during the war, a mere glance is enough: "One turns to
me his appealing eyes—poor boy! I never knew you, / Yet I think I could not
refuse this moment to die for you, if that would save you" (37–38). There is
no saving the boy, but the appeal in his eyes is returned, and the double meaning of "appealing" strangely vindicated. Finally, in "Reconciliation," the
speaker extends the moment of fraternal care to the body of a Confederate
soldier, whose coffin he approaches with slow-motion tenderness: "I look
where he lies white-faced and still in the coffin—I draw near, / Bend down
and touch lightly with my lips the white face in the coffin" (5–6). Again the
gaze engages; again the reiterative rhythm implies both ritual and sweetness.

What all this means musically is a tendency that cuts across the boundaries of style, generation, intention, and influence: a tendency to convey the
epiphanic moment of fraternal intimacy by adding or singling out a unique
expressive thread amid the musical texture. This "thread" may be vocal or instrumental, drawn from within or added from without; its defining trait is its
singularity, a literal or figurative uniqueness that allows it to bear witness to
the unique pain or death it compassionates or mourns. My guess is that this
tendency implies a recognition, however tacit, of the culture of fraternal intimacy fostered by the Civil War, and that this recognition is in turn based on
the persistence of a trope for fallen soldiers with a lineage that goes back to
classical Greece. Before I turn to the music, both the culture and the trope require some comment.

America in the nineteenth century was freer than it would be in the twentieth in giving physical and affectionate expression to close bonds between
men. As David Reynolds has noted, however, before the Civil War these expressions were both tendered in private and privately recorded in diaries and
letters. The war made them public. In venues ranging from press dispatches
to popular poetry to political oratory, the wounds or deaths of soldiers assumed sacrificial, redemptive value in imaginary scenes of comradely intimacy.[7] But sometimes the scenes were real, acted out in the hospitals and on
the battlefields; the press simply helped conventionalize a widely improvised

social script. If the script seems "sentimental" by later standards ("youths . . . pure as the mothers who bore them, and beautiful as their sisters in their homes") that may be because the carnage it had to contend with was unprecedented. Reynolds suggests that the shift to public intimacy involved a displacement of family bonds: "It was normal for a soldier to assume the role of parent, sibling, or spouse for a dying comrade. Since actual family members were rarely present to witness a soldier's death, fellow soldiers or other kindly disposed people filled familial roles, even to the point of expressing deep affection" (428). Another possibility is that by enveloping the soldiers' suffering and death in tender care and "feminine" delicacy, it was possible to assimilate both the physical brutality and fratricidal trauma of the war to the nineteenth-century ideal of the good death—pious, sententious, moving, and exemplary (terms invoked here with no pejorative cast). For reasons like these, Whitman found that the war vindicated his own belief in the sanctity of same-sex love, though he was painfully aware of the cost.[8]

The trope of mortal intimacy involves the paradox that soldiers who die in battle die, so to speak, in two registers: they are one of many, a nameless multitude of bodies on the field, and they are one only, unique beings who have borne a name. Robert Pogue Harrison traces the history of this idea from *The Iliad* ("As is the generation of leaves, so is that of humanity" [6.146]; the one lost in the many) to the Vietnam Veterans Memorial Wall, where "it is the individual who shines in and through the generic multitude of names" (each of the many is one).[9] Whitman's realizations of this trope conjoin the one and the many in terms that Harrison traces to a passage (transmitted from Homer through Virgil) in Dante's *Inferno:* the dead wait to be ferried across the river Acheron "As, in the autumn, leaves detach themselves, / First one and then the other" (3.112–13). Harrison calls attention to Dante's individuation of the falling leaves (182), but this is an individuation of a special kind: each of the many leaves (souls) is one, but none is singular enough to bear a name. In *Drum-Taps* likewise, the fallen soldiers with whom Whitman bonds are all singled out of the many, but none bears a name: each one, in that sense, is any or every one.

"As Toilsome I Wander'd Virginia's Woods" gives this version of the trope in its full traditional form:

> As toilsome I wander'd Virginia's woods,
> To the music of the rustling leaves kick'd by my feet,
> I mark'd at the foot of a tree the grave of a soldier;
> Mortally wounded he and buried on the retreat, (easily all I could
>     understand,)
> The halt of a mid-day hour when up! no time to lose—yet this sign left,
> On a tablet scrawl'd and nail'd on the tree by the grave:
> Bold, cautious, true, and my loving comrade. (1–6)

The intimate bond is double here, performed by the survivor who made the inscription and repeated by his poet-successor who immediately forms an instinctive grasp of the whole situation. The poet comes on the grave amid the symbolic array of fallen leaves, to find among this many the one "leaf" nailed back to a tree, as if restored to its place of crucifixial honor. What he finds is a token of comradely intimacy that, he goes on to say, keeps coming back to him in later years as an involuntary memory. But what he does not find is the identity of the lost comrade; he finds, indeed, the positive form of that identity's loss.

This is the form of the trope that I think I hear in the settings by Vaughan Williams, Rorem, and Adams, and that I think I wrote—without conscious design—in my own settings. I turn to those settings now.

Ralph Vaughan Williams's cantata *Dona Nobis Pacem* was composed in 1936 as an explicit plea to the European powers to avert the war then looming. According to Ursula Vaughan Williams, the music was a response to the "dark picture" formed as Mussolini and especially Hitler declared their intentions, including the first signs of what would become the Holocaust: "The Nazis were dividing the world between Aryans and Jews in hysterical discrimination against some of their greatest citizens. . . . People in every walk of life were suddenly dispossessed."[10] The cantata embeds a miniature Whitman cycle on poems from *Drum-Taps* within a larger whole based on liturgical and prophetic texts. This cantata within a cantata consists of two large-scale movements, "Beat, Beat Drums" and "Dirge for Two Veterans," surrounding a gently elegiac and much briefer centerpiece, "Reconciliation." The first number emits a feverish war cry, a blindly enthusiastic *Carthago delenda est;* the third enacts a public ceremony recognizing the tragic folly of that cry. Both of them can be said to outdo their texts in extremity—and the texts are extreme enough. Only the central song bears some trace of the hope that peace, however unlikely, is possible.

The hope takes root in the mortal intimacy between the poem's speaker and his dead enemy:

> *Word over all, beautiful as the sky,*
> *Beautiful that war and all its deeds of carnage must in time be utterly lost,*
> *That the hands of the sisters Death and Night incessantly softly wash*
>      *again, and ever again, this soil'd world;*
> *For my enemy is dead, a man divine as myself is dead,*
> *I look where he lies white-faced and still in the coffin—I draw near,*
> *Bend down and lightly touch with my lips the white face in the coffin.*
>      ("Reconciliation," complete)

The text of "Reconciliation" turns on a version of the commemorative paradox of the one and the many. The speaker sees the other man's death as a violation of the divine principle incarnate in each of them and on that basis finds beautiful the oblivion that must eventually overtake them both. The deed of carnage can be cleansed only by being lost without a trace. Yet this embrace of oblivion immediately prompts a memorial act, and one that is perpetuated for future remembrance by the poem. Though transitory in itself, the look that bears witness to the loss of the other becomes fixed in the image of the white face with which the poem ends. The light touch of the speaker's transient kiss becomes permanent and marmoreal as the word—not just the word "Reconciliation" but the word in general—indeed becomes that which is over all. The purely contingent encounter between a living and a dead man thus becomes an ideal encounter between all the living and all the dead.

The music seems to recognize this paradox but to reverse its emphasis. For Vaughan Williams, the speaker's intimacy with the dead man isolates the pair of them in a singularity corresponding to the fragility of the hope that their encounter upholds. This singularity crystallizes in the setting of the poem's second half, which is embedded as a unique event within a cycle of quasi-strophic repetitions.

The cyclical process begins with an orchestral introduction distinguished by a lyrical violin solo; the isolated instrumental "voice" helps individualize the intimacy of mortal encounter and prefigures the solo human voice soon to enunciate it. The introduction ends with a melodic phrase that will form the setting for "this soil'd world," the words that close the poem's first half and become something like the motto of the setting. A solo baritone then enters with the first strophe, singing a cantabile line extending from "Word over all" to "this soil'd world." This strophe is immediately reprised (with variations) by the chorus, with the women's voices leading the men's. The full significance of this texture will not emerge until later, but its immediate effect is to enhance the sense of isolation in what follows. The solo baritone now returns to sing the text of the mortal encounter, the poem's second half. He does so in parlando style, and in the virtual absence of orchestral melody. The texture is unlike anything else in the setting, which it as much interrupts as completes; it quietly challenges the comforting lyricism that surrounds it.

When the lyricism returns, it is subtly eroded, haunted by the baritone's absence—he does not sing again—and in need of supplementation. The introduction is the first thing to come back, this time with the solo violin in a less "speaking" role—another departing voice. This is followed by a reprise of the first strophe in its choral version, now adorned with a melismatic halo of high-register women's voices. Given the text, the choral sonority may seem to realize something implicit in it earlier, a transference of the healing work of the hands of the sisters death and night into the female voices of the chorus. But the work breaks down before it can be completed. Just before the expected "this soil'd world," the chorus breaks off, to be supplemented by a solo soprano singing "dona nobis pacem" to a cadential phrase. The chorus follows with the deferred "this soil'd world," expanding on the melodic motto, but then breaks down again. The soprano returns twice more with "dona nobis pacem," the second time ending on a stark, unaccompanied dissonance. Reconciliation remains unachieved as snare drums and tympani intervene with a march figure that leads directly into the ensuing "Dirge."

A word remains to be said about the replacement of the baritone's voice by the soprano's, which is a multivalent gesture. It simultaneously suggests that some external, perhaps sacramental force is required to plead effectively for peace; doubly enhances the once-only solitude of the baritone and his terrible intimacy with a silenced enemy and comrade; subtly diminishes that intimacy by detracting from its intensity of same-sex feeling; and shifts the accent of "dona nobis pacem" from inner to outer peace by merging the liturgical phrase into the ancient trope of the woman who mourns a fallen warrior.

Ned Rorem's *War Scenes* (1971) sets five prose sketches selectively drawn from Whitman's Civil War diaries; the texts give a misleading impression of senseless slaughter unmitigated by the idea of sacrifice so important to Whitman and his contemporaries. Rorem's context, however, is not the Civil War but the war in Vietnam, another conflict of North and South in which the vital interests of America were supposed to be at stake—this time falsely, says the irony formed by conflating the two wars. The cycle expresses the feeling, widespread in the late 1960s and early 1970s, that Vietnam had travestied the idea of sacrifice; the young men sent to this war were butchered in a bad cause, and some had become butchers in their turn. The first song, "A Night Battle," begins with the horrified exclamation, "What scene is this?—is this indeed *humanity*—these butchers' shambles?" The fifth song ends with a vision of "the whole land, North and South," as "one vast hospital," leading to the admonishment: "Think how much, and of importance, will be, has already been, buried in the grave." There is no hint of idealization, let alone redemption, anywhere in the cycle. Yet there is one song, "Specimen Case," that does revert to Whitman's ethos of sacrifice and to its correlative, the sentimental-erotic trope of mortal intimacy. The song is too brief and comes too early—it's the second of the five—to counteract the dominant tone of grim and grisly reckoning. But for that very reason it testifies to the strength of the trope it bears, which is not so much rejected by the cycle as embedded in it in a solitary space apart. Though the sounds involved are very different, in "Specimen Case" Rorem draws close to Oliver Stone's Whitmanesque use of Samuel Barber's *Adagio for Strings* as the theme music for his Vietnam War movie *Platoon*. The movie shrouds its savage action in the sensuously melancholy music; the song shrouds its fallen soldier in an atmosphere of dignified tenderness. The three motives of mortal intimacy—the intimacy itself with its eroticized compassion, the act of bearing witness, and the evocation of singularity—are all present in concentrated form.

The text of "Specimen Case" seems chosen for those motives; except for the prose form, it could well be a lyric from *Drum-Taps:*

> Poor youth, so handsome, athletic, with profuse shining hair. One time as I sat looking at him while he lay asleep, he suddenly, without the least start, awaken'd, opened his eyes, gave me a long steady look, turning his face very slightly to gaze easier, one long, clear, silent look, a slight sigh, then turn'd back and went into his doze again. Little he knew, poor death-stricken boy, the heart of the stranger that hover'd near.[11]

Rorem mirrors the single action of the poem, the arrival and departure of the mutual look, with a long, slowly mounting crescendo that peaks just past the midpoint of the song and ebbs steadily away to the close, with a slight rising of voice at a late moment, as if the vocal persona were reluctant to let the moment go. The process is lucidly framed by cadential passages and, on that foundation, punctuated by two unique events that encapsulate the once-only moment of mortal intimacy between the wounded soldier and his nurse-comrade.

The more dramatic of these events is the *fortissimo* peak of the long crescendo, which initiates the setting of "one long, clear silent look." The moment is melodically as well as dynamically unique: "long" is set to the highest notes reached by the voice, which has been climbing slowly but steadily to this point from a low initial tessitura and will steadily descend thereafter in conjunction with the dynamics (with the same little "bump" near the close). The first high note is attacked via an octave leap, by far the widest vocal interval in the song. Thus singled out, the high note lingers, becomes long itself (the longest sung so far) before dissolving into a melisma, as if both to extend the moment of looking and to enact its dissolution, which inevitably comes too soon. The transparent literalness of the tone-painting adds to the tone of pathos, suggesting less the commemorative power than the futility of the symbolic gesture. The full phrase from "long" to "look," implacably descending by step against melismatic resistance, seconds this impression, musically acting out the loss of the look while verbally announcing its advent.

Less immediately striking, but in the end even more significant, is the setting of "awaken'd" about a third of the way through the song. The wounded man's awakening both makes possible the intimacy to follow and contains it in embryo; the sign of wakefulness and the means by which the caretaker's loving look becomes mutual are one and the same, the opening of the soldier's eyes. The voice intones "awaken'd" just as the dynamic level changes for the first time (from *p* to *mp*) and the piano first releases the soft pedal, which has been in use from the outset. "Awaken'd" also coincides with the song's only genuine cadence, or at least the closest thing to one on offer. Written with a key signature of B♭ minor, "Specimen Case" anchors its harmony in deep-bass oscillations between the tones of the tonic and dominant; these frame the piece, the central portion of which uses harmony more coloristically than structurally. (The way the harmony undulates between relatively stable boundaries perhaps suggests the fluid, ambiguous space of romantic compassion.) Dominant harmony, however, never appears directly. Tonic chords, which arise throughout at critical junctures, are at best approached via dominant substitutes consisting of a dissonant collection over the dominant bass note. The final bass oscillation supplies a partial exception to this rule, telescoping a progression from a dominant-minor chord with added sixth to a tonic seventh. The only full exception occurs at "awaken'd," which moves from a pure dominant six-five—albeit a dominant-minor six-five—to a cadential tonic triad. The triad, moreover, in a kind of modal exchange with its dominant, is in the tonic *major,* imparting to the moment of awakening a sense of brightness and relief with no parallel anywhere in the song, a condition it shares with the tonic-major harmony.

This condition is the more poignant for being fleeting; a tonic-minor inflection supervenes the moment the word "awaken'd" has been uttered. Like the song itself in relation to the cycle, the cadence on "awaken'd" is premature, and too brief to offset the grave realities that envelop it. But like the song, it records a moment of witness anyway, investing the moment with a singularity meant to stand as a memorial sign like the frozen kiss of "Reconciliation" or the scrawled epitaph in "As Toilsome I Wander'd Virginia's Woods." It is no accident that the voice's cadential B♭ begins the rise in tessitura that ends with the climatic setting of "one long, clear silent look."

Unlike most of the *Drum-Taps* poems on the subject, "The Wound-Dresser" does not deal with one particular moment of mortal intimacy but with a proliferating series of them, each singled out by one or two vivid physical details that stick in the speaker's mind. The poem is framed as a recollection in old age; John Adams's 1989 setting of it for baritone and orchestra omits the prefatory verses, beginning in medias res amid the full immediacy of tending the wounded: "Bearing the bandages, water and sponge, / Straight and swift to my wounded I go." Only at the end does the setting reveal that what has seemed so fully present is actually a distant memory: "Thus in silence in dreams' projections, / Returning, resuming, I thread my way through the hospitals." The moment of recognition is doubly marked: in the text by a play on words, whereby the phrase "I sit by the restless all the dark night" refers to both the imaginary act of keeping vigil and its symbolic repetition in the speaker's dreams; and in the music by a grand pause, a commemorative moment of silence in which the reality of absence is concentrated.

Adams individualizes the moments quilted into the fabric of memory by breaking the text up into discrete segments and assigning each one its own distinctive orchestral texture, passing from one patch to another without transition. Or, to change the metaphor with Sarah Cahill, "the instrumental character changes . . . almost like panels of a painted screen."[12] These scene changes, however, occur within a context of overall continuity, even homogeneity, of texture, something created by an emphasis on rich, deliberate string sonority (Barber's *Adagio for Strings* again hovers near as a model) and a kind of continuo on synthesizer. Though fervent, the piece is restrained, indifferent to strong contrasts and grand climaxes; as Adams says of Whitman's poem, "it is . . . free of any kind of hyperbole or amplified emotion . . . a statement about human compassion of the kind that is acted out on a daily basis, quietly and unobtrusively and unselfishly and unfailingly." (On this reading, the statement—both poem and music—widens its scope beyond the war dead to include all the mortally ill, from Adams's own father, a victim of Alzheimer's disease, to the recent generations of those suffering from AIDS.) As the music, too, goes about its work unobtrusively, the character of that work unobtrusively clarifies itself. When the scenes described are acknowledged as memories, the memories, though involuntary, do not appear as traumatic flashbacks: on the contrary, they are strangely consoling, virtual presences to which the speaker gladly and continuously submits. The sequence of distinct patches or panels of memory thus gradually evolves into a single enveloping act of mortal intimacy that is both immediate and commemorative.

Like both Vaughan Williams and Rorem, however, Adams also seeks to separate out a singularity of moment or voice—in this case one of each—in which to embody the core paradox of mortal intimacy, the combination of anonymous universality and absolute particularity. As in *Dona Nobis Pacem*, the voice belongs to a solo instrument playing a lyrical monologue, but with a reversal of symbolic values. Vaughan Williams's violin prefigures the solo human voices, baritone and soprano, the moral or spiritual force of which is immanent and clear. When the baritone first sings "this soil'd world" he identifies the truth at which the violin could only hint. Adams's solo, which passes back and forth between violin and trumpet, is transcendental and mysterious, a "higher" voice of which the baritone solo is only an earthbound realization. This impression can be grounded in both the doubleness of the instrumental solo or solos and their relationship to the baritone line. The violin and trumpet (actually two trumpets, a full-sized and a piccolo instrument) draw on their traditional associations to project the complementary halves of the soldiers' identity, ideally conceived. The violin (which shows a strong affinity for its highest registers) suggests the sensitive, spiritual, "feminine" persona revealed in the young men's keen suffering and the caretaker's compassionate response. The trumpet suggests the warrior persona, but one made remote and elegiac by the disfiguring or fatal wounds that the men have borne away from the battlefield. The two instruments never play at the same time, suggesting the ideal character of the unity they each represent in part. Each takes its turn in a process that surrounds and pervades the voice with an independent melodic line more continuous and more expressively marked than the voice's own. Only at the end, after a second grand pause, does the voice so to speak inherit the full expressive capacity of the solo instruments. There, virtually the only moving thing in a soft and static expanse of sound, the voice gives cantabile utterance to the poem's concluding fusion of eros and compassion: "(Many a soldier's loving arms about this neck have cross'd and rested, / Many a soldier's kiss dwells on these bearded lips)."

This final moment has its own kind of singularity, but the song's center of uniqueness lies elsewhere. With one exception, the segments of Adams's "Wound-Dresser" set Whitman's text without repetition or alteration.[13] The exception occurs at the midpoint of the song when the baritone apostrophizes death, pleading for it to come quickly to those who need it as a deliverance. Here the words "In mercy come quickly" are repeated with the phrases reversed, creating a rhetorical chiasmus: "In mercy come quickly, come quickly in mercy." The vocal line echoes this formation with unusual literalness. The settings of "come quickly" are almost identical; the second "in mercy" reaches for the first but cannot quite grasp it (the mercy slips away). Enclosed at the core of the song, therefore, lies an image of further enclosure, a still deeper core marking the most intimate, least guarded point of contact between the wound-dresser and his dearest charges, those he remembers best because he could help them least.

The texts to my "Three Poems of Walt Whitman" (1984)[14] all deal with music as a form of social energy; their order in the song cycle—"I Hear America Singing" "Dirge for Two Veterans," and "That Music Always Round Me"—is meant to suggest Whitman's preferred postbellum narrative of national unity, traumatic disruption, and the search for recovery, although the framing poems were actually written in the same antebellum year, 1860. "I Hear America Singing" is a utopian text in the spirit of the first edition of *Leaves of Grass*. It depicts a nation of artisans and manual workers united in unalienated labor; the custom of singing at work becomes both a literal sign of contented activity and a new version of the traditional metaphor of social harmony. "Dirge for Two Veterans" abrogates that metaphor as the Civil War has abrogated its world—or its fiction of one. The heavy, formulaic sounds of a military funeral replace spontaneous singing; the music, meant to ease trauma with ritual, instead becomes traumatic itself as it nears the speaker in a steady crescendo. "That Music Always Round Me" recovers the image of social harmony in a new form, but a subtly diminished one. The image is that of a mixed chorus and orchestra, but the ensemble is purely figurative; its music is "unceasing, unbeginning," an ideal sound rather than a real one, utterly remote from the homely realism of "I Hear America Singing." The poem was originally one of the "Calamus" group, suggesting that its musical ideal has an amatory basis; Whitman eventually moved it to the mystical later cluster, "Whispers of Heavenly Death," so my own anachronistic use of it can lean on his. Positioned as the last song, the poem suggests a consoling dream, the tentative beginning of recovery rather than its assured end.

The setting of "I Hear America Singing" (CD track 18) employs a "panel" technique much like Adams's in "The Wound-Dresser." The accompaniment shifts from texture to texture as the scene shifts from one group of workers to another; there also are three "panels" of tempo, each quicker than the last. The piano has spacious opening gestures and an increasingly rich part to suggest the feeling of a broad canvass; vocal climaxes on the open vowels of the poem's last line, "Singing with open mouths their strong melodious songs," seek to convey an utter lack of limitation or inhibition. (There is also a counterelegiac stress on the workers' uniqueness, conveyed by a climax and textual repetition on "none other"—changed, for the vowel, from Whitman's "none else"—in the line "Each singing what belongs to him or her and to none [other]." The effect is anticipated by a repetition of "each singing.") The music proceeds with a lyrical vigor that seems heedless, or wills to be heedless, of the catastrophe to come. By contrast, "That Music Always Round Me" (CD track 20) cannot escape the memory of catastrophe recorded in the preceding "Dirge," even though the music recalls it in no specific way. More homogeneous in texture than "I Hear America Singing," "That Music" seeks to combine rich piano sonorities with a liquid vocal line. It aims at a tranquility that persists even at the most excited moments. But the song carries its lyricism with obvious vulnerability, as if a single wrong note, a single thought, could silence it. The real silence, though, lies in the central song, which, like so many other *Drum-Taps* settings, turns on the trope of mortal intimacy.

My main "expressive intention" in setting "Dirge for Two Veterans" was to avoid imitating the sounds of trumpets and drums; Vaughan Williams's use of the actual instruments was a negative model. What I wanted to depict was not the funeral music, but the act of hearing it. This was to be a difficult act; the poetic speaker was to be so burdened with grief as almost to lose sight of the men being mourned. The external sounds, particularly the drum sounds, were to be persistent but muffled, only occasionally breaking through to a real hearing. I imagined the voice as striving to surpass and finally to silence these aftersounds of war, eventually passing beyond them to a fuller acknowledgment of the fallen soldiers.

That acknowledgment takes the form—it just seemed right it should—of an isolated intimate moment, a singularity that, as a trope, is not singular at all, but communal. As the song draws to a close, the voice and piano separate antiphonically, each making a series of stark, simple statements in the silence of the other. Freed from its bond to the piano, which here "speaks" for the world of history and ritual memory, the voice is free to speak with the dead. Four times, each longer than the last, it addresses them *pianissimo* in a field of silence. Its final statement ("My heart gives you love"), after a premonitory swell on "heart," closes—and closes the vocal line—with a long crescendo and decrescendo, *pp* to *ff* and back, on a single note intoning "love." After a short pause, the piano follows this anguished-ecstatic cry with a short coda, perhaps—though this is by no means certain—with the significance of its characteristic gestures altered by what the voice has gone through.

It seems appropriate to end this volume by discussing my own Whitman songs because they reflect the same long-standing fascination with Whitman, and affection for him, that prompted me to undertake the volume in the first place. What I hope to have suggested both as editor and contributor is that Whitman's role in the shaping of modern memory has a musical dimension that deserves serious attention. What America means—"America" being the ideal, ideological, Adamic name given to itself by the United States—has always been in part a question of what Whitman means, of what it means to have given Whitman the place he claimed as a canonical modern figure. To understand that fully, it's necessary to understand how modern musicians, both Americans and others, have heard Whitman hear America singing.

## Notes

1. "A Backward Glance O'er Travel'd Roads" (postscript to the 1889 edition of *Leaves of Grass*), text from *Leaves of Grass,* Norton Critical Edition, ed. Sculley Bradley and Harold W. Blodgett (New York: Norton, 1973), pp. 567–68.

2. On the mainstream type of male homoeroticism in the nineteenth century, with specific reference to Whitman, see David S. Reynolds, *Walt Whitman's America: A Cultural Biography* (New York: Knopf, 1995), pp. 391–403.

3. Reynolds, *Walt Whitman's America,* pp. 451–63.

4. Quoted in Michael Kennedy, *The Works of Ralph Vaughan Williams* (London: Oxford University Press, 1964), pp. 98–99.

5. "Note by the Composer," prefatory to the score of *The Wound-Dresser* (New York: Hendon Music/Boosey and Hawkes, 1989).

6. This and all subsequent quotations of Whitman's poetry are from the Norton Critical Edition of *Leaves of Grass* (n. 1). For Harrison, see below, n. 9.

7. Reynolds, *Walt Whitman's America,* pp. 426–31.

8. This trope was confined neither to America nor to the Civil War, as the following passage from Émile Zola's novel of the Franco-Prussian War, *The Debacle* (trans. L. W. Tancock [1892; Harmondworth: Penguin Classics, 1972]), illustrates: "Maurice let himself be carried away like a child. No woman's arms had ever held him as close and warm as this. In the collapse of everything, in this utter misery, with death staring him in the face, it was an ineffable comfort to feel another person loving him and looking after him. . . . Was this not the brotherhood of the earliest days of the world, friendship before there was any culture or class, the friendship of two men united and become as one in their common need? . . . And so friendship became a kind of broadening out for both of them: they might not kiss, but they touched each other's very souls, the one was part of the other . . . the two of them making a single being in pity and suffering" (pp. 136–37). From the perspective shown here, the boundary between comradeship, eroticism, and compassion becomes impossible to draw, perhaps even senseless to imagine. On the reservation implied by "they might not kiss," and its paradoxically liberating effect on same-sex love in the nineteenth

century, together with other reflections on music and sexuality with particular reference to Whitman, see my *After the Lovedeath: Sexual Violence and the Making of Culture* (Berkeley and Los Angeles: University of California Press, 1997).

9. Robert Pogue Harrison, "The Names of the Dead," *Critical Inquiry* 24 (1997), 176–90; quotation, 189.

10. Ursula Vaughan Williams, *R. V. W: A Biography of Ralph Vaughan Williams* (London: Oxford University Press, 1964), p. 209.

11. Text from "Some Specimen Cases," *Specimen Days,* in *The Works of Walt Whitman, Deathbed Edition in Two Volumes,* vol. II: *Collected Prose* (New York: Funk and Wagnalls, 1969), p. 32. Ironically, given the paradoxes of naming discussed in this essay, Rorem does not record the name of the soldier described in this passage: Thomas Haley.

12. Note to a recording of *The Wound-Dresser* (#9-79218-4) by the Orchestra of St. Luke's, conducted by the composer with Sanford Sylvan, baritone (New York: Elektra Nonesuch, 1989).

13. I am setting aside a single repetition of "life" in the phrase "life struggles hard," which occurs just before the truly exceptional segment, to which it acts as a prompt.

14. A score of this song cycle, though unpublished, can be found in the Music Research Collection of the New York Public Library, under the longer original title "'That Music Always Round Me': Three Poems by Walt Whitman."

# Contributors

**Byron Adams** is associate professor of composition and musicology at the University of California, Riverside. The first recipient of the Ralph Vaughan Williams Research Fellowship of the Carthusian Trust, he has published widely on the subject of twentieth-century English music in such journals as *Music & Letters, Musical Quarterly,* and *American Music,* as well as in the volume *Vaughan Williams Studies* (Cambridge, 1996), and lectured on this topic on the British Broadcasting Corporation and elsewhere.

**Philip Coleman-Hull** is assistant professor of English at Bethany College in Lindsborg, Kansas. A specialist in American and Great Plains literature, he has been published in *Great Plains Quarterly* and currently is working on a book examining the use of music and art in American and Canadian plains fiction.

**Walter Grünzweig** is professor of American literature and culture at the University of Dortmund; he has published on Charles Sealsfield, Walt Whitman, and European-American cultural and literary relations. **Werner Grünzweig** is director of the music archive at the Berlin Academy of the Arts. He has published on Arnold Schoenberg, Alban Berg, and Kurt Weill, among others, and on the musical reception of Whitman in Germany.

**Kim H. Kowalke** is professor of musicology at the Eastman School of Music/University of Rochester, president of the Kurt Weill Foundation for Music, and the founding member of the editorial board of the Kurt Weill edition. He is the author or editor of four books and a two-time winner of the ASCAP-Deems Taylor award for excellence in writing about music.

**Lawrence Kramer** is professor of English and Music at Fordham University and coeditor of *19th-Century Music*. He is the author of five books and numerous articles on the interrelationships of music, literature, and culture.

**David Metzer** is assistant professor of music at the University of British Columbia. He has published articles in *Black Music Research Journal, 19th-Century Music,* and *Journal of Musicology*. His research interests include American music, gender, and sexuality. He is currently working on a book about quotation in American music.

**John M. Picker** is a doctoral candidate in English at the University of Virginia. He has published articles in *Victorian Studies, English Literary History,* and *Walt Whitman Review,* and is currently completing a dissertation entitled *Hearing Things: Sound in the Victorian Imagination, 1848–1900*.

**Kathy Rugoff** is associate professor of English at the University of North Carolina, Wilmington. She has published several articles on the interrelations of music and literature and is, in addition, a musician who plays a number of woodwind and string instruments and who has hosted programs on classical music for National Public Radio.

# Notes to the Compact Disc

Tracks 1–4. Marc Blitzstein: Four Whitman Songs (recorded by arrangement with Blitzstein Music; ASCAP). First recording.

1. As if a Phantom Caress'd Me—1925 (2:29)
2. O Hymen! O Hymenee!—1927 (1:05)
3. As Adam Early in the Morning—1927 (2:38)
4. Ages and Ages Returning at Intervals—1928 (2:16)

Between 1925 and 1928 Marc Blitzstein composed nine songs to texts by Whitman, most of them celebrating affection between men. Although some of the songs were performed at the time, all remain unpublished; none has been recorded before. The four songs on this compact disc are discussed in the chapter by David Metzer, "Reclaiming Walt: Marc Blitzstein's Whitman Settings."

Tracks 5–8. Kurt Weill: Four Whitman Songs (recorded by arrangement with European American Music and the Harry Fox Agency).

5. Beat! Beat! Drums!—1942 (5:09)
6. O Captain! My Captain!—1941 (4:28)
7. Come Up from the Fields, Father—1947 (6:15)
8. Dirge for Two Veterans—1942 (5:58)

Weill composed the earliest of these songs in the immediate aftermath of Pearl Harbor, followed shortly by two more; as Kim Kowalke shows in his chapter, "I'm an American! Whitman, Weill, and Cultural Identity," the songs reflect both the structure of feeling of wartime America and Weill's strong identification with his adopted country. This recording is the first we know of to include an important revision in the last song to be composed, the addition of which to the set had important repercussions discussed in Kowalke's text.

Tracks 9–17. George Crumb: Apparition (1979; recorded by arrangement with C. F. Peters Corporation).

    9. The Night in Silence under Many a Star (2:51)
   10. Vocalise 1: Sounds of a Summer Evening (0:55)
   11. When Lilacs Last in the Dooryard Bloom'd (1:13)
   12. Dark Mother Always Gliding Near (2:23)
   13. Vocalise 2: Invocation to the Dark Angel (1:31)
   14. Approach, Strong Deliveress! (2:31)
   15. Vocalise 3: Death Carol (Song of the Nightbird; 0:31)
   16. Come Lovely and Soothing Death (7:17)
   17. The Night in Silence under Many a Star (3:28)

Crumb's text is "When Lilacs Last in the Dooryard Bloom'd"; his setting thus follows in the footsteps of (among others) Paul Hindemith and Roger Sessions, both of whose settings are discussed along with Crumb's in the chapter by Kathy Rugoff, "Three American Requiems: Contemplating 'When Lilacs Last in the Dooryard Bloom'd.'" (Hindemith's setting also is the subject of Philip Coleman-Hull's chapter, and one of the topics of the chapter by Walter and Werner Grünzweig.) Unlike his precursors, Crumb treats Whitman's poems as a resource, not an independent artwork; he sets only twenty lines of the poem, drawn from five strophes, but not necessarily in their strophic order. *Apparition* is thus more of a Whitman reflection than a Whitman "setting."

Tracks 18–20. Lawrence Kramer: Three Poems by Walt Whitman (1984; recorded by arrangement with Lawrence Kramer).

   18. I Hear America Singing (6:31)
   19. Dirge for Two Veterans (9:57)
   20. That Music Always Round Me (5:50)

These songs were composed as a cycle in 1984 for tenor Darrell Lauer, and are discussed in the composer's chapter, "Like Falling Leaves: The Erotics of Mourning in Four *Drum-Taps* Settings." All three texts are based on musical imagery, and the cycle in a sense proleptically sums up the contents of this volume by combining the idea of music with the themes named in the volume's subtitle: war, desire, and the trials of nationhood.

This recording could not have been made without the generous help of many people, foremost among whom is Joan Heller, soprano, who contributed her skills as both an artist and an impresario to get the project off the ground and bring it to completion. The recording was partially funded by a Faculty Development Grant from the Meadows School of the Arts at Southern Methodist University to Joan Heller for the academic year 1999–2000. The recording sessions took place in the Caruth Auditorium at SMU's Meadows School of the Arts in June 1999. Paul Phillips was the producer and Curtis Craig the recording engineer; Robert Frank was technical and musical advisor, David Porritt the piano technician.

Soprano **Joan Heller**'s long-standing advocacy of twentieth-century and American music is reflected in her numerous recordings and performances; the latter, both here and abroad, have included the world premiere of more than forty compositions, many written specifically for her. She has given vocal master classes in the United States, United Kingdom, and former Soviet Union, and served on the music faculties of Yale University, Boston University, and the University of North Carolina at Wilmington. In 1994 she was the recipient of an individual artist grant from the National Endowment for the Humanities for her solo compact disc "To the Verge" (Neuma Records), featuring compositions by Luciano Berio, Charles Fussell, Robert Cogan, Milton Babbitt, and Thomas Stumpf. Joan Heller is associate professor and head of the voice department at the Meadows School of the Arts, Southern Methodist University.

Pianist-composer **Thomas Stumpf**, winner of international piano competitions—the Boesendorfer Prize (Vienna, 1970) and the Lili Lehmann Medal (Salzberg, 1972)—took his degrees in piano performance from the Salzburg Mozarteum and the New England Conservatory of Music, and has concertized with the Hong Kong Philharmonic, Boston Pops orchestra, and numerous other ensembles. He has often premiered works by American composers, many written specifically for him; his own compositions have been included on concert programs through the United States and former Soviet Union. He has composed several works for Joan Heller, with whom he has collaborated in concerts and recordings since 1989. Thomas Stumpf has taught at the New England Conservatory, chaired the piano department at the University of Massachusetts at Lowell, and held the position of associate professor and chair of the collaborative piano department at Boston University.

# Index of Names

# Index of Titles

Whitman's volumes appear in SMALL CAPS; titles of settings, where they are not also those of the poems set, are *italicized*.